Praise For

A MOB STORY

"Meet the not-so-goodfellas as they really are in a first-rate first book. You might have read a hundred mob books, but you never read a mob book like this one. Michele McPhee must be lying when she says she is from Boston, because she has Brooklyn down, along with the sixth borough, Miami."

—Mike Daly, *Daily News* columnist
and author of *Under Ground*

"Ace reporter Michele McPhee has jammed *A Mob Story* with more outrages, betrayals, and laughs than three seasons of *The Sopranos*. A very good book about a very bad guy." —Jim Dwyer, Pulitzer prize-winning columnist,
author of *Actual Innocence*

"McPhee is a writer to watch, and I anxiously await the next dark world she covers."

—Raul Correa, author of
I Don't Know But I've Been Told

"A winner! *A Mob Story* is a page-turner with new insight about the wannabe wiseguys that prowl the mad streets of Brooklyn and Staten Island and one who made it to the glitz and glamour of South Beach."

—Jerry Capeci, GangLandNews.com columnist
and author of *Mob Start, Murder Machine,* and *Gotti*

A MOB STORY

MICHELE R. MCPHEE

St. Martin's Paperbacks

A Mob Story was previously published under the title *Mob over Miami*.

A MOB STORY

Copyright © 2002 by Michele McPhee.
Epilogue copyright © 2010 by Michele R. McPhee.

Cover photo of gun courtesy Getty Images/Purestock.
Back cover photo of Chris Paciello © Mitchell Gerber/CORBIS.

For information address St. Martin's Press, 175 Fifth Avenue, New York, NY 10010.

EAN: 978-0-312-94267-0

Printed in the United States of America

Onyx edition / April 2002
St. Martin's Paperbacks edition / July 2010

St. Martin's Paperbacks are published by St. Martin's Press, 175 Fifth Avenue, New York, NY 10010.

10 9 8 7 6 5 4 3 2 1

For Robert Vickerman

CONTENTS

ACKNOWLEDGMENTS

Writing a first book while working trying to keep up the pace working at a New York City tabloid would have been nearly impossible without my *Daily News* colleagues in the "shack" at One Police Plaza: John Marzulli, Alice McQuillan, Patrice O'Shaughnessy, and Richard Weir. My *Daily News* editors, Wendell Jamieson, Dean Chang, Mark Mooney, Jere Hester, and Rick Pienciak, along with Ed Fay, were also generous with their support and guidance. To the entire *Daily News* library staff—a collection of hotshot researchers—I'm entirely in your debt. I would also like to thank Bill Boyle, an editor who has taken pebbles of stories and turned them into gold nuggets.

I am forever grateful to my wonderful and patient agent, Alice Martell, who took a chance on a first-time author and was a constant source of inspiration. Dan Slater, the New American Library editor who labored over this book, is to be commended for his willingness to take every panicked phone call and for the long hours he put into my manuscript. Thanks also to his assistant Ron Martirano.

Without the Brooklyn court reporters—the *New York Times*'s Alan Feur, AP's Tom Hayes, *The Post*'s Chris Francescani, and my *Daily News* coworker Mike Claffey—I would have been lost. I would also like to thank my good friends, *Talk* magazine editor Maer Roshan, *Boston Globe* writer Rick Kahn, and Mike McPadden, a damn fine writer. Thanks also to New York *Post* night-side crime reporter Phil Messing, who shared old mob stories with me.

Being a police reporter has always given me a great respect for cops, but the NYPD went above and beyond the call of duty in helping me track down aging, yellowed documents—especially the DCPI office. Marilyn Mode, the former Deputy Commissioner of Public Information, gave me the green light to talk to the detectives in the Intelligence Division's Investigation Squad, some of the finest cops in the city; Inspector Michael Collins, a hardscrabble Brooklyn guy and an extraordinary cop, lent me his memories; Lieutenant Corey Cuneo got his dad to give us all the right Italian words; Captain Sean Crowley helped keep the flow of information moving smoothly. Thanks also to sergeants Brian Burke, Gerry Falcon, and Andy McInnis, and to Lieutenant Elias Nikas, who along with officers Chris Cottingham, Joe Cavitolo, Gary Cillo, detectives Robert Samuel, Theresa Farello, Walter Burnes, and every other hardworking cop in DCPI, helped keep me on top of breaking stories around the clock. I also tip my hat to Chief Tom Fahey and DCPI commissioner Tom Antennan.

The heroes in this book are the detectives, federal agents, and prosecutors who, while working tirelessly building countless cases, still took the time to answer the questions they were allowed to answer. NYPD detectives Freddie Santoro, Tommy Dades, Michael Galletta, Jimmy Harkins, and Lieutenant Kevin O'Brien, along with investigators assigned to the Staten Island homicide squad led by famous bomb squad cop Charlie Wells, were all immeasurably helpful, along with Sergeant Bobby Losada, Detective Bobby Walsh, and computer whiz Sergeant Tony Luongo. Thanks to Miami Beach Police detective Al Boza for always being just a cell phone call away.

I would also like to thank Drug Enforcement Agency special agent Timmy Foley and Federal Bureau of Investigation special agent Wayne McGrew and former FBI agent Joseph Pistone.

I have much admiration for the prosecutors—assistant United States attorneys Jim Walden and Greg Andres, along with Kings County assistant district attorney Chris Blank. There are also cops and agents who led me to pivotal information, but cannot be named. They have my gratitude.

Jerry Capeci's website www.ganglandnews.com was a virtual wiseguy encyclopedia that I turned to weekly.

Thanks, also, to a group of New York City's most dogged defense attorneys—Ben Brafman, Roy Black, Gerald Shargel, and Vincent Romano—for their time and expertise.

"The Ladies" were also instrumental to this book. They know who they are.

I would like to thank my parents, Sheila and Bruce McPhee, for letting me believe since I was a little girl that I could write a book one day.

This book is dedicated to my dearest friend, Robert Vickerman, and to the memories of two late, beloved journalists who are missed by all, especially those who aspire to follow in their footsteps: *Daily News* columnists Mike McAlary and Lars Erik Nelson.

CAST OF MAIN CHARACTERS

CHRISTIAN LUDWIGSEN, A.K.A. BINGER, A.K.A. CHRIS PACIELLO: A street thug who hailed from Brooklyn, moved to Staten Island, and catapulted himself from small-time hood and wannabe gangster to Miami's nightclub king.

PACIELLO'S FAMILY

Marguerite Paciello: Chris's mother, a onetime hairdresser who insists her son is innocent, a victim of prosecutors who "can't believe someone at his age became so successful."

George Ludwigsen: Chris's estranged father, the former arm-wrestling champion of the world.

George Ludwigsen Jr.: Chris's older brother, an alleged bank robber.

Keith Ludwigsen: Chris's younger brother, who ran the South Beach clubs while his older sibling was incarcerated.

Louis Paciello: Chris's grandfather, who signed away his home as part of Chris's bail package.

PACIELLO'S FRIENDS

Madonna: Pop star who reportedly dated Chris.

Ingrid Casares: Madonna's best friend and former lover who became Paciello's business partner at South Beach hot spots Liquid and Bar Room and the restaurant Joia.

Niki Taylor: Supermodel who dated Chris.

Sofia Vergara: Latin television personality and swimsuit pinup who dated Chris.

Daisy Fuentes: Sultry MTV veejay who dated Chris.

Jennifer Lopez: Voluptuous actress and pop star who reportedly dated Chris.

Love Majewski: Lingerie model and sometime actress from Staten Island who dated Chris.

Shareef Malnik: Famed South Beach restaurant owner.

Jason Binn: Famed publisher of *Ocean Drive, Hamptons,* and *Gotham* magazines.

Lord Michael Caruso: Club promoter who helped Paciello open his first nightclub, Risk.

Vincent Rizzuto: Gambino associate who fled to South Beach and lived with Chris, stealing Lord Michael Caruso's identity.

BATH AVENUE CREW—Bonanno Crime Family

Anthony Spero: Onetime acting Bonanno crime family boss who also held the role of both *consigliere* and captain while overseeing the Bath Avenue Crew.

Joseph Benanti: An elderly Bonanno soldier who pleaded guilty to life for murder, racketeering, and reaping the profits from a south Brooklyn crack gang.

Tommy Reynolds: A Bonanno associate who was the shooter in a botched home invasion that left an innocent woman dead.

Fabrizio Defrancisci: An alleged Bonanno soldier who pleaded guilty to murder, racketeering, and drug dealing.

BATH AVENUE CREW TURNCOATS

Dean Benasillo: A Bonanno wannabe who earned the nickname "Eight Is Enough" because he became the first Bath Avenue Crew member to "flip," or cooperate with the government—in only eight minutes.

Jimmy Calandra: A small-time bank robber who went along with Paciello on a botched home invasion that left a housewife dead. He became a government cooperator.

Michael Yammine: A loopy Bonanno hanger-on who, as a government cooperator, spent much of his sentence at the Butner prison for the criminally insane in North Carolina.

William "Applehead" Galloway: A drug dealer for a Luchese crew and a bank robber with Paciello.

Joey Calco: A "zip" or Sicilian soldier for the Bonannos who was as quick with a gun as he later became with his mouth.

Nicky Tuzzio: A Bonanno associate whose brother, Louis, was allegedly murdered on Anthony Spero's orders.

NEW SPRINGVILLE BOYS—Freelance Criminals

Ray Merolle: The leader of a gang of car thieves that called themselves "the Untouchables" who was burglarized by Chris Paciello.

Gerard "Skeevy" Bellafurie: The leader of the New Springville Boys who became a disc jockey in South Beach at his friend Chris's clubs.

Bekim Fisheku: Paciello's close friend and former cohort indicted for a string of bank burglaries.

Ilber "Billy" Balanca: Bekim Fisheku's cousin and a friend of Paciello's who was found dead in the trunk of his car after a drug deal went bad.

Lee D'Vanzo: Leader of the New Springville Boys.

George Ludwigsen: Paciello's older brother, indicted alongside members of the New Springfield Boys for bank burglaries.

Joseph "Joey Gams" Gambino: A Paciello friend who was indicted for bank robbery.

LUCHESE MOBSTERS

James "Froggy" Galione: A former Bonanno soldier, he made his bones by murdering a wanted felon on the lam and later became a made member of the Luchese family.

Mario Gallo: Froggy Galione's partner who also jumped from the Bonanno family to the Lucheses.

LUCHESE TURNCOATS

Ronald "Messy Marvin" Moran: A Froggy Galione underling who flipped after he was arrested on drug dealing and murder charges.

Michael "Mikey Flattop" Derosa: Cooperated with the government a few months after his arrest, which took place a week after he paid $8,000 for a nose job.

COLOMBO MOBSTERS

William "Wild Bill" Cutolo: A natty businessman who federal investigators say is a Colombo family captain. Paciello was spotted at his social club.

Alphonse "Allie Boy" Persico: Described by the government as the acting boss of the Colombo crime family. He met Paciello for lunch.

Dominick "Big Dom" Dionisio: One of Paciello's closest friends, who is a Colombo associate.

CONTRACT HITS

Gus Farace: A Bonanno drug dealer who killed a Drug Enforcement agent and went on the lam from both the law and the Mob.

Louis Tuzzio: A murdered Bonanno associate, a hit allegedly ordered by Anthony Spero.

Paul "Paulie" Gulino: A Bonanno associate shot dead at his parents' kitchen table allegedly after he tried to take out a hit on his boss, Anthony Spero, and Spero's trusted soldier, Joseph Benanti.

Vincent Bickelman: A drug addict and smalltime crook who was gunned down after he allegedly burglarized the home of one of Anthony Spero's daughters.

Jack Cherin: A Bath Avenue Crew hanger-on who was killed because his cohorts erroneously suspected he was cooperating with the law.

Neil Nastro and Vincent Dipippo: Victims of a double murder by a young Brooklyn man and his uncle, sparked when they aided a murderer on the run. The murderer, Fat Stevie Romano, killed Spero's godson, George Adamo.

PROSECUTORS

Assistant United States attorney in the Eastern District James Walden: A wiry, workaholic prosecutor dubbed "Pit Bull" by the investigators on his team.

Assistant district attorney in Kings County Chris Blank: A focused, headstrong prosecutor who pressed state charges against defendants in the indictments.

Assistant United States attorney Greg Andres: A young, tough, former Peace Corps volunteer who backed up Walden.

DEFENSE LAWYERS

Roy Black: The defense attorney who successfully defended William Kennedy Smith against rape charges, but lost panty-aficionado Marv Albert's case when the sportscaster was accused of assault; had a short-lived stint defending Paciello.

Howard Srebnick: Paciello's friend from Miami who assisted Roy Black in the early stages of his defense.

Vincent Romano: Hailing from Bay Ridge, he was the youngest mob attorney of the bunch, representing Fabrizio DeFrancisci.

Gerard Shargel: An impeccably dressed, quick-tongued New York City mob attorney who has represented a slew of gangsters, including John "the Dapper Don" Gotti—this time Shargel battled for Anthony Spero.

Ben Brafman: Attorney to famous celebrities and famous gangsters such as Salvatore "Sammy the Bull" Gravano (before he turned on Gotti) and rap stars like Sean "Puff Daddy" Combs. Paciello was a mixture of both, a celebrity with mob ties.

FEDERAL JUDGES

Honorable **Edward R. Korman,** chief judge.

United States magistrate **Joan Azrack**.

NEW YORK CITY DETECTIVES

Detective Tommy Dades: A hardscrabble detective from the NYPD's Intelligence Division, investigations squad.

Detective Mike Galletta: The lead detective on the Chris Paciello case from the NYPD's Intelligence Division, investigations squad. He arrested Paciello when he was sixteen for stealing cars.

Sergeant Freddie Santoro: A former narcotics detective and organized crime expert assigned to the Auto Crimes Unit.

Lieutenant Kevin O'Brien: Commanding officer of the NYPD's Intelligence Division, investigations squad.

Detective James Harkins: Lead investigator on the New Springville Boys takedown from NYPD's Intelligence Division, investigations squad.

Inspector Charles Wells: Legendary rough-and-tumble cop who oversaw the Staten Island Homicide Squad.

Detective Robert "Big Boy" Walsh: A seasoned detective from the Staten Island Homicide Squad who made the arrests in the Judy Shemtov homicide.

Sergeant Robert Losada: The lead investigator in the Staten Island Homicide Squad who assisted on the arrests in the Judy Shemtov homicide.

DRUG ENFORCEMENT AGENCY

Special Agent Timmy Foley: Former Chicago detective who was the lead investigator on the Bath Avenue Crew case.

FEDERAL BUREAU OF INVESTIGATION

Wayne McGrew: Former criminal defense attorney who became an agent on the FBI's Bonanno Squad.

1

TALE OF TWO MEN

South Beach, Miami
December 1, 1999

It was after midnight and South Beach was crackling
with electricity. Neon lights sparkled off the dark blue
ocean. Headache-bright convertible Mercedes and brand-
new PT Cruisers crawled down Ocean Drive with their
car stereos pumping bass-heavy Latin beats. Sidewalk
bistros resonated with conversations in a panoply of lan-
guages. Palm trees swayed alongside the strip's hotels
and high-rise condominiums. Leggy models overran
the sidewalks, teetering on strappy high heels in the direction of fancy nightclubs. Buff gay boys strolled hand-
in-hand along cream-colored beaches. Leathery women
with iguanas on their backs hustled tourists for money,
oblivious to the pack of bikers slurping liquor-laden
slushes at outdoor bars.

Even on a weeknight South Beach did not come to life
until now, until the wee hours. Most "year-rounders"—
as the glittery residents of the beachfront area refer to
themselves—don't have anywhere to be come daybreak.
First appointments begin in the middle of the day—
chores like late afternoon photo shoots or workouts with

personal trainers. Posh clothing stores, like Versace and Betsey Johnson, don't even bother to open before 2 P.M. The only people who appeared busy were the paparazzi, vying from helicopters for shots of Madonna jogging along the edge of the waves or of Sylvester Stallone pushing a baby stroller with his wife.

Nightlife is the heartbeat of South Beach, and no one made its heart beat more loudly than Chris Paciello.

Driving on the morning side of midnight, Chris Paciello cruised down beyond-stylish Washington Avenue in his black Range Rover. He had a cell phone clamped to his ear. On the other end of the line was the manager of Joia, the elite Italian bistro Paciello owned on Ocean Drive. Paciello wanted the answer to a relatively straightforward question: What would it take for these guys to shape up and keep that place running smoothly without him? Paciello was steaming. He waited a few impatient moments for an answer, and when he didn't receive one, he hung up in disgust.

The twenty-eight-year-old businessman had just departed from Joia, where he'd dined on risotto sautéed with pungent Parmesan cheese, accompanied by a glass of fine red wine. He ate dinner there four or five nights a week at his personal table near Joia's hostess stand. It was the choicest seat in the house, ideal for those who liked to glance at the beautiful people passing by while nibbling on expensive cuisine. From this vantage point, Paciello could oversee the staff, survey the customers, or focus his attention on the turquoise shoreline with its sunbathers, often topless, across the street. He could even take in the competition at other open-air bars and eateries smattered along the beachfront.

This was his place. These were his people.

You didn't even have to live in South Beach to know Chris Paciello. National magazines had carried photos and profiles of the "hunky club owner." *Vanity Fair* interviewed Madonna and Rupert Everett at Joia, declaring, "If South Beach is the new Riviera, then Joia is the Hôtel Du Cap."

But the elite eatery was just part of Paciello's empire. He also owned Bar Room, Miami's hottest lounge, where Dennis Rodman and Gwyneth Paltrow were regulars, as well as Liquid, another massive nightclub. Paciello's dark moods were always buoyed when he pulled his SUV in front of 1439 Washington Avenue. At this moment, Liquid was the hottest nightspot on the planet.

On this night, more than a hundred decked-out revelers were feverishly trying to beg or bribe their way past swarthy bouncers into the 36,000-square-foot club. The line stretched the entire block.

Each of the area's hotspots hired a crew of buff men with bronze complexions and steely stares standing guard behind velvet ropes. These bruisers had powers far beyond that of mortal doormen. They were the gatekeepers. The givers of "The Nod"—a silent, bobbing-head signal that meant you could join the party inside.

Only then could you enter the realm of South Beach's professional A-list, where Chris Paciello ruled.

Paciello valet-parked his car and palmed a ten into the valet's hand. The valet, like most of his clubs' employees, was an old friend from Staten Island, New York. Paciello always surrounded himself with people he trusted, and usually he only trusted people from the old neighborhood.

Some of the club's regulars, even plain folk who recognized his mug from *People* magazine, spotted Paciello as he strode toward the velvet ropes. He stood six-feet-plus, his frame all muscle, with a boxer's square jaw and blazing black eyes. They yelled his name in vain. "What's

up, Chris?" "Hey, guy, remember me?" "Chris, help me
out here, I'm with my girl." The club's owner just smiled
toward the crowd, whispered to his head bouncer, and
opened the front doors, blasting the hopeful with a few
brief seconds of techno music and kaleidoscopic disco
lights.

Once inside, Paciello was immediately the center
of attention. Svelte women preened for his approval. He
strode through the downstairs lounge, making sure the
candles were lit, the incense was burning, and the vases
were filled with fresh flowers. Everything was in place;
after all, Madonna's brother, Christopher Ciccone, had
designed the club's swank layout.

Paciello twisted through the packed dance floor to his
reserved table in the more exclusive of the club's two VIP
sections. The room was private enough to keep starry-
eyed interlopers out. Before he even took a seat, a waitress set down an ice bucket with Moët champagne and a
bottle of Evian water.

He scoured the surrounding faces with a fixed smile,
curious to see who was in the club. Liquid's guest roster
usually read like *National Enquirer* headline copy. Sean
"Puffy" Combs burst into impromptu concerts there. Cher
was another performer who often packed the place. Starlet Cameron Diaz was a regular, as were Michael Jordan
and Robert De Niro, Matt Dillon and Chris Rock, Naomi
Campbell and Donatella Versace, and James Woods and
Calvin Klein.

America's royalty—the models, the moguls, the movie
stars—had crowned Chris Paciello King of South Beach,
and he wore the title well. He looked regal with his chiseled face and slicked-back hair, a few black strands
highlighted an orange tint by the sun. He wrapped his
toned physique in pricey Prada suits. His face was a sta-
ple in Miami glossies. His every move was monitored

by gossip columnists in tabloids up and down the East Coast.

In a few days Paciello was going to open the fourth outpost of his empire, the West Palm Beach Liquid Room. For the big party, New York business mogul and casino tycoon Donald Trump had agreed to be the guest of honor. The phone was already ringing off the hook. Glitterati from downtown Manhattan to Beverly Hills wanted a spot on the guest list.

As Paciello contemplated the upcoming bash, Miami Heat superstar center Alonzo Mourning passed by his table. Paciello pulled him to the side and invited him to be a guest.

"It's going to be the party of the *year*!" Paciello announced in a gritty New York accent. "This Friday will be one that south Florida will never forget."

Paciello was not even thirty, already a millionaire and a legendary Casanova. He had a hard time keeping his women away from each other. Rumor had Madonna succumbing to Paciello's charm. Sultry MTV veejay Daisy Fuentes pursued him for months until he became her frequent escort. Pop singer Jennifer Lopez deposited her famous derriere into his open palms to ring in New Year's Eve at Ocean Drive's Pelican Hotel one year. Then there was the time he was caught making out with supermodel Niki Taylor in Liquid's DJ booth.

South Beach was a fitting refuge for someone like Chris Paciello. After all, the town's sunny shores had long been a great hideaway for shady characters and B-list celebrities. Al Capone and his cronies wintered on Miami's shores. The FBI has a file stuffed with surveillance shots of Meyer Lansky as he strolled down South Beach. In the forties, Frank Sinatra and Marlene Dietrich made it their own American Riviera.

Yet by the early 1980s, most of South Beach's whimsical buildings stood rotting and near collapse. Biker gangs, drug addicts, and derelicts enjoyed almost complete run of the streets. A decade later, however, savvy entrepreneurs moved in and lured the rich and famous to the dilapidated shoreline with glittering nightlife. Fashion models and their photographers, millionaire rap stars, and surgery-enhanced jet-setters played happy rats to Paciello and his fellow pied pipers. They raised South Beach to a new high. And the best-of-the-best kept coming.

In fact, it might be said that in many ways the revival of this run-down Florida haven paralleled what Jewish gangster Bugsy Siegel and his gang in Murder Inc. did by whipping a pile of desert sand into the money-machine that became Las Vegas. Certainly the guys financing the South Beach renaissance were familiar with Bugsy Siegel's line of work.

Chris Paciello left Liquid just after 3 A.M. He drove past Bar Room a few blocks away, but he did not go in. He just nodded toward the doormen and drove home. At the moment he was living in a rented one-story white stucco house on East San Marino Drive while his $1 million Italian palazzo underwent a complete overhaul. East San Marino Drive was not exactly low rent, though. The small street was one of many dotting picturesque inlets behind South Beach. Paciello lived across the street from an ambassador to Cuba.

As Paciello pulled the Range Rover into the driveway, his faithful rottweiler ran to the front yard and barked a welcome. He patted the dog, walked into the house past his brother, Keith, who had nodded out on the couch, and went upstairs to the master bedroom. He had to get some rest before his boxing coach showed up.

As he slept, Chris Paciello could have stirred restlessly as scenes from his not-too-distant past disturbed his dreams. His future may have looked as bright as a south Florida dawn, but the life he had lived in New York would soon eclipse him, leaving him veiled only in the darkness of his past. The rumors that had swirled upon his arrival in South Beach of his Mafia ties, rumors that had helped fuel his tough-guy image, were well founded. The area's club king had a long list of crimes to his name and an even longer list of criminal accomplices. Those very *paesans* had recently been arrested, and already had been squawking to the government. As Chris Paciello basked in his South Beach empire there was one crime he had to be particularly concerned about: a time bomb that would blow apart the cushy new world he had created for himself among the pastel-hued beaches of Miami and propel him straight back to New York City.

On a dark, freezing February night years earlier, four men in a Mercury sedan headed for a cul-de-sac in Staten Island's Richmond Valley. It was just before midnight and they were looking for a street called Meade Loop.

Nobody said a word as the car crawled past the neighborhood's million-dollar sandstone and brick homes. It was a bitterly cold night even for a northeast winter—the temperature in the daytime had been twenty-seven degrees, but had dropped since. Most people stayed in from the cold, and the street was deserted. The only light emanated from a dozen street lamps dimly flickering over the fallen snow.

A six-foot-one, 195-pound man with dark eyes and brown hair was driving. His baseball cap shadowed the features of his face and luminous brown eyes. To his cohorts he was known as "the Binger" for his propensity to binge on crimes. His robberies and shakedowns also had a nasty habit of turning into broken teeth and splintered bones for his victims. He binged on stealing cars and bank burglaries, ripping ATM machines and night deposit boxes out of brick walls, and random baseball bat attacks.

The Binger was the brains of this bunch.

Next to the Binger sat fleshy James "Jimmy Gap" Calandra, a twenty-five-year-old career bank robber who stood five-feet-eleven and weighed 240 pounds. He was wearing a navy blue Fila running suit, zipped tight over his paunch to hide the 9 mm pistol nestled in the small of his back. He also had on a pair of fake eyeglasses to mask his threatening eyes. In the back seat was Tommy Reynolds, a slight twenty-four-year-old who was considered to be particularly dangerous. He wore a Fila running suit identical to Calandra's except for its white color. He clutched a .45 caliber pistol in his sweaty palms. Sitting next to Tommy was lanky Michael Yammine, also twenty-four, with a boxy, shaved head. Mikey was just along for the ride.

All four men enjoyed ties to the Mafia under the umbrella of the Bonanno organized crime family. They were used to carrying guns, especially Reynolds. This night they were out on business. Everybody understood the gravity of what was at hand.

Earlier that evening, the four men in the sedan had met at a two-bedroom apartment belonging to the Binger on Wellington Court, a very different street on Staten Island.

The Binger lived on the third floor in one of the hundreds of hastily erected, drab-brick condominium complexes all over the island. The building was close to Richmond Hill Road, a main drag routinely filled with traffic from the nearby Staten Island Mall.

That night, about an hour before his friends got there, a state marshal had tacked an eviction notice on the Binger's door. He and his roommate, another young handsome thug named Vinny Rizzuto, had not paid the rent in three months, and his landlord wanted both of them out.

The four men sat on a leather couch and watched a homemade pornographic video. Tommy Reynolds had stolen the tape during one of his home burglaries. When Tommy popped in the tape, the men gasped. They recognized the couple from the neighborhood, but they certainly looked a lot different in lascivious poses.

As the tape came to a climactic end, the Binger spoke. "My buddy Ira told me about this guy. This porno guy, Shemtov. He keeps all his money in a safe built into his basement floor. I'm hearing he has anywhere from fifty thousand to a million bucks in there. I heard he has three hundred thousand in there right now. We just have to wait for the phone call to make it happen. When the guy comes home, we'll get a tip."

The other three nodded. It sounded like an easy score.

"Okay," he continued. "What we are going to do is go in there, tie up the wife, and get the husband to open the safe, take the money and leave. No one gets hurt. Got it?" he added. "No one gets hurt."

A short time later, the Binger's beeper buzzed at his hip, the signal that Shemtov's car had pulled into the driveway. He looked at his cohorts. "That means the guy's home," he said. "We gotta go there right away. I'm going to drive because if they see me, they recognize who I am around here."

The four men were soon driving toward Shemtov's home. It took them about an hour to find the right road.

"Jeez," Yammine said. "How do people find their way home to this place?"

The small enclave of Meade Loop and its dozen-or-so

homes was barely visible from the passing through roads. No signs marked the block. It was tucked behind massive, leafy trees. BMWs and Lincoln Continentals were parked in every driveway.

The front lawns, now covered in snow, were land-scaped with expensive greenery, clipped by hired gardeners. Most of the homes boasted swimming pools, many with accompanying Jacuzzis. For all its wealth, though, Meade Loop was not about glitz. Its residents liked things quiet and out of reach.

Inside 95 Meade Loop, Judy Shemtov was filling a decorative teakettle.

The forty-six-year-old wife and mother worked out regularly and had the taut physique of a teenager. Her flaxen hair ordinarily hung just below her shoulders, but on the night of February 18, 1993, she wore it up, show-casing her bright blue eyes.

Judy's husband, Sami Shemtov, had just returned from a business trip. Sami was an Israeli who had im-migrated to New York in 1967. He'd earned an engineer-ing degree from a prestigious Israeli college, but he changed career paths after arriving in New York. He bought up a string of lucrative businesses—a chain of 99-cent stores and, law enforcement officials say, at least a half dozen pornography shops in Brooklyn and Miami. Sami also owned an electrical supply company based in Cincinnati.

The Shemtovs had been married for just under a year, and they still behaved like newlyweds. Sami's frequent absences just made their relationship stronger. They were planning a new beginning in Florida. Each had three grown children from previous relationships, children who had grown into successful and happy adults.

Even after her children grew up, Judy Shemtov took

pleasure in making sure the house smelled of freshly baked cookies. She'd been a stay-at-home mom who "relished her family," her son Adam would later recall. On that night, the house smelled faintly of cinnamon sugar from a cake she had made earlier in the day in anticipation of Sami's homecoming.

Judy had raised her three children alone after her first husband left, working odd jobs to make ends meet. Her priority was to make sure she was home after school every day for Arlyn, April, and Adam. "She would set aside special time to be alone with all of us," Arlyn says. "The essence of my mother was that she was a really great mom. She made everything fun and special."

Arlyn had introduced her mom to Sami five years earlier. Arlyn was working at the Cherry Tree Boutique at the Kings Plaza Mall in Brooklyn when Sami Shemtov came in with his own daughter, Dena. He was tall, dark-featured, and good-looking. He exuded the confidence of a man who was financially secure. He was also divorced. After Sami stopped back at the Cherry Tree a few times, Arlyn asked him if he would like to meet a beautiful blonde—her mother.

Their first date was like a dream. After that, Sami courted Judy like a gentleman out of a Victorian-era romance novel. He, too, wanted to move out of New York and start a calmer life in Florida. Sami's children, Dena, Richard, and Aaron, were also pleased that their father— who had already been married twice—had lucked into such a sweet, compatible companion.

Sami and Judy dated for four years, and married in 1992. They decorated the foyer of their home with a pink hibiscus tree identical to the ones that grow all over Miami. It was a touchstone to remind them of the sunny days ahead.

The kettle whistled, the water was poured, and Judy carried a cup of tea to her husband. Upstairs, Judy's twenty-three-year-old daughter, Arlyn, was getting ready for a night out with an old friend, Al Bello. Down in the basement, Patricia, the family's maid, was folding laundry. It was around 9:45 P.M.

Ordinarily when Sami and Judy settled in, they switched on the house's elaborate security system, including an alarm and surveillance camera. But tonight they were waiting for Arlyn's friend, and it was too raw to leave him shivering on the brick stoop while somebody fumbled with security codes to let him in. After Arlyn left, Judy figured, she'd turn it on.

Outside, a Mercury sedan approached. "There it is, Ninety-five," the Binger whispered. He drove past and parked a few houses over. The Shemtovs owned a showy ranch home with expensive brick front, the roof dotted with skylights. Sami's Lincoln Continental was parked in the driveway. An outside lamp lit up the front stoop.

Reynolds pulled a face mask over his head, fastened its Velcro backing, and looked at Calandra.

"Okay," he said. "Ready?"

"Ready," Calandra replied, fixing his own mask. Yammine pulled his mask down as well.

The three men stalked to the door, leaving the Binger behind in the car. They crept up the walk, past bonsai trees frosted with ice, and up the few brick stairs to the dark mahogany door.

"Make sure your safety is off," Calandra said to Reynolds. "Cock that thing, will you?" Calandra turned to Yammine. "Mike, you wait here."

Reynolds and Yammine nodded in unison. Calandra pressed on the doorbell underneath a mezuzah, a brass scroll the Jewish family hung to ward off evil. A jingle sounded from the foyer. Judy Shemtov jumped up from the table. "I'll get it," she told Sami. "It's for Arlyn."

There was no peephole or window near the door so she was unable to take a look outside. "Who is it?" Judy asked, as she turned the door's lock.

"The police!" Calandra yelled.

Before Judy Shemtov even turned the doorknob, Calandra and Reynolds slammed into the door like linebackers, knocking the petite woman backward into the foyer.

Inside the doorframe, Reynolds pointed his huge .45 automatic toward Judy's face.

"Where's the safe?" he yelled. "Where's the safe?"

"Where's the money?" Calandra demanded.

Judy was too stunned to speak.

"The money, where's the money?" Reynolds repeated.

Perhaps she didn't even know that Sami had a safe.

"Open your mouth," Calandra hissed. "Where's the fucking safe?"

Reynolds's heart was pounding with adrenaline. His finger tensed on the trigger.

"Are you Ari's mother?" Reynolds asked her. Then there was movement in the kitchen. A tall, slim man—Sami—was making his way to the foyer.

Reynolds spotted the movement and tensed up. His whole body tightened. With that, his finger accidentally squeezed the trigger. The gun muzzle flashed. They had only been in the house for less than ten seconds and the robbery was already botched.

A bullet tore through Judy's left cheek. Her small body flew into the air and slammed backward into the foyer, then dropped to the floor.

Blood splattered all over.

Calandra looked at Tommy Reynolds. "Let's make this one to go," he said, borrowing the line from his favorite movie *Goodfellas,* uttered by actor Joe Pesci after a mob hit scene.

Calandra then raced outside into the snow. Yammine was right behind him.

Sami ran in from the kitchen after the shot had been fired. The close-range blast had hurled his tiny wife nearly into the next room, her head crashing hard against the hardwood panels. Sami looked up and saw Tommy Reynolds running out of the house with a gun at his side. Sami locked eyes with the gunman and then ran over to his wife.

Calandra and Yammine were already at the car.

"I'm going to go to hell for this one," said Reynolds, who was near tears as he slammed the door shut. "This one, I'm going to go to hell for."

The Binger floored the gas pedal and sped off. "What happened?" he asked. But he knew. He had heard the shot.

He got nothing but silence in response. "You fucking idiots," he said quietly to himself.

As they raced back toward the Binger's house, the four men in the car made a solemn pact never to speak again of the incident.

After hearing the shot, Arlyn raced down the steps. "What happened? What happened?" She went to the door and looked outside, but no one was there. Sami was pacing the floor in shock whispering, "Oh, my God. Oh, my God."

Her mother was lying on the hardwood floor, in a spreading pool of blood. Aryln cradled her mother's head. Judy Shemtov could not speak. She only gurgled, choking on a thick gel of her own fluid. There was no exit wound. The .45 caliber bullet was lodged in her brain.

Shrieking at the gory sight, Arlyn picked up the phone to call 911. The emergency operator could not understand what the hysterical young woman was saying over her heaving sobs.

"Send an ambulance. Please!" she finally managed.

The 911 operator demanded she stop screaming so she could take down the address.

"I'm at ninety-five Meade Loop in Staten Island, New York. It's a private house. I don't know what happened. She got shot. My mother just got shot! I don't know how this could happen. My stepfather answered the door and she got shot."

Arlyn cried quietly for a few moments and gasped for air on the phone as the horrible truth sank in.

"Someone shot my mother!"

Again the operator asked where the wound was.

"I don't know. I don't know. Sami? What happened? Tell me what happened!"

The operator tried to calm her down. She told Arlyn to get a clean white cloth and put pressure on the wound.

Arlyn left bloody footprints on the hardwood floor as she rushed to the bathroom for a pile of fluffy white towels. When she got back, she dialed 911 for a second time.

"She's lying on the floor," Arlyn said, holding a towel to the gaping hole in her mother's face. "Please send an ambulance."

The operator told her there was one on its way.

"She's bleeding severely. She was shot in the head."

"Is she breathing at all?"

"She's breathing. She's choking. There is a lot of blood."

The 911 operator yelled into her radio, her voice

broadcasted to ambulances and New York City Police Department patrol cars: "Put a rush on the bus to ninety-five Meade Loop! Repeat. Put a rush on the bus!"

Meanwhile, the four men arrived back at the Binger's house.

"We're fucked," the Binger kept saying. "We're fucked. Everybody knows me around this area," the Binger yelled. "They're going to know I had something to do with this."

When the Mercury pulled up in front of the Binger's house, Tommy Reynolds coldly stared at him. The Binger was a tough guy, but the blank look in Tommy Reynolds's eyes scared him. There had already been one murder that night, and if the Binger said one wrong word, there could very well be another.

"Are you going to crack, you fucking pussy?" Tommy screamed. "Huh? Are you going to crack?"

Reynolds swiftly brought the cold barrel of a different gun to the Binger's head.

"If you pussy out on us, if you open your mouth," he warned, "I will kill you myself."

The Binger stood firm. "Tommy, if you don't trust me, kill me right now. I ain't no rat."

Reynolds lowered the gun. "Nah, nah, it ain't nothing like that." He pulled the clip that held the bullets out of the .45 and tossed it into some bushes nearby.

Then he walked out to the Mercury for the ride back to Brooklyn. "Let's go."

The Binger had got the message loud and clear, and underneath his fear he was furious.

As the three men sped along the lower deck of the Verrazano Narrows Bridge, the two-mile span that links Staten Island to Brooklyn, Reynolds rolled down his window and threw the remnants of the murder weapon into the white-capped waters of the Atlantic Ocean below them.

The flashing lights and sirens of the NYPD's Emergency Service Unit trucks, patrol cars, and ambulances invaded the usual calm on Meade Loop. Neighbors peered out their windows as Judy Shemtov was wheeled out to an ambulance. Detectives poured through the Shemtov house, dusting for fingerprints and collecting evidence.

Crime techs snapped pictures of the bloody spot where Judy Shemtov gulped her dying breaths. Patrol cops searched the area for men who looked like the fleeing perpetrators. A hasty description, given to detectives by Sami, was broadcast over all New York City Police Department radios.

"We are looking for two well-built white men in their twenties," a dispatcher said. "One was about five-feet-nine, five-feet-ten inches tall. The other was a little shorter. Both wearing zipped-up jackets."

Emergency room doctors at Staten Island University Hospital desperately tried to save Judy Shemtov's life. The medical experts knew their efforts would be in vain. Aryln's friend, Al Bello, showed up minutes after the carnage and drove her to the hospital. She had already broken the news to her family and her siblings, and their grandmother had rushed to join her for a bedside vigil.

Her brother Adam came home from a night out to a message on the answering machine: "Call me. Mommy's been shot. Someone shot Mommy."

Adam jumped into a taxi in front of his Manhattan apartment and called his sister April from his cell phone. She left in her own car. They both raced to the hospital in the Prince's Bay section of Staten Island. It was just after eleven o'clock when April rushed into the emergency room wearing sweatpants and a University of Buffalo sweatshirt.

"My mother's been shot. Where is she?"

A nurse led her into a room where her siblings and stepfather were huddled together, crying. The family prayed for a miracle. But on this night, their prayers would not be answered. Judy Shemtov was pronounced dead at 11:36 P.M. An autopsy photograph of the dead woman showed her lifeless blue eyes rimmed with black from the proximity of the fired gun. Her light hair was matted dark brown with dried blood.

Her mouth was still agape in a look of stunned horror.

A few days after what should have been an easy score, the Binger scoured the headlines of the *Staten Island Advance* and the *New York Daily News*. Judy's murder had made the front page of the *Daily News* with the headline: "Death at the Door."

The papers had been covering the ugly murder of the innocent housewife for most of the week, and he was hoping the story would start to die down.

Instead, reporters had interviewed the dead woman's family. Judy Shemtov's funeral service was held that Sunday at the Temple Emanu-El on Fifth Avenue in Manhattan, the largest synagogue in the world. The shaken family was photographed leaving the crowded service in grief, accepting flowers from other mourners. Her daughters—Arlyn, a pretty, petite blonde, and April, a beautiful, statuesque redhead—were wobbly, as if they would collapse if their brother, Adam, was not holding them up.

Adam had a few words from his family that he hoped would reach the ears of his mother's killers. "My sisters, our stepfather, and I are all completely emotionally distraught by this. It's getting worse rather than better. It's bad enough losing someone close, but then to lose them in this way, and even worse, not to know why it happened. . . .

"If there was one aspect of my life that I always relied on to be there for me, it was my mother. She was very happy with Sami. She had a great marriage and great friends. She was never happier."

Judy Shemtov's family offered a $15,000 reward for information leading to the arrest of her killers. Her devastated husband helped cops hang reward flyers all over Staten Island with her photograph and reward information, hoping the photograph of the strikingly beautiful woman would jar the conscience of anyone with information.

Detectives had nothing, said the commander of Staten Island's Crimes Against Persons Squad, Lieutenant Mary Zaleski. "All we know is she got up to answer [the door]. There are two males at the door. There is a brief exchange and then one of the males drew out a large-caliber weapon and shot her once in the face."

The detectives' first priority was to eliminate obvious suspects. Before Judy married Sami Shemtov, she lived with an aging bookmaker and World War II hero named Andrew "Andy Brain" Amato in Sheepshead Bay, Brooklyn. Amato, who earned the Purple Heart as a tail gunner for the air force, became a numbers runner and sometime counterfeiter following his years at war. In the days after the slaying, cops tracked him down and found that he was devastated by his former girlfriend's murder.

Judy and Amato had lived together for almost a decade, but had broken up because Amato could not afford to raise both her family and his own. Amato was so enamored of Judy he had a tattoo of her birth sign, Gemini twins, tattooed on his left arm with her name inked underneath. He was happy that Judy had finally married, but remained suspicious of her new husband. "I don't know much about this Sami," Amato told detectives. "This guy only deals with Jews, Italians, and Spanish people." Amato was questioned thoroughly, and even agreed to take a lie detector test.

Do you know for sure who shot and killed Judy?
"No."
Did you yourself shoot and kill Judy?
"No."
Did you plan or conspire with anyone to kill Judy?
"No."
Do you actually know the reason why Judy was killed?
"No."

Not only did Amato pass the test, he also had an alibi. He was quickly dismissed as a possible suspect.

Investigators pored through life insurance documents but found nothing out of the ordinary. Sami Shemtov had told investigators about the money in the safe. Detectives heard a rumor that Sami's son, Aaron, had bragged about his father's cash at Fillmore's, a Staten Island pub. Unfortunately, many of the young men at Fillmore's were small-time wannabe gangsters—like the Binger. For a time the detectives wondered if Aaron set the robbery up. There was no proof, though. Later the theory was debunked entirely, for it soon emerged that he was a good kid who loved his stepmother and respected his father. Then Sami told investigators his second wife, Carol, had stolen money from him when the couple separated years earlier, a charge that was never proven or even investigated. She was interviewed, denied being involved with the robbery, and was not considered a suspect.

The detectives were coming up empty. And the leads were drying up fast.

Yet the Binger was not comforted. He was constantly sick to his stomach. Try as he might, he couldn't write the shooting off as some woman in the wrong place at the wrong time. The Binger might have been a crook, but he was no killer. He had a mother of his own. Besides all that, what replayed over and over in his head was the gunpoint promise from Tommy Reynolds:

"If you open your mouth, I'll kill you myself."

Six long years passed and the memory never went away.

Even in 1999 the Binger would momentarily mistake attractive, older blondes cruising the street for Judy Shemtov. For a fleeting second, a slight woman with shoulder-length hair would look familiar—the way she carried herself, the unlined face. Of course, it never was. It couldn't be. But he had seen Judy's photo so many times. It was in every newspaper, hung from every lamppost on Staten Island. For a while, he saw her face every time he closed his eyes.

That was then. The Binger was a new man now. It was getting easier to shake off the memory of that horrible night. Today he lived in a waterfront palazzo and vacationed in exotic locales. He had catapulted himself to a very different place than the suburban ranch homes and condominium complexes of Staten Island.

He was Chris Paciello, South Beach nightclub king.

Ultimately, though, that freezing February night would come back to haunt Chris Paciello, and not just as a memory. It would haul him out of the dizzying world he had created for himself on the sunny shores of South Beach for a more familiar locale—New York City. It would drag him back to the company of thugs, including his old pal with the hair-trigger temper, Tommy Reynolds.

Running from the past was a loser's game. Chris Paciello was going to pay.

2

LITTLE CHRIS

Chris Paciello was born Christian Ludwigsen on September 7, 1971, to George and Marguerite Ludwigsen, the second of their three sons raised in a railroad flat on Thirteenth Avenue in Borough Park, a neighborhood in southwest Brooklyn, New York.

The Ludwigsens occupied the first floor of a gray-brick two-family house, one of many identical to it in a row along the avenue. Chris shared a bedroom with his older brother, George Jr., who was one year ahead of him, and younger brother Keith, who was one year behind. Even as a baby, Chris looked like a darker version of his father, with dark brown eyes speckled with amber and curly black hair.

In the early 1970s, Borough Park was largely home to Irish and Italian immigrants who had moved from tenements in Manhattan to apartments or small houses along the elevated train line that runs through Brooklyn to Coney Island. Bensonhurst, Dyker Heights, and Bay Ridge—three Brooklyn neighborhoods that became an extension of Manhattan's Little Italy—lie right around the edges of Borough Park. Brooklyn is part of New York City, but the borough's residents think of themselves as removed from its crowds, noise, and crime.

When Brooklynites travel into Manhattan they refer to it as "going to the city." And, for many, it is a trip best avoided. Still, it was an easy commute to anywhere from Borough Park. Within walking distance were Italian pork stores, clean Laundromats, and decent schools. Catholic churches still served as the heart of the community.

Across the street from the Ludwigsens' row house was St. Frances de Chantal, a majestic church built with marble and stone by Italian masons. The cathedral was decorated with beautiful, kaleidoscopic stained glass windows, and its majestic bells could be heard all the way to the Brooklyn shoreline.

As Chris came of age, the face of Borough Park changed. Scores of strictly religious Hasidic Jews moved in. Palatial temples and storefront synagogues replaced old movie theaters and butcher shops. Yiddish became the primary language on Thirteenth Avenue. The streets were deserted on Saturdays, the Jewish Sabbath. In Chris's neighborhood appeared boys wearing long black coats and sporting *pais*—curly ringlets that hung from their temples to their chins.

The shift in the neighborhood didn't faze the Ludwigsens. They had a nice apartment and worshipped in a nice parish. The streets remained safe. Borough Park was a good place to raise a family until that family could afford to buy a home.

The elder George Ludwigsen stood six-foot-three and weighed 245 pounds. He was a dedicated body builder who worked both as a clerk on Wall Street and as a bouncer tossing drunk and disorderly patrons out of Bay Ridge nightclubs during the height of the *Saturday Night Fever* craze. In fact, the movie was filmed in one of the neighborhood's discos.

Bouncing was a good job and paid well. A doorman had to be courteous and well spoken, since he could never be sure whom he was dealing with. A great number of disco patrons in Brooklyn were made members of crime families, and any slight—real or perceived—could prove dangerous to the club. A place could be torched, shot up, or even closed down by the city if the wrong person was barred entrance at the door.

George Ludwigsen was considered a pro and made a good number of friends standing guard at the discos. Stories abounded about how he had once thrown three rowdy guys out of a club with one arm, and about the time he had broken someone's jaw with a slap. George also became a celebrity as the wrist wrestling champion of the state of New Jersey, and ranked second in the entire country. George Ludwigsen's face became well known to locals during his appearances on *ABC's Wide World of Sports*. When he was on TV, Chris and his brothers cheered in their living room as Dad painstakingly grimaced his way through each victory.

On Saturdays, the days he would take his boys to Dyker Park to toss around a football, other fathers would shake George Ludwigsen's hand or try to finagle free passes to one of the discos out of him. Women would slip napkins with their phone number into his pocket, and, rumor had it, George often called them back.

In April 1975, George Ludwigsen caused a furor in the sports world. Without his having any pro or even college football experience, the famed New York City Giants, impressed with his strength, speed, and reflexes, recruited George Ludwigsen to participate in their summer training camp. To the scouts, George's fifty-three-inch chest, nineteen-inch arms, and thirty-four-inch waist compensated for his lack of a football record. His only real gridiron experience came from being the star of his

New Utrecht High School team, and playing in a park league called the Sixty-eighth Precinct, which was mostly comprised of cops and neighborhood guys.

Giants defensive line coach Floyd Peters explained that Ludwigsen was certainly "fighting a battle" but had a decent shot of a spot on the team's forty-seven-man roster. "He passes every test," Peters bragged. "The only thing I can't answer is, can he play football? The only way we can answer that is to put a helmet on him. To me, the big test is whether you can handle yourself in the pit."

On the first day at camp, Ludwigsen bench-pressed 495 pounds, 75 pounds more than any other player on the team. Then he leg-pressed 1,020—the machine could go no higher. He followed that up with twenty-nine chin ups and forty dips. During a lunch break he excitedly called his wife Marguerite. "The other players had college," Ludwigsen told her, "but I definitely have the desire. I won't quit. I may get beat, but I won't quit. A lot of people kept telling me I could make it. I've been wanting to go out for a while, and people kept saying, 'Why don't you go out?' So I decided to do it."

The Giants never added him to the lineup but, nonetheless, Brooklyn's own George Ludwigsen was still a hero for trying, especially to his little boy, Christian. He was just three years old when his father flirted with fame, but he boasted about it well into his teens.

As for Marguerite Paciello, she had been her husband's high school sweetheart. The small-framed, raven-haired beauty had a flawless dark European complexion and deep-set chocolate brown eyes. She was brazen and outspoken, and George Ludwigsen appreciated her. Most Italian girls from Brooklyn married Italian boys, but George was different. She fell deeply, madly in love with her giant protector. As a trained hairdresser, she sometimes took clients into her home, a common Brooklyn practice, but devoted most of her time to her boys, George Sr., George Jr., Keith, and Chris.

To everyone around them, they seemed like the perfect family.

In time, though, the bouncer circuit took a toll on George Sr. By the late seventies and early eighties he was coming home less and less. Marguerite was barely coping. She stopped cooking dinner most nights. Microwaved Swanson's TV dinners became the norm. When George was home, there were loud, heated arguments. Accusations of infidelity were hurled. Plates were broken, obscenities exchanged. The household became increasingly chaotic.

The disintegration reached a peak when George was shot five times by a patron he had tossed out of a disco called C'est La Vie on Eighty-sixth Street. The shooting happened in the predawn hours in the 1980s, just when cocaine hit the club scene. The discos were flooded with drugs. There were longer lines to get into bathroom stalls than there were behind the velvet ropes outside.

The club was one of the hottest discos in the neighborhood, a gaudy two-floor hotspot with velvet sofas and old-fashioned disco balls. The night he was shot, George had tossed some rowdy guys out. They came back later, and one of them pulled out a revolver and pumped George full of about a half dozen bullets, leaving him critically wounded. After he was released from the hospital, the pain continued to be unbearable. He began taking massive doses of painkillers.

In the age-old pattern of addiction, the prescribed narcotics eventually stopped working. George turned to cocaine and heroin. Before long, he was spotted by Brooklyn cops, the same neighborhood guys who had once idolized him, nodding out on heroin in a seedy doorway in Sunset Park.

By October 1982, George Ludwigsen had become a burglar to keep himself supplied with drugs. He was arrested a dozen times—always on burglary and larceny charges. Once, in May 1989, he was charged with grand larceny and criminal possession of stolen property. He was carrying a dirty hypodermic needle in his back pocket. A month later, in June, he was stopped for driving drunk in a stolen car, and he tried to put up a fight with his arresting officers. In 1992, George was still using drugs and he got locked up for possession of a controlled substance.

As George's rap sheet grew, he also caught the attention of the FBI. The government opened a file on him because of his apparent association with organized crime members. The FBI suspected he was running a sideline as muscle for Brooklyn mobsters. He had even adopted an Italian alias, identifying himself as George Lazzarro.

By then his last name didn't matter. His family wanted nothing to do with him—George Ludwigsen's downward spiral had damaged his children long before his name change.

Chris seemed so angry and withdrawn that teachers at McKinley Junior High School put him in a special education class so he could be given additional attention. He was shy and quiet, but he had a sharp mind, especially with numbers, and was a quick study. He made friends easily. His grades were mediocre, but he made it to high school.

There he started cutting classes, spending much of the day hanging around at the Gateway Car Service, a shop where there seemed to be an abundance of back room meetings held among older men while kids like Chris ran errands for them or washed their cars. At Gateway, Chris befriended two other like-minded young toughs: Enrico "Rico" Locasio arid Dominick "Big

Dom" Dionisio. The three of them made a fearsome trio, especially Dom and Rico, who were so tall. When the two of them were walking down the street, even the tougher men in the neighborhood remarked: "There go the Twin Towers." Chris formed another friendship at the car service that would follow him into adulthood with Gerard "Skeevy" Bellafurie, a rough-and-tumble Brooklyn kid with many connections. Skeevy and Chris were inseparable, but they could not have been more different. Chris was polished, with tight pants and steroid-enhanced muscles and slicked-back hair. He was soft-spoken, though, and had a tendency to stay in the background.

Gerard earned his nickname "Skeevy" because of his questionable personal hygiene. Besides that, he had a face that looked like it had seen a few too many beatings. Skeevy might have been portly and grungy, but he had a charismatic presence and a garrulous nature. Skeevy was the life of any event, spinning stories and telling tales about his escapades ripping radios out of cars or breaking into apartments.

Chris was more the quiet sidekick, but by no means a pushover. By then, Chris had already developed his own reputation for being a tough kid. Other kids began looking up to him at a young age, after he refused to hand his bicycle over to a gang of boys. The way Chris told the story years later, he was pedaling his bike when he got surrounded. "They told me, 'Get off the bike,'" Chris boasted. "No way I was getting off. I just got the bike."

The bike thieves slashed him across the right wrist with a box cutter to loosen his grip on the handlebars. Yet even as his wrist spurted streams of red blood, he held fast. It was not until the muggers physically pushed him to the ground and held him there did he let go of his bicycle. He still had the scar on his wrist as he entered adulthood, and it would become one of the identifying traits, along with tattoos, listed on his rap sheet.

The first entry on that rap sheet was entered around Thanksgiving 1987.

It was a chilly fall night and New York City Police Officer Mike Galletta stood on a corner outside the Alpine movie theater on Fifth Avenue and Bay Ridge Avenue, trying to stay warm. The movie theater marquee lights blazed *Lethal Weapon,* illuminating the cop's handsome face.

"There's no one going to be breaking into cars tonight," Galletta mumbled to himself. "Too damn cold."

Galletta, a plainclothes cop with the anti-crime unit of the Sixty-eighth Precinct in Brooklyn, led his district in arrest numbers. Earlier that evening, his commanding officer had complained that too many cars were being broken into. He wanted it stopped. NYPD brass was especially concerned about the area around the movie theater.

"People are getting robbed over there near the Alpine," the Six-eight third platoon commander instructed his 4 P.M. to midnight shift cops. "We got people parking their cars to go to a movie, and they're coming out to smashed windows and stolen radios. Now, plainclothes anti-crime, I want you guys to fan out around the theater and keep your eyes open."

That's what Galletta was doing. It was monotonous work, but he took it seriously. To him, everyone who lingered too long by a car window looked suspicious, even girls fixing their lipstick in side view mirrors. Finally his radio crackled quietly inside his zipped-up jacket.

"Criminal mis from auto in progress. Repeat. Criminal mis from auto in progress."

That was exactly what he was waiting for. A smash and grab.

"We have witnesses to two white males in a white car seen stealing car radios," the dispatcher announced. "The perps are in the vicinity of Bay Ridge Ave. and Vista Place."

Galletta jumped into his unmarked black Chrysler Grand Fury and raced to Vista Place, a few blocks away. He found a 1978 Dodge with a smashed driver's side window and broken trunk lock. Driving slowly away up the block was a white Cadillac. Galletta threw a red light on his dashboard, pumped his siren, and pulled it over. In the car's back seat were three car stereos and a "slim jim" device used to pop car door locks, and a hammer.

Sixteen-year-old Christian Ludwigsen was behind the wheel. Next to him sat fifteen-year-old Skeevy Bella-furie. Galletta issued tickets that required both teens to appear at the police station, and sent them home. After processing, Chris and Skeevy pleaded guilty to criminal possession of stolen property and paid a $100 fine.

This was Christian Ludwigsen's first arrest, but it would certainly not be his last.

Instead of being deterred from a life of crime after feeling the cold metal of the Smith and Wesson cuffs pressed against his wrists, Chris became a skilled car thief. He made a career out of stealing luxury cars and selling the vehicles and their parts to mob-run rings. As Chris made his start in the criminal world, he also began telling associates his father was dead. He disavowed drug use—except for a daily dose of steroids that he kept in a locked metal box under his bed—and harangued his older brother for getting high. "What's the matter with you?" Chris often screamed at George Jr. "You want to end up like our father?"

Eventually, though, it was Chris's life that most closely mirrored the waywardness of his father's. He became a burglar and a small-time thief. He became a body builder and a womanizer. And he, too, caught the eye of the FBI for associating with made members— gangsters who had been initiated into the upper echelon of New York City crime families.

He did not recognize it in himself, but Chris Paciello was fast becoming the very man he disliked the most: his father.

3

CROSSING THE GUINEA GANGPLANK

In the late 1980s, the Ludwigsen family moved out of their apartment in Borough Park to a tiny house on Staten Island. Among local thugs, this was known as crossing the "Guinea Gangplank," a reference to both the Verrazano Narrows Bridge that links Brooklyn to Staten Island and the area's ethnic population. The island across the Hudson River is fourteen miles at its longest point and five miles at its widest.

The Ludwigsens were one of the many clans who fled Brooklyn for the suburban pleasures of Staten Island. A half century earlier, Italian immigrants moved from tenements in Little Italy and the Lower East Side of Manhattan to quieter neighborhoods in Brooklyn. Now the city's newest émigrés—Chinese, Russians, Middle Easterners—were squeezing into apartments in the once vibrantly Italian enclaves of Bensonhurst, Bay Ridge, and Bath Beach. Among those abandoning the old Brooklyn neighborhoods were the rank and file of Mafia hierarchy.

The Boss of Bosses, Gambino henchman Paul Castellano led the way. Before he moved to Staten Island, he lived on the corner of East Twenty-third Street and Avenue R, in Sheepshead Bay, an ethnically mixed neighborhood of Jewish and Italian families. But as his Mafia clout increased, Castellano crossed the bridge to a sprawling mansion dubbed "the White House" by his underlings because of its stately pillars and high-tech security system and settled on a manicured lawn atop Todt Hill. The Boss lived in relative seclusion with his mistress—a live-in maid—and his wife in dysfunctional family harmony until December 1985 when Castellano was gunned down. The hit on Castellano was orchestrated by John "the Dapper Don" Gotti and carried out in front of Sparks Steak House in Manhattan with the help of another Staten Island resident, Gambino family turncoat Salvatore "Sammy the Bull" Gravano.

Gravano had occupied a tidy brick house in the aptly named neighborhood of Bulls Head before the government moved him and his family to Phoenix with the new name of Jimmy Moran, and gave him a new business, Brooklyn Bagels. Bonanno *consigliere* Anthony Spero, the one-time acting boss of the family, enjoyed a spacious estate in New Springville, lording over his underlings on the other side of the bridge in Bath Beach. Bonanno captain Gerry Chilli, and his son, Joe, a soldier, had a simple home in Bulls Head. Wiseguys from every family had moved in and spread out.

Just as Marguerite Ludwigsen and her sons were settling into Staten Island life, the area became the setting for a gangland drama that would become part of Mafia lore for years to come. From the moment a small-time mob enforcer named Constable "Gus" Farace gunned down Drug Enforcement Agent Everett Hatcher on a dimly lit street, the tale of the murder would be told and retold over card tables in the back rooms of smoky Italian social clubs and in detectives' squad rooms all over the city.

A few months earlier, Agent Hatcher, who was African American, swaggered into Staten Island to spread the word that he was a big-time buyer looking for cocaine.

At that time, the DEA had only a passing interest in Farace. The agency's intended target was Gerry Chilli, the Bonanno family *capo* who had since settled in Florida. Agent Hatcher was smooth, with fancy suits and all the street lingo, but no one, especially a black guy like Hatcher, goes to Staten Island, makes a few inquiries, meets a mob-associated dealer like Farace, and begins buying large amounts of coke off the bat. The whole deal would take time. Introductions would have to be made, identities established.

One of Farace's former cellmates at Rikers Island—where he was jailed on manslaughter charges—provided the first introduction, for a price of course. The inmate's cooperation with the DEA might have earned him a few prison benefits not granted to other inmates, such as conjugal visits, extra phone privileges, or increased gym time. But when an inmate is suddenly treated differently on Rikers Island, people notice. Eventually Farace's friend was moved out of Rikers Island entirely. Word traveled fast.

On February 28, 1989, Farace got a call. "Listen, Gus, you know that guy who introduced you to the black buyer?" a deep voice whispered into the phone. "Well, he went bad. You better be careful." The phone call got Farace riled up. He was about to meet Hatcher, and now he had to figure out whether the guy was an undercover. Just before 8:45 that night, he shoved a .38 handgun into the waistband of his pants, and climbed into a van with his cousin Dominick at the wheel.

A few miles away, Agent Hatcher sat in his unmarked car in their designated meeting place on a lonely stretch of Bloomingdale Road. He took the necessary precautions and conducted a field test by whispering into a wire transmitter taped to his chest. "Testing. Testing." His field team of five backup agents flashed their headlights to let him know he was within range.

In separate cars within a few blocks of each other, the agents waited for an hour. They were about to give up for the night when Farace pulled up in his battered white van. Without saying a word, Farace motioned to Hatcher to follow him. Hatcher used the wire transmitter to say that he and Farace were going to drive to a diner to talk about a deal. Hatcher wasn't worried. He had already bought one-eighth of a kilo of cocaine, a Big 8, and was making plans for a bigger deal.

"No dope, no money, just talk," his fellow agents remember his saying before the Farace meeting. "I've met this guy three times before, and there should be no problem."

The field team gave them a loose tail, worried about being spotted. But it proved too loose. The backup team got snarled in Staten Island's notorious traffic and lost their man. Then, on the way to the diner, Hatcher's wire transmitter inexplicably went dead.

This was the worst-case scenario: the field team losing with the undercover agent as he blindly followed a violent mobster and convicted killer. He could not radio for help. The backup guys could not locate him. Panicked, the backup team screamed into the radio. They beeped him. They beeped him again. A minute felt like an hour.

The field team raced back to the original meeting place—near Route 440 in the Rossville section of the island. The area was so remote that it had become a popular dumping ground for hit men following a piece of work. That's where they found Hatcher.

His body was slumped over the steering wheel. He had been shot twice in the head and twice in the torso at close range. The motor was running and the driver's side window was open.

An hour after the agent's body was found, a massive manhunt for Farace and his cousin erupted throughout the city. A federal task force of four hundred members of the FBI, DEA, and NYPD hit the streets running, pressuring organized crime families to give him up. The dragnet closed the Verrazano Bridge, making virtual prisoners of every person who lived on the island. Searchers kicked in doors and tracked down confidential informants.

President George Bush called Attorney General Richard Thornburgh and ordered prosecutors to seek the death penalty against Farace. It was the first death of a federal drug agent in the line of duty in New York since 1979, and Farace's capture promised one of the largest bounties posted at the time: $250,000.

At six-foot-two, Farace, who had a square, hard body bloated with prison muscles and steroids, had to go to great lengths to hide. He wore long-sleeve shirts to cover his identifying tattoos: a butterfly on his stomach; a green likeness of the Incredible Hulk on his right calf; "mom and dad" scrawled over a heart on his left arm; and a shapely woman with a hula skirt on his left calf. He also dyed his crow-black hair a dirty red, the color of dried blood, and grew a bushy beard. He began telling the few people he spoke to that his name was Tommy, even in calls to his wife.

Weeks dragged on without any sign of the most sought-after murderer in the country. Agents turned desperate and began locking up Farace's friends and family in an attempt to flush him out. His cousin Dominick turned himself in and decided to cooperate against Gus, furious that his cousin had gotten him into such a jam.

The FBI put Farace on their Ten Most Wanted list. The federal government decided to hit the La Cosa Nostra where it hurts—their pockets. Agents became as ruthless as loan sharks, shaking down every made man from South Beach on Staten Island to City Island in the Bronx.

"There has never been as intense an effort to put pressure on organized crime, and we have information that they were indeed feeling it," said Assistant U.S. Attorney Jerry Ross, the lead investigator in charge of the Hatcher murder case during the manhunt.

Farace was terrified. He was too scared to stay in one place too long, and too scared to go far from home. Still, he was brazen enough to hide from the Mob right under the Bonanno family's nose. One of his first hiding spots was directly across the street from the Chillis' Staten Island home. As Joe Chilli, Gerry's son, searched for Farace he was right across the street with Joe's sister, Babe Scarpa.

By most accounts, Margaret "Babe" Scarpa was a love-starved woman. Farace showed up at her place one night and plied her with kisses and caresses. The attention was a drug for her. She had the keys to a neighbor's house and they were out of the country. Farace had a place to hide.

Meanwhile, DEA agents arrested his wife and her brother on pot dealing charges to flush him out. Henry Acierno and his sister Antoinette were charged with running a drug ring that brought huge amounts of marijuana from Texas to New York. Farace's mother, Mary, was forced to put up her Staten Island home to get her daughter-in-law out on $250,000 bail, knowing that her son was the real mastermind behind the drug ring.

Still, Gus was nowhere to be found.

The Mafia, however, was feeling the most intense pressure. The law was pressuring all five New York City crime families around the clock, harassing them in their own social clubs. Card games and prostitution rings were broken up on a regular basis. Even Joker Poker video machines—a chunk of easy money that comes from the rigged games hidden in bars all over the city—were being seized. A mobster could not sneeze on the sidewalk without being hassled by an agent. No one was earning. The bosses decided something had to be done.

Wiseguys all over the city formed an unlikely alliance with law enforcement in hot pursuit of a common goal—find Gus Farace. Soon it seemed everyone was hoping that Gus Farace would turn up the same way Agent Hatcher had—bullet-riddled and dead.

Former New York federal Drug Enforcement Administration boss Robert M. Stutman made a chilling confession in *Dead on Delivery*, a 1992 book he coauthored with writer Richard Esposito. He went as far as to personally visit the Howard Beach, Queens, mansion of Gambino crime family boss John Gotti in an attempt to convince him to order it.

"I broke all the rules that bind a federal agent," Stutman wrote, "in a desperate bid to bring Farace either to justice or into the hands of the mob. I decided to visit John Gotti, the reputed top mobster in the country." Stutman said he drove to Gotti's home months before he retired. He threatened the Gambino boss with more and more "pressure" that would threaten his crime family's earnings from mob rackets.

"Farace whacked our guy. We want him," Stutman told Gotti.

"Maybe," Stutman wrote, "this mob don would also decide that Farace was better off dead."

While Gotti ignored Stutman's plea and refused to take the bait, others didn't.

Just before 9 P.M. on November 17, 1989, Mario Gallo sat in the hodgepodge of graffiti-scrawled wooden benches in a small checkers park at Eighteenth Avenue and Eighty-first Street in the Bensonhurst section of Brooklyn. He had a copy of the *Daily News* tucked under his elbow, but he was not reading it. He was the lookout, ready to signal his cohorts positioned around the corner when he spotted a gray 1982 Pontiac. The car belonged to Joey Sclafani's grandmother, and her grandson had borrowed it for the night.

Weeks earlier, Gallo had accompanied his friends Louie and Nicky Tuzzio to the bar of Forlini's, a restaurant behind the Manhattan Criminal Court on Baxter Street in Chinatown. The trio had gone to Forlini's for a meeting with two high-ranking Bonanno mobsters. When the group sat down and began to talk, the bartender made himself busy out of earshot, dusting the Polaroid pictures of celebrities and straightening a Catholic cross made out of a Palm Sunday reed that were hung over the bar's old-fashioned cash register.

Forlini's was the type of place where conversations could not be overheard, which is probably why the gangsters chose it. The jukebox near the door was loud and their fellow patrons were even louder, but they spoke in hushed tones regardless. This was business that related to all five New York City crime families.

Gallo and Nicky Tuzzio slid into a booth near the door, under a mounted deer head, and barked an order for a couple of beers. Louis Tuzzio approached the two men at the bar. Louis was a well-regarded tough guy built of muscle on muscle. He greeted the two Bonanno men with a European two-cheeked kiss of respect and sat down.

Louis "Louie" Tuzzio was on the verge of getting his "button," or becoming a made member of the Bonanno family. He and Farace had been friends since they were kids, but he was not going to let a boyhood pal stand in the way of getting straightened out, becoming a made man. Hell, he already paid his dues with Farace, throwing him $200 every week for six months while the wanted assassin was on the lam. He even picked up his mail for him. Now Farace was causing problems.

"We have information that he's hiding out in Manhattan with a kid named Joey Sclafani," the soldier added. "When you do this, draw this kid Joey out. His father is with John Gotti and Gotti doesn't want the kid hurt."

The young Sclafani himself was not opposed to gunfire. The year before, a plainclothes NYPD detective named Jimmy Harkins had arrested him for opening fire on a pimp and his prostitute outside the Narrows Tavern, a dilapidated bar he owned in Staten Island. Sclafani told the detective he fired the shots because he did not appreciate "riffraff" hanging around his pub.

The Bonanno associate—who had a reputation for making sure witnesses disappeared—was leery about leaving the Sclafani kid alive. "Ah fuck it, just blow the whole car up."

"No way, the kid he's with, his father is with John Gotti," the soldier argued. "Make sure Sclafani is not hit or we're all going to have even bigger problems."

Perhaps all of that went through Gallo's mind as he sat on that Brooklyn park bench waiting for Sclafani to drive past him in his grandmother's car with Farace in the passenger seat.

Louie Tuzzio waited nearby. Louie, who had a .38 pistol tucked in the back of his jeans and a .45 in his jacket pocket, leaned against his Cadillac parked in front of 1814 Eighty-first Street, just around the corner from the park. Nicky Tuzzio was sitting on a stoop across the street from his brother. James "Jimmy Frogs" Galione left his van, which the crew used for the legitimate job of installing windows, and lurked between two parked cars with a 9 mm.

But these were not exactly the best-laid plans. The van was registered in Galione's name—his real name. The hit was going to happen across the street from the Tuzzios' mother's house. And the Tuzzios' father was a cop.

Nonetheless, the Tuzzios had one thing going for them—Gus Farace's trust. They knew it was only a matter of time until the fugitive reached out to his old pals. Earlier that morning, Louie Tuzzio's beeper had buzzed with a Manhattan phone number. It was Farace. They were in business.

"Hey, it's me, Tommy," Farace said, using his code name. "It's getting hot up here. There's going to be a lot of cops up here for the Thanksgiving Parade. I want to relocate."

"Oh yeah?" Louie said. "No problem. Meet me by my mother's house at nine."

He hung up the phone and gave his brother a high-five. "Let's make it happen."

Just after 11 P.M. that night, a gray Pontiac drove westbound on Eighteenth Avenue, right past Mario Gallo. The driver was Joey Sclafani—the son of a reputed Gambino family wiseguy named Augustus Sclafani, and off-limits for any bloodshed. The passenger was a hulking redhead with a long, tangled beard: Farace.

The car stopped in front of 1814 Eighty-first Street in Brooklyn, outside the Tuzzios' living room window. Louie pointed his finger at the driver. "Joey, come here, I want to talk to you for a minute."

As Sclafani climbed out of the car, Nicky stalked up to the passenger side window, stuck a gun against Farace's head, and pulled the trigger. He squeezed his eyes shut, anticipating the splatter of blood.

Nothing. The gun jammed. The safety was on.

Farace fumbled with his own waistband to grab the weapon he had tucked in his pants, but before he could pull it out, Jimmy came out from between two parked cars, slung his gun hand over Nicky Tuzzio's shoulder, and blasted Farace, pumping nearly a dozen bullets into his head, neck, back, and legs.

Sclafani didn't know the Farace hit was sanctioned by the Mob and opened fire on Nicky Tuzzio and Jimmy Frogs with his own .38 caliber pistol. He squeezed off two rounds before Louie Tuzzio fired back, afraid his brother or Jimmy might take a bullet. Then he jumped into his car and squealed off toward Nineteenth Avenue. Mario Gallo jumped in the work van and sped away.

Nicky Tuzzio, high on fear and adrenaline, slammed the safety off his gun and started firing wildly in the air before Jimmy grabbed him and they ran down Eighteenth Avenue to Eighty-second Street, where they ditched their guns in some bushes.

When cops arrived, Sclafani was burping blood. He told detectives, "I was only trying to help my friend," and passed out.

An ambulance rushed Sclafani and Farace to Coney Island Hospital. Farace was pronounced DOA in the emergency room just before midnight. His pockets were stuffed with love letters to his wife.

"Mob justice isn't always swift, but it's always deadly," James Fox, the former head of the New York FBI office, said after Farace was killed.

Sclafani spent months at the hospital in critical condition, his kidneys seriously damaged. While Sclafani was recovering, the federal government charged him with felony possession of an unlicensed gun and harboring a fugitive. The medical examiner that performed the autopsy on Farace's body found a set of keys in his pocket. The keys belonged to a reputed Cuban drug dealer named Julio Bofill, who was hiding Farace in his apartment at 308 East Eighty-fifth Street on the Upper East Side of Manhattan.

Minutes after the Farace ambush, Jimmy and Nicky ran to Eighty-third Street and Eighteenth Avenue and stashed the retrieved guns with Jimmy's uncle. The uncle gave them a change of clothes, and the duo went to a nearby bar for drinks.

Hours after the shooting, uniformed cops from the NYPD's Crime Scene Unit snapped pictures of the carnage and collected shell casings as detectives canvassed the neighborhood looking for witnesses on the narrow block. As the cops stood in front of the Pontiac with Farace's body, waiting for the city medical examiner's van, a lanky, dark-haired man lifted the crime scene tape, flashed his driver's license to a patrol cop with his mother's address to prove he lived on the block. A patrol cop okayed him. The cop even held up the crime scene tape so he could back out.

Then Nicky Tuzzio revved the engine of his brand-new black Porsche and backed off the block. He drove past detectives as they listened to the block's residents—notorious for becoming deaf, dumb, and blind whenever some sort of mob activity disrupted their sleep—trying to convince the cops they hadn't heard a thing.

Nicky gutted the guns and hurled the pieces off the walkway that passes over the Belt Parkway from Bay Sixteenth Street and Shore Parkway along the brackish waters of the Narrows Bay. As the guns splashed and sank, the only light illuminating Nicky's face—almost blue from the cold winter wind off the water—came from the headlights of cars whizzing by and the beach-glass green bulbs that light up the Verrazano Narrows Bridge in the distance.

As a teenager Chris Ludwigsen had heard the Gus Farace story dozens of times in the months after his family relocated to Staten Island. The story was part of mob lore shared over drinks or coffee in the barrooms and social clubs of his youth. Yet Farace was still a role model to dozens of aspiring wiseguys, like Chris.

Staten Island's spacious lawns and decent schools were not the only draw for mobsters and their families. Guys like Paul Castellano wanted to settle into an area that was insulated from the probing eyes, and hidden camera lenses, of the law. Castellano had watched his underling John Gotti pose for one too many surveillance shots outside his Queens hangout, the Bergen Hunt and Fish Club, pictures that were later used as evidence against him. Also, Staten Island's law enforcement community paled in comparison to the police forces in the other boroughs.

Staten Island contained just three police precincts, with about a thousand cops total. By contrast, Brooklyn's twenty-three station houses supported more than eight thousand officers. The island's homicide squad is a small one, albeit comprised of some of the city's most seasoned detectives. But the patrol cops are often rookies. Even the prosecutor's office is often incapable of handling the sheer number of mob-related stickups and shootings on Staten Island. The Richmond County District Attorney's Office is the smallest in New York City. Some federal prosecutors felt the office could be easily corrupted because a few of its receptionists, filing clerks, and secretaries reputedly had "connections." Information about ongoing Mafia investigations was often kept close to the vest.

Even if there were enough law enforcement investigators for every wiseguy on the island, surveillance in front of single-family homes is a tough trick for even the best to pull off. In addition, younger gangsters preferred crowded, brightly lit bars to Old World social clubs, sites that are harder to bug. Furthering criminal convenience was the borough's geographical position smack between Brooklyn and New Jersey. It functioned as a literal bridge for that state's crime family, the DeCavalcantes, and New York mob organizations.

Still, no one family could claim total control of Staten Island. The criminal enterprises there were run by a mishmash of gangsters from all five of New York City's crime families: Gambino, Colombo, Luchese, Bonanno, and Genovese. That was all right, there were enough profits to go around. It quickly became clear to Chris Ludwigsen that the "Guinea Gangplank" led to a crook's paradise. Virgin territory: a perfect place for "button men" and wannabe wiseguys to earn in a borough where the homes were actually affordable.

The Ludwigsens were looking for a reprieve from the chaos George Ludwigsen's life had become in Brooklyn, and for a nice place to raise their boys away from the city schools crowded with bussed-in minorities. Yet shortly after the Ludwigsens settled into a neat townhouse at 17 Mercury Lane, the marriage dissolved. The drugs and the womanizing had taken its final toll. Marguerite had had enough. George was out, and she was left alone to raise their three rambunctious teenage sons.

Chris immediately stepped into his father's shoes to help his family. His younger brother Keith idolized him. "My brother raised me. My father wasn't around, but we're a strong family," Keith liked to brag. "My brother is a man. He would go to a gunfight with his fists. That's the way we were brought up."

Since Chris had to take on the role of father figure in Staten Island, his days at FDR High School in Brooklyn were over. He barely had a tenth-grade education, but the time was at hand to quit school and make some money. By day, Chris became a smalltime thief. At night, he attended high school equivalency classes at an alternative city-run program called ASHES on Staten Island.

His first order of business was a name change. Ludwigsen was not a very imposing name. Too often, it got shortened to "Luggy." Besides, most of his friends were Italian American young guns whose last names ended in a vowel. Those same *paesans* had already earned monikers, too, like "Gonzo" and "Skeevy," "Joey Gams" and "Big Dom." Chris, skinny and knobby-kneed with a head of black curls the consistency of steel wool, hated his last name.

His mother's maiden name was Paciello. So, at sixteen, Christian Ludwigsen became known as Chris Paciello. By then he had also picked up his nickname: the Binger, because, as one pal put it, "he fiends to rob people." If his friends stole two car radios, he had to steal eight. If they robbed one store, he robbed three. The only time Chris ever used his birth name was when he was arrested. Which would happen a lot.

While other kids his age toiled in high school, Chris

"the Binger" Paciello began spending all of his time in the schoolyard of a grammar school, PS 60 in Bulls Head. The teenage sons and daughters of high-ranking mobsters made it their unofficial clubhouse, a spot where they could lounge around, smoke cigarettes, drink beer, and brag about their fathers. It was just a few blocks away from Sammy the Bull's house. In fact, one of the locals hanging around with the new kid on the block was his daughter, Karen Gravano. The schoolyard was a hub for the offspring of wiseguys, like Vinny Rizzuto, whose father was "Vinny Oil," a reputed Gambino soldier. Jennifer Graziano, the daughter of alleged Bonanno captain Anthony "TG" Graziano, was also a schoolyard regular. So were Danny and Franny Costanzo—cousins whose fathers were connected to the Bonanno family. Roxanne and her sister Ramona, the gorgeous daughters of reputed Gambino soldier John Rizzo, were both in the PS 60 clique. Ray Merolle was another schoolyard regular. He ran a crew of car thieves so adept, they were dubbed "the Untouchables" by the cops on Staten Island.

Karen Gravano was dating one of Chris's good friends, Lee D'Vanzo, New York City mayor Rudolph Giuliani's first cousin. And Chris was dating both of Karen Gravano's best friends simultaneously, Love Majewski and Roxanne Rizzo. Of course, neither knew they were both vying for the attention of the same man. Like their fathers, Love and Roxanne were notoriously secret about their private affairs.

Dating for this group tended to consist of a girl sneaking out of her bedroom window to jump into a stolen car for a cruise to a club in Brooklyn or New Jersey where underage drinkers were not carded. The trick was to dump the stolen car in a remote place and sneak back in the window before dawn.

Both Love and Roxanne were tall, leggy, and voluptuous with long, shiny hair and almond eyes. Both were charismatic cheerleaders at different private schools. And both felt an irresistible attraction to dangerous men. Chris Paciello was a seductive cocktail of simmering rage and swarthy good looks. He usually had a pocketful of cash from robberies and stolen car parts. He was a gifted lover, as it turned out. His skills eventually led him to get a tattoo above his groin reading "Easy Money."

Soon, Chris was picking up Love in his white Buick Riviera, which of course had belonged to someone else before Chris stole it and changed its vehicle identification number. They'd take joy rides, go dancing, and make love. She began spending more and more time at the Mercury Lane townhouse near the Staten Island mall, where Chris lived with his mother and two brothers.

By this time, George Ludwigsen was gone. Feeding a habit somewhere, in all likelihood. When Love or any of his other friends asked Chris about his dad, his blunt answer was always the same: "He's dead."

Mr. Chris Paciello was the boss of the household now, ordering everyone around, even his harried mother. He fashioned a basement apartment for himself, with a freezerful of Swanson TV dinners. Love even saw Chris stab his brother Keith in the hand with a fork in a fight over a frozen meatloaf.

Chris and Love hung out at Fillmore's, a popular Staten Island bar. When Love could not make it, Chris went with Roxanne. The bar seemed an unlikely place for the minor league wiseguys that had overtaken it. It was more Irish pub than Italian social club. Still, numerous crimes were planned at the small round faux mahogany table in the back of the club. Unbeknownst

to its law-abiding owners, the bar became a virtual headquarters for Staten Island's break-in squads, burglary
teams, and stolen car rings.

Fillmore's was also where Chris Paciello got tight
with Ray Merolle—the leader of the Untouchables, at
the time the largest stolen car ring in the United States.
Merolle was only in his early twenties, but he had made
his operation a nationwide enterprise. Rumor had it he
often loaded stolen cars into massive ship containers
docked in Red Hook, Brooklyn, to send overseas. Ray's
specialty was "switching tags" or transferring a vehicle
identification number from a junked car to a stolen car
so it could not be tracked.

Chris earned Ray's respect first by selling him stolen car parts—the hood of a Mercedes or the bumper
off a Beemer. Then he graduated to selling him whole
cars, vehicles he sometimes stole from his next-door
neighbors.

"Chris could steal your car in the middle of the night,
then shake your hand over the bushes the next morning,"
Ray remembered with a sly smile. "He would rob his
friends' cars. His girlfriends' mothers' cars. That's when
we started calling him the Binger. He was the Mad
Robber."

Another duo that would become important to Chris
was Danny and Franny Costanza, cousins who were
aspiring wiseguys that masterminded a spate of ATM
robberies up and down the eastern seaboard. Theirs was
a simple, if brazen, enterprise. The Costanzas would
steal a bulldozer or a cement truck from a construction
site or a Con Edison work yard, plow it into an ATM
machine or night deposit box, grab the cash and flee
on foot, leaving the vehicle smashed into the side of a
bank.

The Costanza cousins, along with Paciello and Chris's

close friend from Brooklyn, Gerard "Skeevy" Bellafurie, formed the bulk of a ragtag crew of burglars that
called themselves the New Springville Boys—the name
they took from both the neighborhood they lived in and
the touch football team they played on.

By now Skeevy, who was only in his late teens, ran
his own car cleaning business across the bay in Bath
Beach. During the day, the Fillmore's crowd would hatch
their criminal plans there.

The New Springville Boys began robbing night deposit boxes and ATM machines regularly. The smash
and grab crews soon graduated to safecracking. Chris
proved to be adept at it, and in 1988, stealing safes out
of homes and smashing them open was almost a nightly
event, one friend remembered.

"Just hit it on the end, don't smash it," Chris whispered to another New Springville Boy after they had
robbed a safe out of Blockbuster Video on Hylan Avenue. They had burned the lock with a blowtorch and
during one rampage used a small metal tool to twist the
opening back and forth. "Nice and easy."

When their patience ran out, Chris picked up a sledge-
hammer and swung it. Finally the lock snapped and
sprang open. Money-filled envelopes poured all over the
floor.

"Nice." Chris nodded. "Very nice." He handed a wad
of twenty-dollar bills to one of the New Springville
Boys. "Hey." He grinned. "Go buy some new clothes.
Sergio Valente jeans went out ten years ago."

The more money Chris made, the better he treated
Love. What was in his wallet became extremely important to him. Yet he was prone to violent mood
swings, fueled in part by his increasing use of steroid
injections.

At one of his low points, he got into an argument

with Love. Afterward, he telephoned her incessantly, enraged that she refused to speak to him. In a fit, Chris went to her house and rang Love's doorbell. Her mother, Lorraine Majewski, answered it. "Chris," she said, "she doesn't want to see you right now. Go home until this blows over."

Chris ignored Lorraine and instead shoved her out of the way and stalked up to Love's bedroom. He threw his girlfriend over his shoulder "like a Neanderthal," Love later remembered, and took her outside to the Buick.

"I was crying," Love later told a friend about the incident. "I was kicking, screaming. It was horrible. My mom was separated from my dad. She didn't know what to do, so she called the cops. Chris was livid. He kept yelling, 'That cunt, that cunt!' The cops just brought me home and after a few days we both forgot about it. I was in love."

As gorgeous as Love was with her lingerie model's figure, bee-stung lips, and long highlighted blonde hair, she was just as insecure. Chris was a constant source of compliments. She was not willing to let him go, even as the fights and his bizarre behavior escalated. "He was my first love," she remembered. "I would have died for him."

Love might have forgotten about her mother calling the cops, but Chris didn't.

A few years before, Love's mother had reached a longtime goal. She had saved her hard-earned wages from a part-time job at the cosmetics counter in Macy's to buy her own car, a 1983 white Cadillac convertible Coupe DeVille with a black ragtop. She had taken the separation from her husband hard, and the car was her way of reinforcing her independence, to feel like a woman on her own.

One night Chris was dropping Love back off at home when she noticed two of the New Springville Boys screeching away from her house.

"What are they doing here?" she asked Chris.

"How the hell do I know?" he barked back. "What do I look like? A fucking psychic?"

Love ignored it and went up to bed.

A half hour later she heard her mother screaming. The smoke detector in her hallway had erupted in an earsplitting alarm. Love looked out the window and saw clouds of smoke billowing out of the garage. The entire house smelled like burned rubber and smoldering wood. Her younger sisters' bedroom was filled with gaseous fumes. She and her mother grabbed the crying girls and ran outside. As they stood in the front lawn in their pajamas, Love's mother spotted the source of the blaze.

Her beloved Cadillac had been torched.

"Who would do this? Who would do this?" she screamed. She turned her anger onto her eldest daughter. "This has to be your no-good friends! Who else would set my car on fire? Your sisters could have been killed. We all could have been killed. You have to get out of here."

In the confusion, Love completely forgot that she had seen Chris's friends pull away from her house. She called her boyfriend in tears and he raced over to pick her up. Love packed a bag, buried her face in Chris's chest, and moved out of her mother's house and into the basement at Mercury Lane. Chris did not have to ask his mother's permission. By then, he ruled the roost.

Not until years later did one of Chris's friends tell Love that Chris was the one who set her mother's car ablaze.

Then she remembered how strange it was that he

had begun driving a Cadillac only about a month after her mother's exploded. She remembered that Chris had given her mother $500 to "take care of the car" for her. He also gave Lorraine Majewski a bill of sale that stated the car had been sold to a junkyard.

Love had been around enough car thieves by then to suspect Chris had burned her mother's car for its vehicle identification number. It certainly was suspicious that he began driving a Caddy a short time later. But she was so deeply in love she didn't want to believe Chris could hurt her or her family.

Chris was hurting many people in those days. Determined to bulk up his lanky frame, Paciello had made the Richmond Avenue Health and Fitness club a second home. He worked out daily and began ingesting larger doses of steroids. He kept his injections and a needle hidden in a locked metal box, stashed alongside the illicit cash garnered from home and store break-ins, his latest form of employment. As his muscles expanded, so did his ego. Chris took to walking around like he was invincible, throwing himself wildly into fistfights sparked by the smallest slight. His burglaries grew more and more reckless as well, graduating from video-store break-ins to home invasions.

But unlike most of his *paesans,* Chris Paciello did not align himself solely with one crew for his crime sprees. Instead he jumped from one group of compatriots to another. In Brooklyn, he aligned himself with both the Twentieth Avenue Crew in Bensonhurst, and the Bath Avenue Crew in Bath Beach. In Staten Island, he hung around with the Untouchables and the New Springville Boys. Whoever was going to help Chris Paciello make money was his friend for the night.

And whoever crossed him was in line for a bloody beating with the hands and baseball bats of Chris's entire network of friends. Paciello usually emerged the victor in street brawls. But sometimes Chris picked the wrong target.

September 9, 1989, offered up such an occasion. That was the night that Paciello assaulted a police officer.

Danny Massanova was a plainclothes cop assigned to one of the most dangerous details in the NYPD, the narcotics squad. That September evening he was at his Staten Island home when the phone rang. His brother Anthony was in a panic.

"Danny," he said from a cell phone in his car, "guys are chasing us. Someone is ramming my car from behind. I can't lose them. We're on Hylan Boulevard. They're in a black Buick Grand National."

"Drive to the precinct, Anthony. I'll meet you there."

Tough, brawny Danny Massanova jumped into his personal car. His blood was racing, a reaction honed from years of protecting his younger brothers when they were kids. As he drove toward Hylan Boulevard he thought about how violent the teenagers around him had become.

We used to just get into fistfights, he thought. *No guns, no bats, no trying to run each other off the road.*

He spotted his brother's car in front of the One Hundred Twenty-second Precinct, Staten Island's busiest police station. Luckily, no one was hurt and Anthony had a trailer hitch hooked up to the back of his car, so the damage was minimal. Nevertheless, Massanova was furious.

He wanted to have a talk with the driver of the black Buick. Anthony knew where they could find him. The driver and his pals were notorious thugs in the neighborhood who had made themselves comfortable settling into the corner of Hylan Boulevard and Armstrong Avenue. When the Massanova brothers pulled up, a crowd of young toughs were leaning on luxury cars lined up at the curb.

In the thick of them was a muscled guy they called the Binger.

"What's going on?" Danny Massanova yelled. "Why are you guys chasing my brother?"

Silence.

"Listen, you idiots. I'm not leaving here until this is straightened out."

The Binger stepped out of the crowd, grabbed Massanova by the elbow, and pulled him aside. "We're not after your brother. Your brother did nothing wrong," he explained. "It's the guy he's with. He's got a problem with us."

Massanova was seething. "You could have killed somebody. What, you didn't care that you were smashing up the front end of your car? What the hell kind of sense does that make, ramming someone with your own car?"

"What, are you slow or something?" The Binger laughed. "It wasn't our car. It was a stolen car."

"I think you're the stupid one, asshole." Massanova reached for his badge. "I'm a cop."

"A cop?" The Binger's fist clenched.

Massanova didn't see it coming. The Binger sucker punched him in the face. Massanova hit him back. The fisticuffs flew for a few seconds before Paciello took off on foot, fleeing down Hylan Boulevard.

"Get the bats!" Paciello yelled over his shoulder as he booked down the street. "Get the fucking bats!"

Danny Massanova, still numb and bent over from

the exchanged jabs, looked up just as another muscle-head came at him with a Louisville Slugger from behind. As he spun around, he zipped open a fanny bag around his waist and pulled out his gun. He pointed the revolver square at his assailants. The bats clinked to the ground.

By then witnesses had started calling 911. A call was broadcast over police radios. "Assault in progress at Hylan and Armstrong."

A radio patrol car screeched toward the corner. Massanova jumped in front of it. "I'm a cop!" He held up his silver shield.

Off-duty fights are always messy for cops. There is plenty of explaining to do, and lots of paperwork to fill out. Massanova was in the back seat of a patrol car scribbling out his version of events when he glanced up and saw that Paciello had returned.

"I can't believe it. This kid has got *some* balls. That's him. That's the guy."

A sweaty Paciello had sauntered right past the patrol car, the keys to his white Cadillac El Dorado dangling from his hand. As he twisted the key into the door lock, a patrol cop cuffed him.

"You're under arrest for assaulting a police officer."

The Binger smirked. He was only eighteen years old and it was his third arrest. This time it counted. He just earned the first entry on his rap sheet charged with assault in the third degree and harassment. He pleaded guilty and was given a conditional release, or probation.

Now Paciello had to keep a low profile. If he got arrested one more time, even for spitting on the sidewalk, he would be thrown in jail.

By then, Chris tried to take a step back from the New Springville Boys and the Untouchables and began cultivating a new group of friends, guys from Bath Beach. The Bath Avenue Crew had already moved on to bigger things than smash and grabs. They were making money and they had Mafia clout. Chris wanted to know them.

4

BATH AVENUE CREW

While little Chris Ludwigsen first flirted with gangster life via the knock-around boys who hung around outside the Gateway Car Service in Borough Park, a few miles away in Bath Beach some other young hustlers made their bones at Nick's Candy Store, an arcade and baseball card shop. Nick's was located at Bay Sixteenth Street and Bath Avenue, next door to the Pigeon, a Mafia social club where Bonanno associates and made men checked in with the area's onetime boss who was now being described by the government as the family's *consigliere*: Anthony Spero.

When the kids from Nick's were not playing Pac-Man at the candy store, they were running simple errands and washing cars for the older guys who played cards and got into animated debates in their native Italian over cups of espresso served on rickety tables in the Pigeon.

Over time, as they matured, the youngsters' assignments escalated into numbers running, thievery, drug trafficking, and loan-sharking. The older men in the Pigeon had begun calling them *il malandrini*, or wannabes. But by then the boys had given themselves their own name: the Bath Avenue Crew.

Bath Avenue is the main thoroughfare in Bath Beach,

and has long been described as one of the Mafia's historical Main Streets, a hotbed of criminal activity. For more than thirty years, it has been home to wiseguys and their families, a host of mob-run social clubs, and more than its share of gangland hits.

The tranquil bayfront neighborhood began as a booming resort town complete with sandy beaches and surf a century ago. Then, during the postwar building boom, the beaches along the bay were wiped out and replaced with single and two-family brick houses.

Bath Beach, less densely settled than neighboring Bensonhurst, boasts both the world-class Dyker Golf Course and a waterfront park that bustles year-round with skaters, joggers, and bicyclists. It was a nice place to raise children. It was also a great place to be a wiseguy.

The Pigeon could be missed if someone did not know where it was, which was precisely the point. It was a small store on the ground floor of a brick apartment building marked only with a tiny sign that read HPC—an acronym for Homing Pigeon Club. But everyone just called it the Pigeon.

Anthony Spero was an expert at the sport of raising and racing homing pigeons. He built an elaborate coop—which housed some extremely rare birds and was the envy of fellow racing pigeon aficionados everywhere—on the roof of the Big Apple Car Service, a business owned and run by his daughter, Diana. Spero was a gray-haired man who barely stood five feet tall and preferred cardigan sweaters to tailored suits. Quiet and unassuming, he often sought out the company of his birds rather than the conversations of his much younger underlings. During his years as a Bonanno kingpin, Spero learned from his flashy friend John "the Dapper Don" Gotti how to avoid the government's wiretaps and surveillances. "Baseball, football, women," is what Spero usually liked to talk about remembered one aspiring wiseguy. "Organized crime, Mafia—anything like that has never come from his lips."

The father figure for the Bath Avenue Crew was an Old World-style gangster, Joe Benanti. He was a nattily dressed tough guy who used to hold court in tailored silk suits and fedora hats with a glass of J&B Scotch clutched in his meaty fingers. Back in his day Benanti had been the king of the heists, mostly commercial robberies with no victims and no witnesses. He had done some time as a young man and had mellowed when he got out of prison, even counseling his young underlings to stay away from "The Life." Spero, too, seemed to loathe unnecessary violence, and often tried to be a peacemaker when the young mob wannabes got out of hand. But his warnings often went unheeded, especially in regards to the members of the Bath Avenue Crew who were determined to immerse themselves in the gangster lifestyle. The unofficial leader of the crew was a dark-haired handsome thug named Paul "Paulie Brass" Gulino. His boys numbered about a dozen in all, but there were about six key players "on record" with Gulino: Chris's old friend Tommy "TK" Reynolds, as well as Jimmy "Gap" Calandra and Mikey Yammine, Fabrizio "the Herder" DeFrancisci, Georgie Adamo, and Little Joey Dellatore. And just as they looked up to the older guys at the Pigeon, *malandrini* like Dean Benasillo looked up to them.

Like the Staten Island youngsters Paciello was running with, the Brooklyn boys spent a lot of time cutting school to smoke cigarettes and drink beer in a schoolyard, the park at Public School 200 in Bensonhurst. They spray-painted their "tags" or graffiti names on the sides of trains and brick walls. On the weekends they competed on a flag football team for money on a field at Bay Fiftieth Street, wearing T-shirts emblazoned with

"Bath Avenue," a street so entrenched in the Mob, the shirts deterred other teens, even those who lived outside of Brooklyn, from bothering them. They ate dinner at each other's houses, and went on dates together. Most Saturday nights the crew would drive into Manhattan to dance at the hottest discos, hotspots like the Funhouse and Webster Hall.

Dean Benasillo was a promoter at the Tunnel and threw "Bath Avenue Crew" parties there on Thursday nights in the nightclub's Shampu Room. Jimmy "Gap" Calandra's brother John was the doorman, and made sure even the toughest-looking thugs got in without any hassle. Where there was one member of the Bath Avenue Crew, there was always another. The crew was inseparable. They did everything together, including a plethora of crimes: drug deals, burglaries, and shakedowns. They were stealing cars, collecting gambling debts, and giving beatings, anything to make a buck. When they traveled in a pack, they were a fearsome group.

One of the crew's first forays into the crime world came when the members were barely sixteen years old. They had come up with a scheme to shake down the owner of a used car business in Gravesend, Brooklyn. The owner of the business had reportedly been turning back the odometers of his used cars before putting them in a lot. So the boys decided they would threaten the owner, and force him to turn over cars and protection money using extortion tactics they had learned from watching the older guys at the Pigeon.

"We talk to the owner," Mikey Yammine later remembered. "We said, 'Listen, we're taking this car, and we're taking this car, and plus we want money every week because we know what you're doing, you're messing around, and we don't want to hear it.'" The terrified owner told his tormentors he would have to talk to his partner, and to come back later. They did. The second owner of the business was not about to be shaken down by a bunch of teens. "Get off my lot! I ain't paying nobody nothing."

"We're arguing back and forth," Yammine said. "We're threatening him, saying that we're going to break every window in there and firebomb the place if we have to. We're not leaving here with empty hands. Then the [NYPD] Anti-Crime Unit pulls up to the place. They tell us lift up our shirts to see if we have weapons on us. They search us."

As the cops questioned the young thugs, the second owner became so incensed that he pulled out his own gun and aimed it at Yammine. The cops quickly moved to calm him down. As they put the car dealership owner in cuffs, the cops turned to the members of the Bath Avenue Crew. "Beat it," one officer told them. "Go pull this shit in your own neighborhood."

Members of the Bath Avenue Crew cohorts went on to follow that cop's advice.

At an early age, Paulie Brass Gulino took on the leadership of the crew, using his namesake "big brass balls" to boss around the others. Gulino was not all bluster. He was swarthy and charismatic, and quick with both his fists and his mouth. He came up with the idea for crew members to have "shooter tattoos"—tiny numerals—inked into the their ankles, signifying both crew allegiance and a willingness to take on any assignment for the Bonannos, including murder.

Paulie "Brass" Gulino got a tiny 1.

Jimmy "Gap" Calandra inked a 2.

Tommy "TK" Reynolds was 3.

Fabrizio "the Herder" DeFrancisci tattooed the 4.

Mikey Yammine had 5.

Anthony "Gonzo" Gonzales was 6.

Joey "Crazy Joe" Calco was 7.

Calco was the last to be inked. He thought it was a stupid idea, and mumbled to anyone who would listen: "Mafia people don't get no tattoos."

"We were like the hit squad," Yammine later remembered. "The tattoos meant you shot. We carry guns, and whatever we had to do. If we had to go shoot somebody, we'll go shoot somebody."

The Bath Avenue Crew ingratiated themselves with Anthony Spero through Bonanno soldiers like Joe Benanti. One by one, members of the crew were "put on record," officially paying proceeds from most of their crimes to liaisons who funneled the money to the top— Spero himself. The reward for these payoffs was mob protection, the ability to drop mobsters' names if things got hairy on the streets. *"Hey, you know who I am? I'm with Joe B."*

Tommy Reynolds and Georgie Adamo were the closest of crewmembers. Every day after school, Tommy would walk home with Georgie to help his little sister, who was handicapped, get off her school bus. Georgie's mother was out working, raising her children alone after her husband was murdered in October 1975. Little Georgie had been just an infant when the police came to the Adamos' Bensonhurst home to tell his mother that they found her husband and another man slain gangland style in the back of a stolen van parked in Brooklyn. The two had each been shot in the head, and their bodies were wrapped in a blanket and tied up with cord.

Investigators believed the elder George Adamo had ties to the Gambino crime family, and may have been involved with a $30 million heroin ring. Adamo also may have been close to a high-ranking Gambino guy, Carmine Consalvo, who had died a month earlier after he mysteriously fell from the twenty-fourth floor of a New Jersey high-rise apartment building.

After George Sr.'s demise, Anthony Spero immediately stepped in to take care of the dead man's widow and children. Little Georgie Adamo was christened Spero's godson and Anthony cherished him. Georgie and his friends grew up under the watchful eye of the Mob. As the boys got older and entered their teens, they graduated from running errands and washing cars to committing crimes. The mothers of most of the crew wanted their sons to have nothing to do with the gangsters, but they were powerless.

The early 1990s brought busy days to Bath Avenue.

Paulie Gulino, who by then was in his late teens, had started a cocaine and pot business using an elaborate system of beepers to keep track of his dealers and his customers. His bases of operation became public parks in Bensonhurst and Bath Beach. Dealers would stand in the park with $10 bags of marijuana, while younger kids—called Chickees—acted as police lookouts.

Paulie was making a lot of money, and so were the upper echelons of the Bonanno family. He raised the cash factor by extorting money and drugs from dealers who were not protected. He also became obsessed with elevating himself in the ranks of the Mob. His friends and family remembered that every move Gulino made was an attempt to get "straightened out" to become a "button man," a made member of the Mafia.

Paulie's rank in the Mob reached a new level September 17, 1991, when he had to carry out his first Mafia contract: the murder of a twenty-five-year-old burglar named Vincent Bickelman. Bickelman was a small-time hood and a junkie who fed his drug habit by robbing Bath Beach homes. Months before he was killed, Bickelman robbed the wrong house. It belonged to Anthony Spero's daughter, Jill.

Bickelman gave himself up when he showed up at PS 200 hours after the robbery wearing a thick gold chain offering to sell a dog collar made out of gold and beset with diamonds. "He looked all stoned out," Yammine later remembered. "He comes over to us and says, 'I got all this jewelry for sale. I'll take drugs or money.' We come up with the plan that we're just going to beat him up and take the jewelry from him. We beat him up badly and left him like for dead on the floor. We took all the jewelry."

After the crew divvied up the proceeds from Spero's home, a problem emerged. The boys had told Gulino about beating and robbing the young burglar and their leader immediately became nervous. "By any chance did there happen to be a round pendant, like a dog collar?" Gulino asked.

"Yeah," Yammine answered. "Mario's got it."

"You're going to have to get it back," Gulino said. "Spero's daughter's house got robbed last night for jewelry and they took a pendant off her dog's neck."

Gulino collected the jewelry from his underlings and handed it over to Joe Benanti. A short time later, Gulino paged the Bath Avenue Crew shooters, including Yammine and Calco, who later recalled their leader's words: "Listen," Gulino said. "I just got the order to kill Vinny Bickelman from Anthony Spero. All right? They want to make an example out of him."

Gulino could barely contain his excitement. It would be his first contract hit and carrying it out correctly could be a step toward becoming straightened out. Gulino sent Yammine and Gonzo around the neighborhood checking crack spots, and roughed up other addicts looking for the young burglar. They knocked

on doors and asked around. Their orders were to find
Bickelman and beep Gulino when they did. Gulino was
intent on being the gunman.

On September 17, 1991, Gulino got his wish.

Bickelman was leaving a Bath Beach bar when he
spotted Gulino and Jimmy Calandra coming toward
him. He took off running with the two men in close pursuit. As Bickelman darted toward his Bath Beach home,
Gulino closed in and shot him six times.

The following day Gulino met Yammine in a Bath
Beach park. "I got him last night," Gulino said. "I killed
him. I shot him through his hand, then I shot him five
more times in the chest area." Then Gulino shoved a
heavy Ziploc bag in Yammine's hands.

"Go get rid of these," he said. In the bag were six
empty shell casings.

Without a word Yammine took off on his bicycle and
pedaled along Shore Road. He hurled the bullets off a
footpath crossing the Narrows Bay and into the ocean.

With Bickelman's murder, the Bath Avenue Crew's
Bonanno crime family clout had been cemented. But
before the crew could celebrate their new status, one of
their own was killed.

On December 30, 1991, a crack cocaine dealer stabbed
Georgie Adamo in the heart.

Like many of the younger Brooklyn kids, Georgie
had developed a drug problem. Detectives were told
Adamo tried to rob a drug dealer named Fat Stevie Romano at knifepoint. The dealer grabbed the knife from
him and plunged it into his heart. Then the dealer went
on the run. He knew whom Georgie Adamo was connected to.

Georgie's death devastated the crew. Paulie Gulino
immediately vowed vengeance. "We got to get revenge,"
Gulino told the crew. "It's our friend. It ain't right what

happened." With that, the Bath Avenue boys scoured the streets looking for Fat Stevie. They told Fat Stevie's friends: "You got to bring this kid in and they got to get killed." Months went by, but he was nowhere to be found.

Mobsters from other families approached the Bonanno family on Fat Stevie's behalf, asking for mercy, swearing that the fatal stabbing had been a mistake. But there would be no mercy.

Then Crazy Joe Calco got word that twenty-one-year-old Neil Nastro was helping Stevie hide out. Calco and Tommy Reynolds decided to send Fat Stevie a message by whacking Nastro. They reached out for him.

"Hey, Neil, I need to pick something up from you," Joey Calco told Neil over the phone. "Meet me at the corner of Bay Seventh Street and Cropsey Avenue. I'll be there around two o'clock."

It was October 18, 1992—almost a year after Georgie Adamo had died. Still, Neil Nastro was nervous and brought along his uncle, Vincent DePippo, a tough forty-five-year-old Vietnam veteran, in case there was trouble. The two arrived in a 1988 burgundy Pontiac at the meeting spot. Tommy and Crazy Joe climbed into the back seat.

"What's the matter? What's going on," Nastro asked Calco when he spun around and saw the glares the two men were giving him. "Are you all right?"

Without saying a word, Tommy pulled out a gun, grabbed Nastro's neck, and ordered him to hand over his cash and cocaine. Terrified, Nastro reached under the seat and handed a package and a pile of bills to Reynolds.

"Where's the rest of it?" Reynolds asked.

"I don't have any more," Nastro answered. He was nearly crying. Then his uncle turned around. "What the fuck do you want?"

Reynolds answered him by putting a gun to his left cheek and pulling the trigger. The gunshot blast killed DePippo instantly. Nastro began to scream, "Oh no!"

Reynolds turned the gun to Nastro and blew off the back of his skull with a single round.

Tommy and Crazy Joe fled the scene in a getaway car driven by Willie "Applehead" Galloway, whose nickname stemmed from a large head and a tendency to flush hot red when excited. As they raced back to Staten Island, they pulled over on the Verrazano Bridge where Calco got out of the car and hurled the murder weapon and his own gun into the water below.

The night before, Calco had shaved bullets fitted for his .38 Special with a razor so he would not leave traces of the barrel of the gun. He had also engraved a cross on the front of the rounds—actions he said he had "seen on TV and in magazines."

Cops and reporters identified Nastro and DePippo as low-level associates of the Colombo crime family. Everyone wrote the murders off as two more casualties of an ongoing Colombo war. That took the heat off Tommy and Crazy Joe. They were not even suspects. Their names would not come up until much, much later—at least not to law enforcement.

The Mob, however, was another story. Nastro had worked for a Luchese soldier named Frank Gioia who was livid that his underling was murdered and saw it as a sign of "disrespect." He immediately ordered that Nastro's killers be whacked. Bath Avenue Crew leader Paulie Gulino stepped in, telling Gioia: "Reynolds and Calco meant no disrespect by their actions." After a number of sit-downs, the matter was squashed.

As the Bath Avenue Crew became more entrenched in the Mafia, they merged with Chris's crew from Staten Island—the New Springville Boys, also affiliated with the Bonanno crime family, but reporting to reputed *capo* Anthony "TG" Graziano.

Applehead Galloway, who grew up in Brooklyn but moved to Staten Island in his teens, oversaw the merger. Galloway was close to guys in both crews, and introduced them to each other at clubs and parties.

At that time, Chris Paciello was part of the Bath Avenue scene during his days hanging out at the Gateway Car Service, but he was not an official crew member. To them, he was just the Binger, the Mad Robber, a car thief and small-time burglar. He was merely a kid who hung around the neighborhood once in a while. He did incur the ire of Crazy Joe Calco. Every time the crew got together, there was tension between both hulking, handsome men.

Still, Bath Avenue guys tolerated Chris because of his childhood friend Gerard "Skeevy" Bellafurie. "He wasn't our friend," one Bath Avenue Crew gangster remembered. "But he liked to keep us a phone call away. He would never keep a close friend because of money. The Binger did not want to share his money."

The Binger might not have shared his money, but he was good at making it. With the New Springville Boys, he continued to mastermind strings of ATM robberies, night deposit box thefts, and home invasions. He was also stealing cars with abandon.

"These guys are earners," Applehead bragged to the Bath Avenue Crew.

Soon after, Applehead, Jimmy Gap, Paciello, and Skeevy started robbing commercial establishments. They stole a safe out of Fillmore's, one of their hangouts. They broke into a pet store on Staten Island. They smashed open dozens of night deposit boxes. True to form, Paciello would grab any opportunity to rob, even if the victim was someone he considered his friend. Once, he had hotwired his next-door neighbor's Ferrari, making off with it just eight feet from his own front door.

Perhaps Chris felt some remorse, because in the summer of 1991 he helped Ray Merolle—the leader of the Untouchables—pull off his most dangerous escapade yet. It started one day when Merolle stopped by to inspect a car Chris had stolen. Chris greeted Merolle and waved him over to a Cadillac in his garage.

"So," Chris asked, "know anybody looking for a beaut like this?"

Inside was a fully loaded blazing white Seville. Before they could talk about price Merolle's pager vibrated. It was his father who had a message that a hurricane was heading for the marina where Ray's cigarette boat, *Petty Cash,* was docked. Somebody had to go batten down the hatches.

"Hey, Chris," Merolle said, "wanna take a ride? I have to take care of my boat, and you can help me out. I just have to pick up my brother Keith. He can hook us up with some rope."

They left to pick up Keith. As they made their way to the Nichols Marina on the Staten Island shoreline in Great Kills Park, the overcast sky gave way to a misty drizzle. Storm clouds the color of newsprint rolled in hard and fast. A downpour was imminent.

It was July 23, 1991. As they approached his boat, something made Ray look around. Maybe it was criminal instinct.

A handful of men in wool caps and yellow slickers darted around the decks of other boats, arranging fishing equipment. Ray nodded to one guy wearing a black wool cap with white sneakers, a dead giveaway that he was no fisherman.

"What are they going to fish for around here?" Ray whispered. "Dead bodies?"

"Who knows?" Paciello quipped. "Maybe they're looking for Jimmy Hoffa."

The moment Paciello and the Merolle brothers boarded *Petty Cash* the "fishermen" surrounded them.

"Freeze mutherfuckers! It's the police!"

The hurricane warning called into Ray's father's home was a ruse to lure his sons to the marina. By then, Ray Merolle had really made an enemy out of the NYPD, and the commanding officer on Staten Island, Chief William Allee, wanted him taken down.

"Don't move! Don't move!"

Chris Paciello and the Merolles put their hands in the air. Their wrists were quickly cuffed behind their backs.

"You are under arrest," one cop yelled as he pulled his detective's shield out from under his yellow slicker. "Possession of stolen property. Altered vehicle identification numbers. We've been watching you. You're in some serious shit now, Merolle."

Paciello did not even have to ask why they were under arrest. He never thought Ray Merolle would spend $60,000 on a boat when it was just as easy to steal one. The boat had been reported missing months earlier by a Staten Island union official.

At the police station, Ray immediately took responsibility for the stolen boat. He told the district attorney repeatedly that it was he alone, and not his brother or Paciello, who was responsible.

The district attorney didn't buy it. All three men were charged. And this time it wasn't petty-ante charges, like a stolen radio or a fistfight. They were facing long sentences. Paciello saw only one way out: get rid of the evidence.

Ray Merolle found out *Petty Cash* had been towed to a city impound dock at Randall's Island in the Bronx. The dock, part of the NYPD Harbor Unit's launch re-

pair shop and taxi unit, was located behind the city's
fire department training academy.

Paciello took the better part of a week to stake out the
Harbor Unit's cops. He memorized their faces and when
they took their breaks. He took note of which cops spent
their shifts reading the paper and who seemed the most
alert.

Finally, on a Friday night, they were ready.

Dressed head to toe in black, complete with a black
wool face mask, Paciello cut a hole in the chain-link
fence that circled the Harbor Unit's dock. Chris and the
Merolle brothers crawled on their hands and knees
through the brush and dirt until they reached the boat.

Chris Paciello took a deep breath and waded into the
rank-smelling water. He held a tiny blowtorch over his
head as he sloshed toward *Petty Cash*. When he got to
the side of the boat, he applied the small flame to the
vehicle identification number. Then he used a knife and
scraped off whatever was left of the digits. The scratched-
away numbers took care of the altered VIN charge.

Over coffee at the Victory Diner on Staten Island,
Ray Merolle continued to be worried. "There's still the
boat," he said. "They can still prove it's a stolen boat."

"Then I guess we light it up," Paciello said. "I've
been saying that all along."

Three days later, the Merolle brothers and Paciello
went back to Randall's Island. The hole in the fence was
still there. Apparently, no one had noticed that *Petty Cash*
had been tampered with. Dressed all in black again, the
three boldly crawled along the dock directly to the boat.
The cop in the security booth had his face buried in a
copy of the *Daily News*.

They quickly doused a seat cushion on the boat with
kerosene. Ray Merolle lit a match. As the boat began to
smoke, the three hurried back to their car and raced to

the Triboro Bridge. When Ray rolled down the window to pay the toll on the bridge, everyone heard a boom.

"By the time we got to the toll booth, the flames were huge," Ray remembered. "The whole boat blew up. You could see the flames shooting up in front of the fire academy. It was nuts."

Of course, Ray would have to still do some jail time for being on the stolen boat. With no evidence, his lawyer could make a nice deal. And Chris Paciello was off scot-free.

After the boat job, Chris Paciello figured he could do anything. And he was about to put his theory to the test.

He wanted to pull off an armed robbery of the Chemical Bank inside the Staten Island Mall. His Bath Avenue Crew cohorts would make perfect accomplices. It was very early on December 14, 1992, when Paciello and four other Bath Avenue Crew guys gathered at his Mercury Lane townhouse, less than a mile away from the mall. Chris's mother had moved out months earlier, and he had taken over the entire house. Sitting on his black leather sofa were Skeevy, Jimmy "Gap" Calandra, Tommy Reynolds, and Applehead Galloway. Sledgehammers, walkie-talkies, and black wool ski masks were laid out on a coffee table in front of them.

"Okay," Chris told the assembled men. "Everyone meet back here when it's over. This is what we are going to do."

For weeks Paciello had maintained an around-the-clock surveillance on the bank. It was directly across from a tuxedo rental shop and a small boutique and near an entrance to the mall. He memorized the movements of the bank's employees, and the comings and goings of the tuxedo shop customers and boutique owners.

Every morning, an hour before the bank opened, a

Chemical employee wheeled a cart to the night deposit box, where many of the mall's businesses dropped their daily earnings. The teller put the cash in burlap bags and wheeled them to a spot right near the front plate glass windows, where they sat for hours until a bank manager tallied up the contents.

The bank had unwittingly set up the perfect score.

Just before 8 A.M. that December day, Chris Paciello took up position inside the mall with a walkie-talkie in his hand. He had a clear view of the teller and the burlap bags choked with money. The coast was clear. He calmly pressed the talk button and barked a single word: "Go."

Reynolds, Calandra, and Galloway smashed the bank's plate glass window with sledgehammers, climbed through the broken glass with guns drawn and grabbed the cartful of money. The two bank employees inside screamed as the robbers hustled the loot into a stolen Chevy Blazer in the parking lot outside. Skeevy Bellafurie was behind the wheel. Once the cash was loaded, Skeevy hit the gas and they tore off.

The robbery netted the newly united Bath Avenue Crew and the New Springville Boys a total of $262,000 in cash. The stolen Chevy Blazer was found days later, still smoldering after it was set ablaze. The cash was never recovered.

The bank job was a substantial score, especially in La Cosa Nostra circles. Of course, a portion of the proceeds had to be funneled up to the Bonanno family. The robbers also chipped in and bought Paulie Gulino a brand-new Corvette.

The Binger was quickly making a name for himself as a go-to guy. But at the same time, he was also earning a reputation for someone who would rip off his friends.

On May 24, 1991, while Ray was on Rikers Island serving time for the stolen boat, his family's home was burglarized. His father's safe was stolen right out of the Staten Island house.

Ray Merolle Sr.—a member of the NYPD's elite Emergency Services Unit—had just borrowed $40,000 to pay for his daughter's wedding. The cash was in the safe. So were a .22-caliber Beretta and a .25-caliber Beretta, NYPD service revolvers licensed to Ray Sr. and his daughter Linda, a patrol officer assigned to a Brooklyn precinct. The family most regretted the loss of their heirloom jewelry, pieces that had been handed down for generations.

Months later, the .22 ended up in the small town of Forest Acres, South Carolina, in the hands of nineteen-year-old John Wesley Crumpton. The smalltime crook was arrested with it after a failed holdup. It never became clear how the gun made its way so far south.

Prior to the break-in, Ray had been grousing to his friend Paciello that his father was going into debt to pay for an extravagant wedding that his sister wanted. "It's ridiculous, all this money," Ray had complained. "I'm going to help him pay for it, but he didn't want my money."

Chris listened close, ever the attentive friend.

After Ray went to a cell on Rikers Island, one of Paciello's pals called Keith Merolle and asked him to come hang out with him. When Keith left the house, the robbers moved in fast. They used a hand truck to roll the safe right out of the garage.

It did not take long for Ray to hear that Chris was one of the robbers. "Chris was the kind of guy who would steal your wallet and help you look for it," Merolle said. "He had us all fooled with his nice guy act."

The Bath Avenue Crew had enough of its own problems to worry about Chris Paciello robbing his own friends. Their leader, Paulie Gulino, was on his way out.

After executing the burglar who had robbed Jill Spero, Paulie Brass began thinking he had done the Bonanno family a favor, and he wanted it returned. His Bath Avenue drug business had burgeoned into a productive money machine. He sold cocaine directly on the street. He had his beeper business, in which other dealers were allowed to sell drugs themselves, as long as they paid a weekly fee to Paulie. And he was also extorting money from other dealers who were not under the protection of a Mafia family.

Before long, another crew aligned with the Colombo crime family wanted a piece of the drug-dealing action, but Paulie Brass did not want to share the turf. The Twentieth Avenue Crew—a larger group that worked under Colombo protection—was trying to spread out its own business, even on the Bath Avenue Crew's territory.

One night in 1993, the two crews got into a shootout after a fight at the Vegas Diner in Brooklyn. During the brawl, Tommy Reynolds stabbed a rival in the eye with a fork. Then the two crews opened fire on each other in broad daylight on the corner of Bath Avenue and Twentieth Avenue—the Twentieth Avenue Crew's territory. After that Calco took to roaming the streets carrying an Uzi.

The final straw came days later when one of the guys in the Twentieth Avenue Crew slapped a Bath Avenue Crew member's sister across the face. Then the dispute exploded into almost weekly shootouts. Casualties piled high on both sides. Gulino ordered his underlings to stay armed at all times. He was preparing himself for war. Crew members even converged on Calco's upstate home for target practice. Calco had an old Jeep outfitted with cardboard figures and would make his cousin, Charles, drive the car at full speed while crew members shot at the targets.

Despite all their preparations, all was not well in

gangland. Anthony Spero was said to be furious with
Paulie Brass for sparking a dispute that could bring heat
on the whole family. He wanted the bloodshed stopped
immediately. Paulie, however, believed he was entitled
to undying support from the Bonannos. When he didn't
get it, he wanted out of the Bonanno family and tried to
bring his drug business to the Luchese family.

That was Paulie's first mistake.

South Brooklyn is a small place. It was only a matter
of time before word of Paulie's plans made it back to
the ears of the Bonanno family. Spero summoned Gulino to the Pigeon. Heated words quickly escalated into
threats. Paulie Brass lived up to his nickname. He shoved
respected soldier Joe Benanti outside the Pigeon. Then
he laid a hand on Anthony Spero, smashing his palm
into the elderly gangster's face in a movement called
"mushing" on the streets.

That was his second mistake.

Spero was so enraged by the breach of respect he
silently spun around and walked back into the Pigeon
without uttering a sound.

With the shove, Paulie signed his death warrant. He
was terrified. He ordered Mikey Yammine to stay with
him as an around-the-clock bodyguard armed with an
Uzi. Gulino hoped that the Luchese family would step
in and save his life by squashing what had happened
with Spero. Until then, he would have to be careful.

When the Luchese family did not make any move to
help him, Gulino decided to try to preempt any move
Spero might make against him by trying to coax the
Bath Avenue Crew into helping him kill Anthony Spero.
"We're going to get rid of the old man," Gulino told
Crazy Joe Calco.

Calco was stunned. He listened to the plan and then
quickly alerted the bosses. The following morning, an

order was passed to Calco through Benanti. "Paulie's got to go. He's got to be killed. That's what the old man wants. He's got to go today."

On July 25, 1993, Paulie Brass was eating breakfast at his parents' kitchen table. He had sent Yammine home the night before because he had a date. Sometime after eleven o'clock that morning Calco and Tommy Reynolds stopped by. The music at the Gulinos' home was quickly pumped to full volume. A neighbor remembered hearing a dog barking, then he heard about a dozen shots.

"Hey Paulie, can I have something to drink?" Calco asked.

When his friend turned around to walk into the kitchen, Calco and Reynolds followed him. "I walked behind him and pulled out my gun and shot him in the back of the head," Calco told his cohorts. "He fell, and I went up to him and put the gun to the side of his head and shot him again."

The Gulinos—hardworking, humble people—came home from a Catholic Christening Mass to find their son slumped over the table in a pool of his own blood.

Later that day, the Bath Avenue Crew gathered at Fabrizio DeFrancisci's home, frantic about the hit.

"What are we going to do?" they asked one another. Then Dean Benasillo noticed brownish red splotches on Tommy Reynolds's sneakers. His face drained of blood as he stared at the stains. Everyone was looking at Reynolds's sneakers. Reynolds shrugged his shoulders. "Whatever happened, happened," he said.

After Gulino was killed, the Bath Avenue Crew received another order from Joe Benanti. None of his friends were allowed to attend Paulie Gulino's funeral. But a Mass card fat with cash would be pressed into his mourning father's hands at the wake. The Bonanno family hierarchy had also decided that Gulino's close friends—Anthony "Gonzo" Gonzales and Mikey Yammine—should be banned from Bath Avenue.

"As far as those other two kids go," Yammine later recalled Joe Benanti as saying, "they're on their own. That's it. Let them get jobs. They died with Paulie."

Before long, Crazy Joe Calco began to fill his victim's shoes as the Bath Avenue Crew's leader. He was awarded Gulino's drug business and quietly began working toward becoming a made man. A few months after the murder, Spero himself embraced Calco, kissed him on both cheeks, and whispered, "You're a good boy."

Gulino was not the only Bath Avenue guy who died by his friends' hands. In the winter of 1995 Crazy Joe Calco killed another crew hanger-on, nineteen-year-old Jack Cherin.

Cherin was a onetime drug dealer for the Bath Avenue Crew. After he was arrested for dealing drugs, he decided he had had enough of the criminal life and refused to go back on the streets with his crack beeper. This made Calco suspicious. "This guy is a rat," Calco told the crew. "He's gotta go."

Calco was mistaken. Cherin had never cooperated with the law. But he died on a cold winter afternoon anyway.

On January 18, 1995, Cherin was standing on a Bath Beach corner in broad daylight when Calco and Fabrizio DeFrancisci yelled to him, "Jack, come here."

"Are you ratting on us?" Calco asked him when he walked over.

"Nah, I'm not ratting on you," Cherin answered.

"I think you're ratting on me," Calco said. Then he pulled out his gun and fired six shots, killing Cherin in broad daylight. The shots scattered small children who had been walking home from school. Cherin, who was slated to enter a rehabilitation center to kick his drug habit the following morning, was pronounced dead at the scene.

With that, the crew had caught the attention of the New York City Police Department. Detectives began following the activities of the crew. Their history was so violent, it led NYPD Chief of Detectives William Allee to remark: "The most dangerous thing to do around the Bath Avenue Crew is to be their friends."

Chris Paciello would find that out soon enough.

5

REACHING A DEAD END

Jumping from crew to crew was never a problem for Chris Paciello. He hung around with everybody but trusted no one. He'd take no pledges of allegiance, let alone get a tattoo on his ankle. The New Springville Boys were his *paesans*. The Bath Avenue Crew were his business associates.

The cash was rolling in from his smash-and-grab ATM robberies. The Chemical Bank number at the Staten Island Mall had earned him big-time success. He never paid sticker price for his luxury cars anymore. Paciello's life was also looking good, and he wanted a new romantic partner to share in his success. Lately he had taken up with Love Majewski's best friend, Roxanne Rizzo.

At first Chris and Roxanne tried to hide their affair, meeting secretly to make out and sneaking off to Long Island nightclubs to party. But Staten Island is a small place. Word travels fast. And soon enough, Love couldn't help but notice the way Chris was looking at Roxanne as of late.

Friends remembered that she confronted Chris more than once. He denied seeing Roxanne. "You are a psycho, you know that, Love?" was his usual response. "Now give it a rest, will you."

But Chris came around a lot less. He had begun to treat Love awfully. In response, she clung to him. Her neediness was the push that he needed to let her go. Chris dumped Love and soon he was publicly courting Roxanne, telling people she was the love of his life.

Love lost her best friend and her boyfriend in one fell swoop. Her relationship with her own family had soured after the Cadillac incident. She felt completely alone. Chris Paciello had destroyed a piece of her, and to make matters worse, it looked as if he had fallen hard for Roxanne, and she for him. Love turned to Ray Merolle for friendship. His initial comfort quickly culminated into something more, and Love and Ray landed in a full-blown relationship. Chris was dating Love's best friend, and she was dating one of his close cohorts. Besides, by then, Ray had begun to hear the accusations that Chris Paciello was one of the thieves who had robbed his home. Of course, Chris and Ray still did some business together. The Staten Island soap opera continued.

Like everyone else in Chris Paciello's life, Roxanne seemed to serve a financial purpose. Her father, Johnny Rizzo, was reputedly a respected Gambino soldier who had interests up and down the eastern seaboard. If Paciello ever wanted to make a move, whether it would be in South Beach, Staten Island, or in South Beach, Miami, Johnny Rizzo was a good guy to know.

While Chris courted Roxanne's love and her father's respect, he was infuriating a lot of other people in Staten Island. He was growing so wild he was antagonizing even his close friends. Legitimate businessmen who had acquaintances with underworld ties began to complain about him. The Binger's criminal activities would soon be curtailed by his disloyalties.

In September 1992, a Staten Island restaurateur named Anthony Deandra fell prey to a pack of burglars. Paciello was eventually fingered both as one of the armed thieves and as the mastermind of the plot.

Deandra, who owned the Road House, a popular pub Paciello frequented, was at home with his wife, Josephine, when the doorbell rang at around 11 A.M. The couple was not expecting anybody, but their daughter had just had a baby. Maybe it was a friend stopping by to see pictures of the infant.

Anthony Deandra opened the door. Three men stood on his stoop, their faces hidden behind a giant basket of fruit and a large vase of fresh flowers. He thought it was strange three grown men were making one delivery, but before Deandra could shut the door, the strangers pushed their way inside. They had pulled nylon stockings over their faces and were wielding guns.

"Where's the money?" a muffled voice yelled.

The Deandras were having work done on the house and a hired painter in a back room hustled Josephine outside and to a neighbor's house to call for help. As Josephine called the cops, the intruders beat her husband, punching him in the stomach, kicking his knees, and tying him up with duct tape. The assailants then ransacked the premises in search of the earnings from the previous night at the Road House. They quickly found a locked steel cabinet in the basement and smashed it open.

The cabinet contained $60,000 in cash. The robbers broke it open and loaded the stacks of money into a plastic laundry basket they found in the basement. Their swiftness made it obvious that it was not their first home invasion.

But Deandra, whose brawn equaled his business acu-

men, had broken free from the duct tape and grabbed a
licensed handgun. Detectives later heard a story that he
had fired two warning shots in the air to scare the burglars. Another rumor surfaced that had Deandra grab-
bing one of the robbers, holding a gun to his head, and
letting the pathetic punk go after he started crying. That
punk, detectives later alleged, was Chris Paciello.

Deandra's gun jammed and Paciello bolted.

Whatever the true story was, Deandra refused to say.

Cops did know that the would-be crooks in their
panic dropped the laundry basket full of cash on the
ground and ran helter-skelter to a dark-colored car before police arrived. When a patrol cop pulled up in front
of the house, tens and twenties were flying all over
Wetmore Road. Nonetheless, the would-be robbers got
away.

As detectives began investigating the robbery, one
name came up over and over: The Binger. The Binger
set up the robbery, street sources told detectives. He carried it out. And he was angry when his cohorts dropped
the cash. Yet the police could not come up with a real
name to go with the nickname. But wiseguys in the
neighborhood had heard who set up the robbery, too, and
they knew exactly who the Binger was. He was getting a
reputation as a "real ballsy guy."

Danny Costanza was one of the New Springville gang's
most active members. He was a skilled burglar and drug
dealer who had slowly climbed the Mob's ladder. By the
early 1990s, when he was still in his twenties, Costanza
was being proposed for a button by the Bonanno family.
He usually ran with his cousin, Franny, another rough-
and-tumble Bonanno associate. Both cousins were considered gutsy, even brazen, and organized crime law
enforcement authorities had been keeping tabs on them.

Once, when they were arrested after a gunfight outside a Manhattan nightclub that left their friend wounded, the cousins did the unthinkable in a downtown police precinct once the detectives left the room. Detectives had made a fresh pot of coffee in the precinct's interview room, and then left for a minute to consult with a commanding officer. Franny Constanza smiled at his cousin, walked over to the brewing coffee, and took a long piss into the cops' java. Then the cousins sat back and smiled as the cops came back, poured two piping cups, and took big gulps of the rank mixture.

The Costanza cousins were always up to something. Sometime in the late winter of 1992, the Costanza cousins came up with a big score and needed Chris Paciello's help.

Danny had caught word of a shipment of pot coming into the New York area from Arizona. A Spanish drug cartel was supposed to receive the delivery and then transport it by a tractor-trailer to New Jersey. Costanza did a little poking around and came up with the exact location of the drop-off. When the shipment arrived on a rented truck, Danny was there, hiding along with his cousin and two other New Springville Boys, Beck Fisheku and Lee D'Vanzo.

As the truck rumbled into a secluded spot in New Jersey, the foursome watched as bales and bales of marijuana were loaded into a smaller U-Haul. Then the delivery men drove away. They were leaving the truck right on the street.

What luck, they thought.

Breaking into the truck itself, though, turned out to be impossible. They would have to steal the entire truck.

Danny Costanza knew whom to call—Chris Paciello, master car thief. He dialed the Binger's number. "Chris, we need you to come to New Jersey. We have a

problem here, and if you can take care of it, it will definitely be worth your while."

The Binger scribbled down directions and was on
his way.

"A U-Haul?" Paciello said upon arriving. "Piece of
cake."

When he arrived at the scene, Chris went over to the
U-Haul truck, jimmied the door open, and slid inside.
He ducked low in the seat as he fiddled with the wires
under the dashboard. The New Springville Boys kept
close watch. After a few minutes the engine roared to
life.

When they unloaded their take in Staten Island, everyone was stupefied. They'd scored nearly two thousand
pounds of pot. It had a street value of about two million
dollars. The bonanza was to be split five ways. Everyone would walk away with about 400 pounds, about
$400,000 worth of product to do with what he wished.

Unknown to the others, however, Paciello decided
that for whatever reason Franny Costanza should not
get his share. His beef with Franny was unclear, but
more than likely stemmed from old resentments over a
woman or money—the cause of most disputes between
aspiring gangsters.

Later that same night, Paciello picked up several elaborate electronic tracking devices at a spy store in Manhattan. He planted the bugs in Franny's bales of pot.
When Franny secreted his share away in his Staten Island home, Paciello knew just where to find it. In no time
it disappeared.

Rumblings circulated that once again Chris Paciello
had ripped off one of his own friends.

The Costanzas were agitated and very upset with
Paciello. He knew he was going to have to clear out of
Staten Island before long. He took a trip to Miami, then

another one. He was spending a lot of time vacationing along the shore on South Beach. With each trip, he was formulating a plan that would help him leave New York City for good.

After planning one last big score, Chris Paciello was going to get out of town and head to sunnier climes.

Just after New Year's Eve in 1993, Chris Paciello got a tip from a pal named Joe Eisenberg that someone in Staten Island kept the windfall of his pornography businesses at his home in a safe built into the basement.

Eisenberg had dated Sami Shemtov's ex-wife, Carol, and said she was complaining that she had to squeeze every dime of alimony from him, even though he was wealthy. She had been tossing around numbers in the hundreds of thousands, all kept in Shemtov's basement safe. The safe had a face dial, and Sami was the only one who knew the combination.

Shemtov kept this a secret from his new bride, Judy. Her children insisted she did not know the combination to the safe, and may not have even known about its existence. She never knew that adult video stores were among the businesses her husband owned and ran.

To Judy, Sami was a businessman who sometimes traveled to Cleveland for his electrical supply company. He had an engineering degree and was a decorated Israeli soldier. He made a very good living and treated her well.

Judy's only son, Adam Kidan, had his doubts. The instincts that made him a good attorney made him wary about Sami, but he bit his tongue. After all, his younger sister, Arlyn, lived at home with them and she seemed to like Sami. Judy's other daughter, April, was away at college, but she was elated that her mom had finally found a nice man.

Sami's youngest son, Aaron, also lived with them. His

oldest son, Richard, and daughter, Dena, were adults and lived on their own. In fact, Dena and her father were feuding because she was dating a man who was not Jewish. During the summer, though, most of the kids stopped by on weekends to swim in the backyard pool or sit in the Jacuzzi. It was a tight-knit family. That is, until the night of February 18, 1993, when their world was blown apart.

As soon as Paciello heard about the Shemtovs' safe, he tried to make amends to his cohorts in the New Springville Boys by bringing them in on the robbery. He asked Skeevy Bellafurie to come in on the piece of work. Skeevy said okay, but he dragged his feet. Impatient, Paciello brought the job to the Bath Avenue Crew.

Consummate bank robber Jimmy "Gap" Calandra was in. So was Tommy Reynolds. Paciello agreed they needed a fourth member, so they brought in Mikey Yammine. No one was supposed to get hurt. The wife was not even supposed to be home. It should have been a simple score. Tie up the husband, along with his son Aaron, if he was home. Get the combination to the safe. Grab the cash and go.

But everything went bad really fast. First the woman answered the door. Then Tommy spotted movement in the kitchen and tensed up. His whole body tightened. When his finger accidentally squeezed the trigger the pretty blonde lady was hurled backwards with the blast. Everyone ran out of the house empty-handed.

The bullet that tore through Judy's face had the same impact on her loved ones' lives. Her daughters were absolutely destroyed. Arlyn still became a successful interior designer, but she had changed. "It was more than a loss," Arlyn told people who asked about that horrible night. "Part of me died."

Judy's other daughter, April, found a career as a

financial advisor and got married, but the wedding was a lackluster affair without her mother. When April had to pick out her wedding gown, she collapsed in tears inside the boutique, devastated that her mother was not there to bask in her happiness. When April walked down the aisle, she whispered to her brother: "I wish Mommy was here." Judy's own mother aged overnight, her body shriveling as if her daughter's death had drained her of blood. She told her grandchildren she felt like she had nothing to live for.

"She was our best friend," Arlyn said. "We were all closer to her individually than we were to each other. It's hard enough to lose a parent, but to lose your only parent."

Adam Kidan later went on to start a lucrative business of his own, Dial-A-Mattress, and relocated to Miami where he entered into a partnership with a Miami casino mogul to run a lucrative string of offshore betting boats. He quickly became a millionaire.

Less than two months after Judy's murder, Sami Shemtov, too, relocated to Florida. He moved in with an old girlfriend in Hollywood and opened an adult video store on South Beach. Sensations Video was at 1317 Washington Avenue, just two blocks from the site that would later become Liquid, the nightclub that would make Chris Paciello a very rich man. "It's something horrible that happened right in front of my eyes," Sami Shemtov later said when tracked down to Sensations. "She was killed right in front of me. It took me a long time to get over it. I really went through a hard time trying to get over it."

Still, Sami never spoke to Judy's three children again. They had even hired private investigators to see if he had anything to do with their mother's death.

Chris Paciello spent the day following Judy's murder in utter panic. He met with the three other participants at a Staten Island hotel to talk to the Bath Avenue Crew leader, Paulie Gulino. He feared repercussions from the Bonanno family, but Gulino told them he would quash it. No one would ever know they were the culprits, he promised.

At least not for a long time.

6

MAFIA BEACH PARTY

For all his mistakes, Chris Paciello still had supporters. His girlfriend Roxanne's father—Johnny Rizzo—liked him. Staten Island attorney Dennis Peterson, who was a longtime friend of the Paciello family, also watched out for Chris. Peterson could understand how someone so likable had such a rough persona, since his brother had been jailed in Florida. Peterson's wife, Emily, was enjoying a hot run of success as an interior designer in South Beach, Miami, with a string of celebrity clients, including Donald Trump. Rizzo had some connections on South Beach, too.

It was as good a place as any for Paciello to make a new start. He had been spending a great deal of time there on vacation, crashing with friends at the Clevelander on Ocean Drive. The Clevelander is more fraternity house than hotel. It has a huge outdoor bar around a built-in pool with a stage for live music and a DJ that pumps pop into the street all night long. It was perfect for a pack of guys from Brooklyn looking to crash in a place with a view of both the waves and the steady flow of scantily clad beautiful women that passed by their window.

Chris had already decided that he wanted to move to

South Beach. The question was what to do once he got there. Chris thought long and hard about opening a nightclub. He could do it, but not alone. He'd need help.

At the same time, a club promoter in New York City was looking for a fresh start. It would prove to be a perfect merger.

Lord Michael Caruso was a sought-after promoter at two of Manhattan's hottest clubs, the Tunnel and the Limelight. He was also the leading peddler of marijuana and the designer drug Ecstasy. He also had a seamy background that included kidnapping and drug dealer robberies.

Caruso grew up on Staten Island but he felt completely at odds with his Italian neighbors so he dated black women and surrounded himself with gang members from the projects instead. "Staten Island was all guidos and goons and bubblegum-gangsters," Caruso said. "I was sick of it, so I moved into the city."

Lord Michael Caruso, who, even in his twenties, sported a spiky highlighted haircut and baggy clothes, was a flamboyant club kid who peddled his dope in dancehalls owned by New York City club kingpin Peter Gatien. Lord Michael's crowd consisted of omni-sexual Ecstasy fiends, most dressed in drag, all with freak names like "Rah Shaky," "Loungin," "Vel," and "Ghost." If he wasn't hanging around with gay cross-dressers, Lord Michael preferred the company of black rappers, who often were members of their own violent street gangs.

His income as a club promoter was good, but his real profits were derived from his sideline as a drug dealer. That, of course, made him a target for gangsters who robbed drug dealers; young mobsters who were much like Chris Paciello.

Lord Michael watched Chris develop a reputation as

a tough guy. When punches were thrown, he was almost always the one who got up, brushed himself off, and walked away. Caruso needed that kind of muscle behind him.

He quietly spread rumors that he was "with Paciello" or that Chris was his protector. Before long, Lord Michael's claims made it back to Chris Paciello. But instead of getting angry with Lord Michael, Paciello saw an opportunity. He was making plans to get out of Staten Island for good and open a club in Miami. Caruso was an ideal partner.

The unlikely duo began hitting the nightclubs together.

To Manhattan club hoppers, Paciello was a member of what was referred to as the "bridge and tunnel crowd"—suburban cowboys who spill in from places like New Jersey and Staten Island, packing bars and dance floors, decked in mall duds and out-of-date hairstyles. Over the summer of 1994, the bridge and tunnel crowd converged on hotspots such as Webster Hall in the East Village and the Sound Factory on the West Side.

Chris Paciello thought he'd check out Sound Factory on a hot July 4th in 1994. With him were Lord Michael and childhood buddies Rico Locasio and Big Dom Dionisio, the "Twin Towers."

Like everybody that got an invitation to hang around with Chris Paciello, Lord Michael's being there had a purpose. Lord Michael had juice in the club world, something that Chris Paciello and his intimidating crew did not have. Lord Michael could get them in most places with a nod at the doorman.

The odd couple would become closer friends after a fight at the Sound Factory that night. The club was too crowded for the holiday weekend, and the bouncer at the door did not need any more single guys roaming the dance floor. That night, Lord Michael had no juice. It was a story Lord Michael liked to tell over and over.

"We were waiting on line, waiting, and then a security came over and said, 'Guys, you are not going to get in tonight,'" Caruso recalled. "A few minutes later security came back again and told us, 'Guys, I told you to get off the line. You are not going to get in tonight.' Well, Chris didn't like that. He took off his Rolex watch and slipped it into his pocket. Out of nowhere, another security officer, Alex, a guy whose last name we never knew, came up to Chris, pushed his arm, and said, 'Listen pal, get off.' Chris just whaled on the guy. He punched him in the head, then smashed him in the head with a metal velvet rope stand."

Lord Michael's version of events matched that of eyewitnesses at the Sound Factory that night. One bouncer remembered the aftermath. He came on the scene just as Paciello and Caruso marched into the club. A gang of other party crashers followed.

Bedlam came with them.

Infuriated security guards blasted the intruders with Mace and fire extinguishers. When the foam ran out, the bouncers hurled the empty tanks. Alex, the bouncer hit in the head with the stand, lunged at Paciello with an ax handle. Paciello yanked it away and cracked it over Alex's skull.

Unbeknownst to him, Alex was in the infamous Outlaws biker gang. Before doctors at St. Vincent's Hospital in Greenwich Village finished stitching his wounds, Alex vowed revenge. "I want to get my licks in," he told his friends.

Lord Michael and his new pal Paciello sauntered out the front door past their dazed victims and went home.

Lord Michael had been around the club scene in Manhattan for a long time, though, and even if he did not know Alex's last name, he knew what his reputation was. He was anxious about what Alex might do.

Besides all that, his boss, Peter Gatien, was getting into his own trouble with the law. The cops began raiding his clubs constantly, cracking down on dealers. They just didn't know that the biggest infusion of Ecstasy and marijuana was coming from the club's promoter, Lord Michael.

A few weeks after the fight at the Sound Factory, Lord Michael felt someone tug his elbow as he leaned against the bar at Gatien's other club, the Limelight, located inside an old Gothic church.

"Hey Mike," Paciello said. "What's up? I have this business proposition for you."

"I'm up for anything right now," Caruso told him. "It's getting hot around here."

"Have you ever been to Miami, to South Beach?"

"Ah, once, I think," Caruso answered.

"It's booming down there," Paciello said. "Booming. I've been partying down there all year. Now I want to open a club down there. Would you be interested in coming down and taking a look?"

Chris Paciello needed a face man for his new club, and Lord Michael needed a new job.

"Listen, Mike, people know you from the club world," Paciello said. "You've been the face everybody knows; you know how to deal with people. I'm a goon. I'm not a high-fashion pretty boy."

So on Labor Day weekend in 1994, Lord Michael and Chris Paciello landed in Miami. They headed to Ocean Drive, South Florida's most famous waterfront strip, dotted with art deco hotels, pricey high-end shops, and open-air bistros.

Chris had the keys to a friend's apartment a block off Ocean Drive, across the street from the Armani store. They dumped their bags in the living room and then went directly to a real estate office.

Within hours, the two aspiring club tycoons were looking at rundown storefronts and vacant buildings. Nothing appealed to them. It was a long, frustrating day, and Lord Michael began missing his girlfriend back in New York.

Later that night in the apartment, feeling Lord Michael's tension, Paciello told him he might have another option. "Listen, I have this friend. He has a club. Let's go take a look at it," he said.

The next morning they walked to a failing barroom called Mickey's Place at 1203 Washington Avenue— directly across the street from the Miami Beach Police Station. The hole-in-the-wall bar, named after its owner, the pugilist and actor Mickey Rourke, was nicknamed "Mickey Rats" by South Beach denizens because of its seedy interior. Usually there was a group of elderly men who held animated debates in Italian as they pitched pennies against the bar's wall during the day waiting for the bar to open.

But it had a steady clientele of workaday types who popped in for a draft beer and tourists who hoped to spot the sexy star of the film *9½ Weeks* and *Angel Heart,* at least until Mickey Rourke was busted for resisting arrest after a melee outside the club and made himself scarce. The bar was decorated in a boxing-club motif, made up to look just like the interior of Gleason's Gym, the Brooklyn boxing club where Mickey Rourke got his start.

When Chris and Mike walked in they headed to the bar. Sitting there was a thickset white-haired man wearing bright orange swim trunks and a white tank top—Carlo Vaccarezza. Mickey Rourke's name was on the sign, but it was public knowledge that Vaccarezza, an alleged Gambino crime family associate, managed the place. According to oft-repeated rumors, John Gotti gave Mickey Rourke the bar after he supported Gotti during his 1992 racketeering and murder charges. Vaccarezza had been sent down to make sure things ran smoothly.

Lord Michael immediately noticed that the bar's walls were festooned with photographs of the Dapper Don. Law enforcement officials described Vaccarezza—a native of Genoa, Italy—as Gotti's driver back when the boss of bosses held court at the Bergen Hunt and Fish Club in Howard Beach, Queens. When Gotti was in the mood for a good espresso, he would have Vaccarezza escort him into Manhattan to visit with underlings at his second hangout, the Ravenite.

Vaccarezza was a loyal man, a stand-up guy, and when the boss was sentenced to life imprisonment in 1992, he decided it was a good idea to fly south. Besides, the government had seized Vaccarezza's restaurant in Manhattan, a posh spot called Da Noi—Italian for "Our Place." The government charged that the eatery was nothing more than a money laundering front for John Gotti. Even the restaurant's corporation "existed merely to provide the appearance that John Gotti and other Gambino family members have legitimate income," they chimed. The government stopped hounding Vaccarezza when Gotti was locked up for life.

Chris and Lord Michael looked around the place. They nodded to each other. But to Lord Michael, it seemed that Chris had already sealed the deal long before they had even set eyes on the place. Vaccarezza excused himself to round up paperwork. He was eager to get rid of the place. He wanted to retreat to a more remote part of Florida to work with his thoroughbred-training facility called Break of Dawn Farms. He was banned from New York racetracks when state gaming officials had denied him a license to own racehorses because of his reputed connection to organized crime. Instead he had become part of the Gulfstream racing scene.

"This place is like a John Gotti shrine," Lord Michael hissed out of the side of his mouth.

"We don't have to leave them up there," Paciello whispered. "What do you think of the location? Do you think it's workable?"

Despite its obvious underworld overtones, Lord Michael thought the location was ideal, and he began mentally picturing the club rehabbed. He measured the dance floor with his trained eye and looked at the ceiling rafters to see if it could hold a disco ball.

This should work out great, he thought.

He shook Paciello's hand. "Let's do it."

On Tuesday morning, after the long weekend, Lord Michael and Chris Paciello flew back to New York to plot their next move.

They sat down with a friend of Paciello's, Rob Currie, owner of the Staten Island Fitness Club. Currie was a financial whiz and quickly drew up a budget for nightclub essentials. Lord Michael knew Chris had a reputation for burglaries and obviously he had some connections, so he never questioned where his new partner's share of the money would come from. Michael had sold his Harley-Davidson and used the proceeds from a drug rip-off for his share. Currie owned the gym on Richmond Road, so he had his own money to invest.

A month later, with no down payment, Paciello took

over Mickey's and its $400,000 debt. They also hired
Janet Navarro, Mickey Rourke's sister-in-law, to do the
club's books. The trio flew to Miami to seal the deal.
They walked around the empty bar slapping each other
on the back. They were going to be club tycoons.

After a day of passing the papers, the partners decided to stop in at one of the no-name bars that dotted
the neighborhood behind South Beach. They were
grubby and tired and did not want to dress up.

Lord Michael noticed Paciello staring at a group of
Latin men drinking beers in the corner. "These guys
keep looking over here," Paciello said. "What's their
fucking problem, huh?"

Lord Michael realized his friends did look out of
place. Paciello was wearing denim cutoffs and white
sneakers with socks. Lord Michael was wearing baggy
pants and a tight silk T-shirt. Rob Currie was dressed
in a sweat suit. They had unwittingly wandered into a
club where they didn't belong.

The four Latinos may have had too much to drink, or
maybe Chris and his friends looked like troublemakers.
Whatever the reason, the eyeballing escalated into exchanged punches and smashed bottles. The fight spilled
outside, got uglier, and one of the Latino guys pulled out
a gun and pointed it squarely at Paciello's head.

"Stick the gun in my mouth if you want to shoot
me," Paciello yelled. "Go ahead, shoot me. But you'll
spend the rest of your life in jail. And you'll die. Sooner
or later, you'll get yours."

The gunman trained the barrel on Paciello for seconds. Someone inside called the cops. Upon hearing the
sirens in the distance, Paciello's assailant pocketed the
gun and fled.

Rob Currie had seen enough. For Currie, who initially planned to be one of the club's partners, the

damage was done. He had seen enough of his friends get tangled with the wrong type. There were plenty of bubblegum gangsters out on Staten Island who did stupid things that culminated in long jail sentences. Rob Currie was not going to become one of those guys. He had a legitimate business at home and did not need problems.

"You two are nuts," Currie said angrily to his blood-ied friends. "I'm out. Anyhow, to me the place is a white elephant. And on top of it, you two still want to be thugs. Count me out."

Rob Currie left Miami on the first flight to New York the following morning. He never came back.

Paciello was not deterred. Currie's leaving was not a deal killer. The papers were signed. Things were mov-ing right along. On a later State Liquor Authority ap-plication, Paciello told authorities that Rob Currie lent him more than $100,000—a claim the gym owner hotly denies to this day. Few were aware that Paciello had plenty of money.

Lord Michael sometimes wondered if his partner had to put up any cash at all. He had already spotted Paciello holding a number of private backroom meet-ings with a couple of characters who introduced them-selves as "the Nose" and "Big Johnny." Their real names—Johnny Rizzo and Jackie D'Amico—were well known to prosecutors back in New York City. Both men were reputed associates of the Gambino crime family.

Mike also heard that Chris would bring in another partner from Staten Island, a member of the New Spring-ville Boys, Lee D'Vanzo. D'Vanzo had vacationed in South Beach but, after a few days, he backed out as well. "This guy is involved with some sharks," Lee apparently told Mike. "I don't want any part of it."

Lord Michael didn't ask many questions. He stuck to his business, planning the grand opening of the new club. It would be named Risk.

Lord Michael had a feeling it was going to be hot, and he was right.

7

HOT ENOUGH TO GET BURNED

The grand opening for Risk was scheduled for the third Thursday in October 1994. The problem was that another nightclub, Groove Jet, had planned its own grand opening for the same night. When Chris Paciello found out, he decided Groove Jet would have to suffer a delay in their plans.

Groove Jet's owners had been making renovations and they left a construction Dumpster parked on Washington Street near the building. Chris Paciello made an anonymous call to report the code violation, hoping a hefty fine might slow them down. It didn't. Then he and Lord Michael decided to take matters into their own hands.

As night fell on a late fall evening, Mike Caruso filled a five-gallon gasoline tank and carried it to the roof of the Groove Jet building. There was a long steel pipe that snaked from the roof into the club itself. Mike poured the gasoline down the chute, followed by a book of lit matches. After ten minutes, smoke poured from the pipe. Pleased with his work, Mike gave Chris—who was on the ground acting as a lookout—a thumbs up. Yet seconds later he heard a loud siren. Directly across the street from the Groove Jet was the Miami Beach fire station.

The fire was doused in a matter of minutes and the damage was minimal.

Risk's owners decided that if they could not shut the Groove Jet down, they would blow them out of the water with the biggest bash South Beach had ever seen. They planned to put two bottles of champagne on every VIP table and have an open bar all night long to pack in the crowds.

The trick was to find a liquor distributor willing to open an account of that size with new club owners. Chris and Mike were not exactly upstanding citizens with a long line of credit.

Paciello, ever enterprising, came up with an idea. A friend of his owned the nearby Le Baines, an upscale lounge on Washington Avenue. He gave Chris, the South Beach newcomer, a courtesy tour of his operation—including the alcohol storage facility about two blocks away. "Mike," Chris said when he got back from the tour. "I think we've solved our liquor problems."

Late that night, they kicked in the door of the storage room and emptied it.

That's what friends are for.

On opening night in October the booze flowed freely at Risk. Club goers found the floor carpeted with a plush zebra print. In a bay window, women slicked with glowing body paint gyrated to hip-hop music. A smoke machine made the bartender look like he was serving drinks from the mouth of a volcano. At the back bar, a constant shower trickled so when the dancing throngs got too hot, they could cool off under the sprinkle.

Lord Michael had built an "opium room," which was really just a corner sectioned off from the rest of the club with bamboo screens and lined with silk pillows. It would quickly become the "heroin room," popular with the skinny, sunken-eyed fashion models that filled magazines in the mid-1990s.

Risk was the closest thing Miami had to a decadent New York City nightclub, which is exactly the effect Chris and Michael were after. It was a cross between the swingers' sex club Trapeze and the swanky Palladium. It took off so fast that crowd control became necessary. Patrons were given the phone number of an answering service that, when you called, whispered a password to get into the club. If you couldn't get the password to get into Risk, you were a South Beach nobody.

Its Monday night event, Fat Black Pussycat, a theme party that spun funk and soul, immediately attracted a huge following. Risk was the first Miami club to play hip-hop, thanks to Lord Michael's rap connections back in New York. Its gay night titled "Risk Your Anus" was packed every weekend. The club changed the whole nightlife scene on South Beach, bringing together rich kids, drag queens, gays, straights, strippers, drug dealers, and gangsters.

Before long, rumors started swirling around the beach about Chris Paciello, but no one was concerned. "We heard all these rumors that Chris was connected to the Mob back in New York, and that the Mob was taking over South Beach, but we didn't care," said club kid Kirby Jean-Joseph. "He was throwing the best parties in town. When Risk got hot, Chris got hot."

With Risk's makeover so successful, Chris Paciello knew he needed one as well. He heard the whispers when he strolled around the club in his old New York City clothes. "Hey, who's the guido?" He was also aware he was the only guy going to the beach in cutoff jeans. He turned to Lord Michael for help and they began shopping together.

They went to Armani and Versace for pants. They bought leather belts at Gucci and tight black T-shirts at European import boutiques. Suits were hand-tailored by a Japanese designer. They picked out hip Patrick Cox shoes. He grew out his hair, then had it expensively coiffed and began taming it with shiny pomade. Even his underwear had to be perfect. Chris wore only Calvin Klein tight boxer shorts, the ones that showed off what he felt was his most valuable asset, which had already earned its own reputation on the beach.

Women were soon vying for his attention. Reporters and writers chronicling South Beach nightlife began profiling the newcomer, praising his abundant charm and business acumen. Still, no one really thought Risk would become as hot as it did. These clubs came and went. But every week Risk kept packing them in.

No one was more surprised than Paciello. "I was a big guido from New York," he told the reporters. "Everyone thought I would be out of business in a year."

Everybody on the beach loved Chris Paciello, except for his business partner, Lord Michael. The duo were soon grating on each other's nerves.

For the first six months in Miami, they shared an apartment to save money. But Lord Michael could not stand the way Chris lavishly spent money on $100 bottles of wine or picked up other people's bar tabs and left him holding the bag on the rent. Mostly, though, Caruso had tired of all the "goons and guidos" packing Risk every night. They were either working for Paciello or ripping him off. Swarms of Staten Island and Brooklyn guys with thick gold chains came to Miami by the planeload. They showed up at Risk, amassed huge tabs, and then left without paying, citing their friendship with Chris.

By then, the feeling was mutual. Paciello was barely

speaking to Lord Michael. He preferred the company of his two brothers, George and Keith, who had moved to Florida and were helping him run the business. Lord Michael got his own apartment and began spending all his free time with the few blacks on South Beach, playing basketball and listening to rap music.

Also, Lord Michael had begun to hear rumors about Chris that made him nervous. He heard that Paciello had ripped off some big-time mob drug dealers back in New York, and that they were looking for him. He heard Paciello had robbed a few banks. He had witnessed firsthand Paciello's handiwork with his fists, and had heard about even bloodier incidents. He may have transformed himself from a street thug into a suave impresario, but at heart he was still the Binger.

Even though Risk was raking in the dough, Lord Michael felt he was sitting on a powder keg.

The final straw came when Paciello stole their neighbor's car.

Just before 4 P.M. on December 9, 1994, Dr. Edward Neff pulled his shiny four-door BMW 740i into Seacoast Towers, the luxury condominium building he lived in at 5151 Collins Avenue, overlooking the beach. The Coral Gables cardiologist handed the keys to the building's valet, Bill Kent, then went upstairs to get ready for a night out. He did not notice that one of his neighbors was lurking in the garage.

Chris Paciello had admired Dr. Neff's forest green BMW for weeks, especially after he had gotten into an accident and smashed up his own black Beemer. The accident in front of the Seacoast Towers left Chris's BMW totaled and he was so upset he left the hood of the car, the only part intact, in his parking spot.

Two weeks after Dr. Neff's BMW vanished, the day before Christmas Eve, Chris Paciello zoomed into the garage with a brand-new green BMW. Then he got rid of the old hood. Valet Bill Kent walked up to the car for a closer look.

That looks a lot like Dr. Neff's BMW, he thought.

After Chris parked it and got into the elevator, Kent examined it more closely.

It *was* Dr. Neff's car. Only with tinted windows. He picked up the phone and called the Miami Beach cops.

Detectives showed up a short time later. First they did a computer check on the BMW's vehicle identification number. The VIN on the BMW parked in Chris Paciello's spot was assigned to a 1989 car. The BMW parked in Paciello's spot was obviously a 1994 model.

The detectives knew they had grand theft auto on their hands, a felony. The two detectives set up surveillance just outside the posh building.

An hour later, Chris drove out of the garage and headed toward Risk. He was pulled over at Twenty-eighth Street and Pinetree Street and arrested. The stolen car was towed and impounded nearby by Tremont Towing. A little later, Lord Michael bailed his partner out of jail.

The next night George Fernandez was manning the impound lot for Tremont Towing, Just before midnight a tow truck beeped to signal he wanted to leave the lot. Fernandez pressed the button that electronically opened the gate. As the tow truck drove out of the lot, it was followed by a green BMW. Its headlights were off. Fernandez could not see the driver because of the tinted windows.

Chris Paciello had stolen the stolen car back.

A few days later, the police found it torched on a desolate street in Miami. The evidence needed to pin Chris Paciello to the stolen car had gone up in smoke.

The seasoned detectives were furious that Chris had made fools out of them. They decided to press the case anyway. But Dr. Neff, despite being contacted by the State Attorney's Office numerous times both by certified letter and by phone, never showed up in court and refused to return calls. He had clearly decided not to press charges, whatever his motivation.

Assistant District Attorney Daniel Farkas allowed Chris Paciello to plead to lesser charges. Chris wrote Dr. Neff a check for $800 for damages, and the case was closed. Lord Michael was furious. He had been in the garage with Chris shortly before the BMW was stolen, and was nervous that he would be implicated in the theft.

"A stolen car," Michael bemoaned to his girlfriend back in New York. "I don't need this."

To make matters worse, word traveled all the way to Florida that Alex, the Outlaw biker who had pledged to "get his licks in" after the Sound Factory brawl, was looking for them. Alex had a reputation of shooting first and asking for explanations later.

Lord Michael bought a round-trip ticket to New York, telling Paciello he wanted to see his girlfriend and would be back in a few days. Mike Caruso would not return to South Beach for a long time.

Chris, however, tracked him down in New York City.

After a few weeks back in New York, Mike Caruso got word that Alex was still "looking to slice him up." At the same time he had approached his old boss, Peter Gatien, asking for his job back.

"First you have to take care of this thing with Alex," Gatien said.

Caruso worked up his nerve and arranged a meeting with Alex. The two men met at the trendy Union Square

Coffee Shop in downtown Manhattan. Things went better than Caruso could have hoped.

All Alex wanted was Chris Paciello's address, phone number, and his daily routine in South Beach. That, and some money to pay for his hospitalization. Caruso was relieved. Besides, it was Chris and not he who had smashed Alex over the head with the velvet rope stand.

"Listen, Alex," he said. "I'm not a tough guy. I'm not even that tight with him. To tell you the truth, I can't stand Chris. He's a snake. I'll tell you anything you want to know."

Caruso gave him $2,000 in cash for his hospital bills. Within the wad of money was Chris's address, where he worked out, the location of his clubs, and some of his favorite haunts. But it was all a setup. Alex had recorded Caruso's every word with a hidden tape recorder, and as soon as Lord Michael left the eatery, the tape was on its way to Miami. Caruso may not have been tight with Chris, but Alex was. They had become friendly in the past few weeks. Chris had blamed Caruso for Alex's injuries.

Weeks later, Lord Michael—who had been reinstated at Gatien's club the Tunnel—imagined that the whole incident was behind him. His mind changed when suddenly Chris walked into the club and ordered a bottle of expensive champagne. He looked good, but he seemed distant. Lord Michael approached him, thinking Paciello was still angry that he had not come back to Miami.

"Guy," he said. "Listen, I'm sorry. My son, my girlfriend. I couldn't deal with the scene anymore. I should have called, but I had a lot going on."

Paciello seemed appeased. "No problem, Mike." Then he added, "I gotta talk to you about some other things. You gonna be home tomorrow?"

The next morning, Paciello rang his doorbell in Staten Island. He walked in and shook Caruso's hand. He walked around the house to make sure no one else was home. The next thing Lord Michael knew, Paciello came at him with his fists whaling. In a flash, the barrel of a gun appeared between his lips.

"I'll fucking kill you, you rat," Paciello seethed. "You set me up. You set me up with Alex. I should kill you right now."

Lord Michael clenched his eyes shut, waiting for the blast.

But instead Paciello smashed him in the face with the butt of his gun, over and over. Caruso's blood splattered the walls. Then, as quickly as the beating started, it stopped. Paciello sauntered out of the house. One of the neighbors who had heard Caruso's screams called the police.

Caruso was taken to the hospital where his wounds were cleaned and stitched. He never saw Chris Paciello again, at least in person. Nor did he give up his assailant's name to the police.

Later that night, as he huddled in bed with his girlfriend, Gina, she harangued him to turn Paciello in. She knew how violent Paciello could be. She had briefly dated him during a short breakup with Caruso. He refused. Even after everything, Caruso could understand what made Paciello tick.

"Criminals don't give each other résumés," he said. "I knew what he was about before I even went down there. In Chris's heart, I think he wanted to get away. He truly wanted to do something legitimate. He did care about his friends. At one time he even helped me out.

"There was this night that he caught me doing drugs," Caruso remembered. "He slapped me right across the face, a bitch slap, and screamed in my face, 'You want to kill yourself like my father did?'

"He had a good side," Caruso said. "He wanted purification, he wanted a pure heart. But he would just go mental. You have to remember, I did screw him over a little bit, leaving Miami and all that."

He paused, deciding not to tell her about the meeting with Alex. He stroked her hair. "He could have clipped me. He didn't."

Paciello soon got over Mike Caruso. He did not need him anymore. He had met a genuine South Beach celebrity, Ingrid Casares, a button-cute openly bisexual club hopper. Casares had connections. She had dated Madonna, Sandra Bernhard, and k.d. lang. She was already a mover and a shaker on South Beach. And she was gorgeous.

Paciello had shrewd plans to bring Ingrid Casares in on running his nightclub. Casares could be the bridge to the celebrity world while he could be the moneyman. Together they could catapult themselves into a type of stardom a street kid from Staten Island and the daughter of a Cuban businessman could only dream of.

Risk, however, would be coming to an end in a hurry.

The crowds at the club had dwindled. Its newness had faded, and with it, its allure. Fat Black Pussycat was still packing them in, but the club was empty the rest of the week. Chris Paciello knew how to take care of that problem.

At 8:58 A.M. on April 21, 1995—six months after Risk opened—Miami Beach police officer Paul Nagel was driving to work at police headquarters across the street from the club when he noticed smoke billowing out the club's back door and called the fire department.

The blaze had been burning for hours in the windowless building. By the time firefighters arrived, it had raged into what is called a "flashover fire," a full-blown inferno.

By the time Miami Beach Fire Department investigator A. J. Anderson arrived to investigate, the place was gutted. "The nightclub is comprised of three distinct but non-divided rooms. The fire room is in the rear or east. It measures approx. 26 feet wide by 24 feet deep. Two semicircular couches 4 feet by 8 feet are against the north wall and two are against the south wall. A bar approximately 18 feet long by 7 feet wide is at the east wall. The origin of fire lies within the northeast portion of the seat cushion of the west couch on the north wall. Fire extension exists to the contents of the entire room most probably due to flashover," he wrote in his report.

Anderson determined the fire was started after someone shoved a lit cigarette into the cushion of a plush couch in the back VIP area of the club, sometime after the bar backs closed the club at 5:20 A.M. Though it looked like an arson blaze started by the building's owners to collect insurance, Anderson couldn't prove it.

"It always bothered me that the fire broke out long after the patrons went home," he said later. "In our minds it was a suspicious fire, but it was ruled accidental after we couldn't prove it was set."

Rumors abounded on South Beach that Paciello had torched his own club, but those close to him didn't believe it. Gilbert Stafford, a well-known doorman who worked for Chris, remembered going to the club after hearing of the fire and seeing his boss sitting outside the ruins on a barstool, his head in his hands. "The man was devastated," he said.

Chris Paciello's insurance company paid out over $250,000. It was just enough money for the twenty-four-year-old to start another club. He would call it Liquid.

8

ON THE LAM

It was just as well Lord Michael Caruso had left South Beach. Paciello's old roommate Vinny Rizzuto was coming to town. Now he would have a place to stay.

Rizzuto, a Gambino crime family associate, was wanted for murder. He had whacked the son of a Colombo family *capo,* and there were a lot of people looking for him, including the NYPD, the FBI, and the Mafia.

South Beach was as good a place as any for someone on the lam.

Vinny Rizzuto's gangland odyssey started with a simple robbery in Brooklyn on January 20, 1995. Rizzuto and two buddies—Joey Scarpa and a guy they called Jay—decided to rip off a marijuana dealer named Paulie in Bensonhurst. All three men were in their early twenties, bulky with dark hair and olive complexions, and ran around with a drug-dealing crew named after a favorite Brooklyn bar: First and Goal.

It was January 20, 1995. The young guns kicked in the door of an apartment at Ninety-fifth Street and Twenty-third Avenue where Paulie, whose last name was not released by authorities because he is cooperating against the Mob, lived with his girlfriend. All three intruders were armed, but they didn't need their weapons. The only person home was the girl. She was tied up just in case she tried anything. No one wanted the girl getting herself killed.

"Where's the money, bitch? Where is it?" Scarpa demanded. His finger tensed on the trigger of his gun. "Just tell us where it is, and no one gets hurt."

She refused to talk. The men ransacked the apartment and left with $10,000 in cash and more than $30,000 worth of marijuana. But before they even split up the bounty, the aspiring mobsters faced a very big problem.

Paulie was said to be a drug dealer protected by Frankie Fappiano, reputedly a made man in the Gambino family who was a feared and respected member of a crew run by underboss Salvatore "Sammy the Bull" Gravano. The bandits had inadvertently robbed someone protected by their own crime family. Even if Paulie was aligned with a different crew, it was still a problem. By daybreak, word was on the street. Fappiano was said to be very unhappy that his earners had been ripped off. Someone was going to pay.

Of course, Paulie could not call the cops. So he'd conduct his own investigation. He went to the cafés, the social clubs, and barrooms in the area. Was anyone flashing cash? Had anyone opened his mouth about robbing a drug dealer? Before long he picked up a name: Joey Schiro Scarpa.

Joey was on the streets dealing Paulie's pot. Yet just a couple of weeks before the robbery, Scarpa had tried to make a deal with Paulie and it didn't go through. So how could he have drugs to deal now?

It was not the first time Joey Scarpa had gotten into trouble. Three years earlier, he needed the help of his stepfather, Colombo *capo* Gregory Scarpa, who became infamous after his death when it was revealed that for almost thirty years he was a secretly paid FBI informant.

The elder Scarpa was an odd mix of Sicilian gangster and American patriot. In the 1960s J. Edgar Hoover used Scarpa as a mole in the Ku Klux Klan to find the bodies of three civil rights workers in Mississippi. Scarpa was sent south at the height of the tensions of Freedom Summer in 1964. He was told to use mob tactics to shake down a local Klan member who owned an appliance store for information about the murders. The plan worked, leading the FBI to the bodies of the civil rights workers, buried beneath seventeen feet of Mississippi clay. The incident was later memorialized in a movie called *Mississippi Burning*.

But even as Scarpa led a secret life as an FBI informant, he was still a wiseguy. A captain, no less. And why not? He had the FBI as a backup team. They tipped him to raids, gave him information on rival mobsters, and got him out of jams. In the 1980s, Scarpa's crew had flooded South Brooklyn with crack cocaine, making him extremely wealthy. One of the dealers was his stepson, Joey.

Being a crack kingpin is a stressful job, though, and Scarpa was more brutal than most. He used to brag to his cronies that he loved the smell of gunpowder and would punch the numbers 666 into his pals' beepers after he killed somebody. Most days he would sit on beach chairs on Thirteenth Avenue in front of his storefront, the Wimpy Boys social club, where his crew met to discuss business and whistle at young mothers as they walked by. Scarpa's crew, which numbered about half a dozen, spent their days lined up on the sidewalk on beach chairs taking in the sun while wearing dress pants and "wife beater" white undershirts, neighbors remembered. They always wore gold rope chains adorned with diamond-encrusted Playboy bunny charms, and rubbed oil into their shoulders to ensure dark tans.

Ultimately the anxiety of the drug business landed Scarpa in the hospital with a bleeding ulcer. He needed a blood transfusion, but he was not going to take one from the hospital's supply. After all, the die-hard racist reasoned, he could get a foreigner's blood or an African American's. A member of Scarpa's crew stepped forward to give a transfusion. Ironically, the underling's blood was infected with AIDS, and with the transfusion, the deadly virus was passed along to the boss.

By 1992, the virus had wracked his body. Greg Scarpa, though bedridden, was under house arrest awaiting trial on murder and racketeering charges. Even the FBI could not protect him. But when Joey Scarpa needed his help after he got into a brawl with rival drug dealers in Bay Ridge, his father jumped off his deathbed, his electronic monitoring bracelet sounding an alarm, and raced to his son's aid.

Joey had tried to take over drug turf belonging to two rival dealers who were protected by the Luchese family. Encroaching on another mobster's territory proved dangerous, and soon enough, Joey was being threatened by two Luchese associates, Mikey "Flattop" DeRosa and Ronald "Messy Marvin" Moran. Joey had gone to Mikey Flattop's doorstep to try to work something out, but had been chased off the stoop with a baseball bat.

Joey Scarpa was furious and went home to get the real muscle—his father.

"Get in," Scarpa said as he jumped behind the wheel of his son's red Ford Escort. Then he squealed off toward Thirteenth Avenue to the house where DeRosa lived with his mother. Next to him in the passenger's seat was his son. In the back seat was Joey's friend Joe Randazzo.

Mikey Flattop and Messy Marvin knew they were in for trouble. "Hey Marvin," Flattop yelled as the Escort pulled up and double-parked in front of his house. "He's back. He brought his father."

Flattop handed a 9 mm Taurus to Marvin and gave another underling a .22-caliber Beretta. The three men walked outside to greet their uninvited visitors.

Randazzo had pulled the hood of his sweatshirt over his head. Flattop stalked up to the elder Scarpa, who did not get out of the car.

"I don't need an audience," Greg Scarpa snarled. "I came here to speak to you."

"Marvin, you two go back in the house," Flattop ordered.

As Flattop's friends turned around to go back inside, they heard two booms. Flattop had fallen to the ground screaming, shot in the neck and the back.

Messy Marvin—a giant, overweight man with a puffy face—hustled back to the Escort and emptied his clip through the back window of the car, firing sixteen shots in all. The windows blew out. Blood splattered the windshield.

As Joey Scarpa jumped out of the passenger seat, Messy Marvin ducked behind a tree for cover. Flattop had crawled into his mother's house, and was lying on his mother's kitchen floor with a gunshot wound in his shoulder and stomach.

His mother was on the phone, calling 911. The emergency operators could barely hear her over the guns exploding in the background.

Outside, Greg Scarpa's head slumped over onto the steering wheel. The horn blared nonstop. Blood oozed from a hole in Scarpa's head. His right eye had been blown out. But miraculously, he was still alive. Randazzo, though, was dead in the back seat.

After a few minutes, Greg Scarpa crawled out of

the car and walked three blocks home. He left the blood-soaked Ford Escort with its shot-out windows and Randazzo's corpse in the back seat double-parked in front of the DeRosas' house.

By then pretrial service officers were calling the house to find out why the prisoner's ankle bracelet had sounded an alarm. When he walked in, Scarpa's daughter handed the phone to her father.

"Here he is. He is out of the shower now," she told the officer.

"Hello," Scarpa answered smoothly.

He held a dishrag to the gaping, bloody hole in his head and poured himself a healthy portion of Scotch. He poured an equal amount of the booze on the wound.

"Nope, boys," Scarpa assured them. "Everything is fine. I was in the shower. You know how these bracelets go off."

Pretrial services believed his story, until Scarpa was arrested at an upstate hospital later that night. Two members of his crew drove him to the hospital forty-five minutes out of the city after his efforts to staunch the pain himself failed.

Scarpa was in jail until his death of AIDS complications on June 8, 1994, in a federal medical center in Minnesota. He was sixty-six.

His twenty-three-year-old stepson, Joey, would die less than a year later.

A few weeks after the robbery at Paulie's house, Joey Scarpa was driving in Brooklyn with two female friends when a car pulled in front of him and cut him off. Paulie jumped out of that car and pulled Scarpa right through the driver's side window.

"You little fuck! I know you robbed us! It was you! Who were you with?" Paulie said. "You better open your mouth before I kill you!"

Terrified, Scarpa mumbled a name. "Vinny."

"Vinny who? Huh?"

"Rizzuto. Vinny Rizzuto."

The name was funneled to the upper echelon of Frankie Fappiano's crew. Now even bigger problems emerged. Rizzuto's father, Vincent "Vinny Oil" Rizzuto, was also an alleged Gambino soldier. He, too, was respected and ran with a tight crew.

Just to make sure Rizzuto really did have something to do with the robbery, a crew of Fappiano's underlings broke into his Brooklyn apartment. They ripped off anything worth more than five dollars. Just to send a message, they tied a huge pink bow around Vinny's watchdog's head.

When the burglars left, they also took a bag of Rizzuto's trash with them. In the bag was a photograph negative. They had it developed. It was a picture of Vinny, which they showed to Paulie's girlfriend to see if she could identify if he was one of her attackers. She took one look at the photo and nodded. "Yeah, that's him."

Later that night, Vinny answered the phone. The caller did not identify himself.

"I know who you are. I know you robbed us. If you don't believe me, come to the phone booth outside your house."

Vinny rushed to the corner. Resting on top of the pay phone was a picture of him.

He knew he was in trouble, so he reached out to his father. There was a sit-down. Something had to be done. The money, and the pot, had to be returned. And further reparations had to be made.

On March 20, 1995, Joey Scarpa called his friend Vinny Rizzuto. He was oblivious to the Mafia politics swirling around him.

"Hey Vinny, want to bang out some credit cards? I can give you back some of that cash I owe you."

"Where are you?"

As he talked on the phone, Joey's three-year-old daughter, Linda Marie, clamored for his attention.

"I'll come get you," Joey answered. "We'll take a ride to Sheepshead Bay. I got a guy over there. I'll pick Jay up. We'll be right over."

Joey picked up his daughter.

"Daddy, Daddy, don't leave," the little girl squealed.

He kissed her goodbye and squeezed her to his chest. "Daddy will be back later," Joey told her. "Daddy will bring you back a big doll."

He put on his leather jacket and left the house, looking back at the window as Linda Marie smiled and waved goodbye.

Soon the red Ford Escort pulled up in front of Rizzuto's house. Behind the wheel was Joey Scarpa. Jay sat in the passenger seat. Vinny slid into the back seat.

As the Ford pulled away from the curb, a black Buick Century followed it. In the Buick were Vinny's cousins, Ronald and Russell Carlucci. It was still daylight, around 5:30 P.M., when the car reached 2737 Brown Street in Sheepshead Bay.

"Hey, pull over," Vinny said.

When Joey turned off the engine, Vinny reached over the back of the seat and pressed a gun to the right side of Scarpa's head. He pulled the trigger twice, shooting Joey once above the ear and once in the back of the skull. The blasts blew out the driver's side window. Then he turned to shoot Jay.

But before he could squeeze off a round, Jay rolled out of the car and fled. He ran straight into the arms of an NYPD cop on foot patrol.

"He tried to kill me!" Jay screeched hysterically. "He killed my friend."

Vinny was already gone. He jumped into the Buick with his cousins and sped off.

Vinny knew he could not go home. The cops had already been there within an hour of the shooting. He couch-hopped for a few days. But he knew he had to get out of New York City.

And he knew he could count on Chris Paciello to put him up in South Beach.

The police are unsure exactly when Vinny arrived in South Beach. They believe he stayed a few months. And they know he did not leave empty-handed.

When Lord Michael Caruso left South Beach and flew back to New York, he had accidentally left his wallet in a metal box on his bureau in the Miami apartment.

Vinny found it. The wallet contained Michael Caruso's driver's license, social security card, and a plethora of picture identification. He was no longer Vinny Rizzuto, wanted murderer. He became Michael Caruso.

He made his way to Minnesota, where he took up with a stripper, began dealing drugs, and went underground for nearly three years. Even when the television show *America's Most Wanted* featured Rizzuto on its program, no one noticed. He was Michael Caruso. When Vinny was arrested for dealing cocaine out of a Minnesota motel room with his cousins, he was let go. Minnesota cops did not find a warrant for Michael Caruso.

But nothing lasts forever. After he had been on the lam for three years, he debated resurfacing only when the Feds threatened to indict his dad. Vinny Rizzuto eventually turned himself in to the Sixty-first Precinct house in Brooklyn on June 29, 1998. Waiting for him was DEA Agent Tim Foley, NYPD detectives Tommy Dades and Mike Galletta, and the FBI.

On January 28, 2000, Rizzuto was sentenced to twenty-four years in prison. His sentencing at Brooklyn federal court in front of Judge Edward Korman was an emotional and dramatic climax to a gangland slaying.

Rizzuto's family was in the courtroom. So was Linda Schiro, Joey's mother. Schiro's daughter-in-law Maria, Joey's widow, was also there with the couple's little girl, Linda Marie. Over the objections of Rizzuto's lawyer, they were allowed to give a victim's impact statement to the judge.

"My son Joey stands beside me today as he always does," Linda Schiro began, sobbing. "You can't see him, now, Vinny. But you saw him the night he was killed and sitting alone in a car to die by himself.

"Vinny, you didn't even give me a chance to hold and comfort Joey the way I did when he was born and put in my arms. I watched him laugh and I watched him take his first step. I was with him when he was married and I stood beside him as we both cried looking at his beautiful baby daughter that was born to him. Because of you, Vinny, his life is over. And I couldn't be there for my son to comfort him and hold him in my arms one more time. I couldn't be there for my son."

Linda Schiro paused to wipe at her tears.

Vinny Rizzuto's mother glared at her. Then she mumbled to her relatives. "Look at her. She's such an actress. She should get an Academy Award."

Rizzuto, himself, saved his venom for Brooklyn's toughest federal prosecutor, Jim Walden.

"Good job Walden," Vinny said in open court. "Good job. Twenty-four years you want to give me. You're threatening to indict my father. That's blackmail if you ask me."

By the time Rizzuto was sentenced, Chris Paciello

was already in jail himself, dealing with his own weighty legal problems.

Those problems would soon land him in the exact same place where Rizzuto stood, in front of Judge Edward Korman at the Brooklyn federal courthouse with prosecutors Jim Walden and Chris Blank seated at his right elbow, facing a charge of murder.

9

INGRID

One Monday night before Risk burned down, Chris Paciello was squeezing through the bodies packing the bar when he spotted a woman gyrating on the dance floor. He was immediately struck by how beautiful she was. She wore her raven black hair in a short, spiky cut that accentuated her almond eyes and café-au-lait skin. Her full lips gleamed with gloss and just a hint of brown lipstick. Her physique was toned and tanned. She wasn't wearing the South Beach uniform—miniskirt and tight halter—but a pair of men's tailored black slacks and a silk camisole. In one hand she clutched a pack of Kool Lights. In the other, she carried a cell phone in lieu of a purse.

The beauty's name was Ingrid Casares.

She was a sometime fashion model and party booker. She flitted about the globe, off to Milan, Paris, Ibiza—wherever the "it" place of the moment was. She was South Beach's glamour girl and Chris Paciello had never met anyone like her, especially not at the clubs back in Brooklyn and Staten Island.

Ingrid was famous among nightlife denizens, and in South Beach there is little else but the nightclub scene. She had even taken to calling herself the Mayor of

South Beach. "This is my town," she often laughed. "Going to Miami without seeing Ingrid is like Christmas without Santa Claus."

When Chris met her, Ingrid did not have a day job, or any job for that matter. She had college-hopped for a while, before she finally earned an English and public relations degree from the University of Maryland. She had lived in Los Angeles, booking pretty faces for Wilhelmina Models when she was not jet-setting around Europe. Finally, in the early 1990s, Ingrid came back to Miami and settled in South Beach for good.

Raul Casares, Ingrid's father, was a Cuban refugee and Miami businessman who'd made a fortune with an aluminum window and door company—RC Aluminum Industries. As his fortune grew, the family became more committed to anti-Castro exile causes and Cuban charities.

In the course of building up his business, Raul Casares had earned a reputation as a tough guy himself. When some of his foreign employees—most of whom made $5.25 an hour—tried to join a union, Casares was accused of making death threats to the organizers. The case was serious enough that the Florida Council of Churches and the South Florida Interfaith Committee for Worker Justice sent him a strongly worded letter.

Raul Casares was not worried. Nothing could hurt RC's profits. Business journals put its yearly earnings at around $21 million—plenty to keep Ingrid in the Gucci sunglasses and trim Versace double-breasted suits she favored.

For a while, Ingrid's only real job was to stay looking beautiful, taut, and tan. She spent her days jogging, practicing yoga, and buying clothes. She also attained minor celebrity status the world over as the girl who landed the ultimate prize—Madonna.

Ingrid's name had initially appeared in the gossip columns in 1992, when she was romantically linked to comedian Sandra Bernhard. The way the story was often retold, Bernhard introduced her pretty young girlfriend to Madonna at a birthday party, and the star singer stole Ingrid away. Within months of the breakup—and the demise of Bernhard and Madonna's friendship—Ingrid was photographed by Steven Meisel tongue-kissing Madonna and cuddling up to Italian beauty Isabella Rossellini in the singer's 1992 softcore porn book, *Sex*. Next to the lascivious pictures in the book, Madonna kept a written diary of the randy liaisons, often as "Dear Johnny" letters to another lover. In an entry scribbled inside a suite at the Ritz-Carlton Hotel in Cannes, France, Madonna wrote:

> *Me and Ingrid are laying naked on the sundeck rubbing suntan lotion on each other. I'm feeling very relaxed. . . . Now Ingrid is calling down to the sailors below while straddling the railing. I hope she's careful and doesn't slip and fall because her pussy is so wet right now it's dripping and she's kind of leaning over too far. Of course, I don't mind cause I get a perfect view of her ass, which is pretty fucking righteous. I wish I could stop playing with myself and thinking about sex. I'm going to have to go now because I have to finger fuck Ingrid or she's going to freak.*

By the time Chris Paciello met Ingrid, her affair with Madonna had come to an end, even though their friendship was still strong. But it was Madonna who kept Ingrid in the limelight. "I could discover a cure for cancer," Ingrid often complained, "and I'd still only be known as Madonna's girlfriend."

Ingrid loved Chris Paciello's gritty nightclub, Risk. She had even brought Madonna with her to the club. From the moment he saw her, Chris became enchanted with Ingrid Casares. In time, she invited him to dinner and they became fast friends.

Madonna and Chris Paciello were soon more than that. The *National Enquirer* photographed them coming out of Risk together one night and declared that the Material Girl had found a new man.

Even with his introduction to celebrity and high society, the old Chris Paciello still lingered under the surface. He behaved wildly, and acted like he was too important to suffer any serious consequence. Occasionally, though, the cops could slow him down.

Just before 6 A.M. on July 7, 1995, Miami Beach police officer Michael Vernon spotted a white Range Rover speeding down Collins Avenue. The four-by-four was going so fast, he knew he could not start his engine and gain enough speed to pull the driver over. Vernon was left shaking his head.

A half hour later, Vernon spotted the white Range Rover again. He couldn't believe his luck. This time the truck was weaving all over Collins Avenue near Twenty-first Street. Officer Vernon turned his lights on and pulled the truck over.

When ordered, Chris Paciello stumbled out of the driver's seat. He was barefoot, and he nearly walked into the northbound lane of Collins Avenue into the path of oncoming cars. The cop grabbed him, and was overcome with the smell of stale booze.

"I know you," Paciello said, his words slurred. His eyes were glassy and red-rimmed. Paciello tried to walk back to his truck, but he tripped over the curb and nearly fell.

"Sir, can you touch the top of this pen, please?"

Paciello reached out, but his finger missed the top.

"Close your eyes, sir." No problem.

"Raise your hands." Paciello threw his muscled arms in the air.

"Raise your left foot." Paciello put one sinewy leg in the air, then another. Again, no problem.

Then the cop asked him to count to ten out loud.

"Ah, one, two, three . . . four, five, six," Paciello burst out laughing. He could not walk in a straight line, and he had to grab a fence for balance. Then he missed the tip of his nose, instead smashing his finger into a nostril.

"Sir, you are under arrest for driving under the influence of alcohol. Hands behind your back, please."

Paciello told the cops his address was an apartment above Risk and gave them a false date of birth and social security number, just in case anyone back in New York was looking for him. He had backup for his lies. By then, Chris Paciello carried two driver's licenses. One identified him as Christian Paciello born on January 1, 1970, and living at 2025 Brickell Avenue in Miami. The second was in the name of Christian Ludwigsen with a birth date of September 8, 1971, and a Miami Beach address at 1439 Washington Avenue.

It was Paciello's second arrest in South Beach in less than a year. His third would come a month later when he threatened to kill the manager of a rival South Beach nightclub.

On August 7, 1995, four months after Risk burned down, Chris Paciello could stand the boredom no longer. He'd collected the insurance and wanted back in the nightclub game. And he would use the tactics he honed in Brooklyn to get what he wanted—he would strong-arm anyone necessary.

One of the hottest clubs on South Beach was Glam

Slam, a dancehall backed in part by the pop star Prince. It drew in hordes of tourists, who convened nightly outside the velvet ropes hoping to catch a glimpse of Prince or any of the other Miami celebrities.

That sweltering August afternoon, Paciello walked into Glam Slam at 1235 Washington Avenue and tried to make the manager, Paul Butler, an offer he could not refuse. "Let me rent the place," Paciello insisted. "I'll make us both a lot of money."

Butler refused. He was making plenty of money, and he did not want to get tangled with some guido from New York City.

"Oh yeah?" Paciello said, steaming. "Greediness is going to get you killed!"

Butler was scared. He had heard the rumors swirling around the beach that Paciello was connected. He had seen the hulking goons in gold chains that worked at Risk. When Chris stormed out of the club, Paul Butler called the cops.

"Can you just wait around here for a while in case he comes back?" Butler asked the responding police officer. He later dropped by the stationhouse and asked about hiring an off-duty cop to work at his club.

They tracked Chris Paciello down and arrested him for assault in the third degree, but the charges were later dropped. Paciello realized he had to come up with a softer image. Too many people thought he was aligned with New York City mobsters.

Ingrid Casares was the perfect front person for his image makeover. He asked Ingrid if she would be interested in helping him open a new club in what seemed a most unlikely location—a big space wedged in next to a Payless shoe store. But he knew he could make it work, especially with Ingrid.

She was soon convinced as well, and came on as a paid consultant making five thousand dollars a month. They would call their venture Liquid.

"We're a lot alike," Chris later told a *Details* magazine writer about joining forces with Ingrid. "We think about the same things: money and women."

Ingrid chimed in: "If I were a boy, I would be Chris."

"If I were a girl, I'd be Ingrid," Chris said. "She's one of the guys."

Chris might have used Ingrid for her connections, but she used him to give her life a sense of purpose, her friends say. Ingrid showed Chris a whole new world, and when she did, he used it to get away from his past.

Liquid opened on the Friday night after Thanksgiving in 1995. Outside, swirling spotlights announced that the two-story club was open for business. Limos lined the curb in front of the club disgorging a steady flow of beautiful people who were swept inside by chiseled doormen. First-night revelers included movie mogul David Geffen, fashion icon Calvin Klein, supermodels Naomi Campbell and Kate Moss, and pop star Gloria Estefan. Actor Michael Caine stopped by, as did Barry Diller. The celebrities crowded the dance floor with south Florida sports figures and South Beach socialites.

Chris Paciello had packed them in. He had made it all happen. This was his big night. "I don't believe the success achieved by my associates and myself is just a coincidence," he told a nightclub chronicler. "Everything in this world can be accomplished through hard work."

At some point, the scene outside Liquid got out of hand. People dressed up in their best Armani and Prada only to ogle the club on line for an hour or more began to get restless, then angry. When it became clear they were not going to get in to the most exclusive South Beach party of the year, they tried to crash the velvet ropes. Some even spat at the bouncers.

Inside, the bash raged on. Liquid's dance floor scarcely contained the throngs that gyrated to a slamming DJ known as Lord G. At another time, back on Staten Island, people called the man in the booth Skeevy. Gerard Bellafurie, Paciello's closest childhood friend, had transformed himself in the Miami heat, becoming one of the most sought after DJs in North America, and competed with brand names like club king Hex Hector and Madonna's music man Victor Calderone.

Skeevy and the Binger. Together again. A long, long way from home.

10

THE GOOD LIFE

Liquid's grand opening success was no one-night fluke. The club continued to do booming business among both the "bridge and causeway crowd" from all over Miami, and the celebrities who vacationed or kept homes on South Beach. The club never shut down—on slow nights it hosted fashion shows and special events.

"We wanted to create something different so that people can't easily forget and will want to experience this again," Chris Paciello told a writer two months after the club opened. "South Beach has seen a large number of restaurants and clubs open and close their doors. We know that Miami Beach is not an easy market; the competition is tremendous, however, we also know that there are incredible opportunities here."

Shortly after the opening of Liquid, *Variety* magazine labeled Chris Paciello the "hunky impresario" in a story about the glitzy nightlife world of Miami. And Lord G—that man who'd been branded with the moniker Skeevy because of his lack of personal hygiene—was suddenly ultra-desirable, sipping distal champagne out of gold-rimmed flutes and surrounded by voluptuous women.

Paciello could even take credit for much of the salsa-

house rhythms the crowd gyrated to: he and South Beach
pal Michael Capponi owned a small music production
company, C & P Music, that mixed and released it. Capponi and Paciello were good friends. Capponi still insists
that his partner was responsible for getting him off heroin by sending him to a detoxification center, and even
paid for it out of his own pocket.

Chris Paciello soon moved out of his condominium
with a view of the beach and bought a million-dollar
waterfront Italian palazzo and began to rehab it. In the
meantime, he was staying in a posh home on San Marino
Island, a small inlet in North Miami Beach.

The owner of South Beach's most happening hot spot
possessed a deep, mysterious appeal. He was good-
looking, with bulky muscles and smooth skin and dag-
ger black eyes. But it was more than his looks that drew
people to him. Chris strode the beach like the epitome
of the old-time gangster cliché—a big bad guy with a
heart of gold. He looked like he could knock a mook's
teeth loose with one punch, and in the next breath lay
his coat down over a puddle for his girl to walk on. He
got laid constantly and the cash was rolling in.

"I've seen women come up to him grind against
him," said fellow club impresario Gerry Kelly who had
once worked with Paciello. "He was a star. There was a
steady flow of women who showed up at the door claim-
ing to be his girlfriend. Usually, they were. He was hot,
hot, hot!"

Roxanne Rizzo had followed Chris to South Beach.
She settled into a luxury high-rise in Miami Beach and
was a regular at Liquid. Everyone remarked to Chris
about how beautiful she was, but it was not enough. She
began to get plastic surgery—larger breasts, sultry lips,
anything to fit in with the models that strutted the beach
around her. Before long, Chris had begun to date other

people. Eventually, so did Roxanne. Their relationship dissolved, but Roxanne stayed in Miami Beach and they remained friends. "I'm still close to his family," she said when asked about the relationship. "I love his family."

Madonna was reportedly the first "name" to fall for his goombah charm. The *National Enquirer* wasted no time in chronicling the pop star's fascination with the brawny club owner, and the two were photographed holding hands. Later, Paciello dated Daisy Fuentes, the shapely MTV veejay. After Daisy (though some say while he was still dating her), supermodel Niki Taylor dropped by Liquid for a Halloween party. One look at Chris was all it took. She joined him in the DJ booth for a late-night make out session and declared to her publicist that Paciello was "a great kisser." Friends spotted them canoodling in the pool at the Delano Hotel. Even Chris appeared to be shocked by his allure. Friends remembered him raising his eyebrows and giving them the "thumbs up" sign every time he slung his meaty arm around Niki.

On the heels of Niki, Paciello got comfy with Sofia Vergara—a big-breasted Colombian goddess, a swimsuit model, and a Latina television superstar with long blonde hair and full lips. She was the sizzling Univision television personality who had become famous for dating singer Enrique Iglesias and was often spotted with Mexican fighter Oscar De La Hoya. Her swimsuit calendar sold more than a million copies, and her website had received more than twenty million hits when Chris Paciello first laid eyes on her.

"Chris is the nicest person I have ever met," Sofia gushed in halting English. "I trust him completely. I like Chris a lot. He is my friend."

Even Jennifer Lopez fell for Paciello's charms at a New Year's Eve party at the Pelican Hotel in 1998, before she started dating Sean Combs. Paciello and Lopez had been photographed together at the *Vanity Fair* Oscar party earlier that year. "Chris Paciello was the King of South Beach nightlife," said his friend Michael Capponi. "If you're the king of nightlife, you're the king of the city. Women loved him."

While Chris was becoming a superstar on South Beach, it was business as usual among the young thugs on Staten Island. On January 3, 1996, one of his close friends was murdered back in his old neighborhood.

That night, two patrol cops working a midnight shift in Staten Island came across a tan four-door Oldsmobile on Johnson Street, a rarely used dirt road. The car was covered with ice and snow, all its windows were smashed in, and the keys were still in the ignition. The cops, thinking they had just another dumped stolen car, drove it back to the precinct. At 7:15 the next morning, they ran the license plate and saw that the car was reported missing five days earlier when Ilber "Billy" Balanca failed to pick his sister up for work.

They called the Oldsmobile's registered owner, Ilber Balanca Sr., Billy's father.

"Sir, we think we have your car here," Sergeant Pat Reilly told the elder Balanca.

"My son, he took it and never came back. Where is it? I'll be right there."

When Balanca came to pick up the car, Sergeant Reilly opened the trunk. What was inside made both men jump back and scream.

"There was a body in there. It was completely frozen. You could have picked him up with a crane and dropped him and he would have shattered into pieces. I looked at Mr. Balanca and asked him, 'Is that your son?' He just nodded."

After the body thawed, a medical examiner determined the twenty-six-year-old had been stabbed repeatedly about five days before his body was found. Detectives began interviewing his family and friends. The last time the six-foot-two bodybuilder had been seen was at the Manhattan nightclub the Tunnel.

Balanca's sister, Ganga, gave detectives a list of her brother's friends. One of the first names on the list was Chris Paciello, accompanied by his Miami telephone number.

Reilly reached out to Chris in Miami. After Reilly told the busy club owner about Balanca, Paciello sighed and said, "Yeah, I know. Listen, it's a shame what happened to Billy, he was a good guy. I want to help you, but I'm dealing with some problems down here. I'll call you next week."

Paciello never called back. Instead, Staten Island homicide detectives got a call from his friend Dennis Peterson, a well-known lawyer. "I'm afraid Mr. Paciello has nothing to say to you."

With no evidence that Paciello was involved with Balanca's homicide, he was under no obligation to talk to police. Besides, the word on the street was that Lord Michael Caruso, who at the time controlled most of the drug deals going down at the Tunnel, was the killer, not Paciello. But Caruso told the government that Paciello had killed Balanca because the Albanian failed to make good on a $50,000 drug deal. "He killed Billy to protect his name," Caruso said.

Paciello denied that account, telling a *Village Voice* reporter he was "dumbfounded" by Caruso's story. "Caruso is either lying or as delusional as an informant as I knew him to be as a promoter," Paciello said. "After he's admitted to being a liar, a drug dealer, and a thief, it

Chris "the Binger" Paciello after a 1994 arrest by New York City detectives. *From the library of Michele McPhee*

The Bath Avenue Crew, who tattooed "shooter" numbers on their ankles, from one to seven, to allegedly signify their allegiance to the Bonanno family as hit men. They are as follows:

#1 Paulie "Brass" Gulino after a 1992 arrest. He was later killed.

From the library of Michele McPhee

#2: James "Jimmy Gap" Calandra, one of the masked gunmen who took part in the Shemtov robbery, shown here at the Metropolitan Detention Center before he began cooperating with the government against his former cohorts.
From the library of Michele McPhee

#3 and #4: Fabrizio "the Herder" DeFrancisci with his arm slung around the shoulder of another crew member, Tommy "TK" Reynolds, inside the Metropolitan Detention Center. Reynolds was the shooter who accidentally squeezed off the bullet that killed Judy Shemtov inside her Staten Island home.
Reprinted with permission of Maryanne Reynolds

#5: Michael "Mikey" Yammine, who was also along for the ride the night Judy Shemtov was killed.
From the library of Michele McPhee

#6: Anthony "Gonzo" Gonzales after he was rounded up in a 1999 Mafia takedown dubbed "Operation Little Caesar" by investigators.

From the library of Michele McPhee

#7: Joseph "Crazy Joe" Calco in a mug shot.

Reprinted courtesy of www.GangLandNews.com

Michael Caruso, Chris Paciello's former business partner at his first nightclub, Risk.

Reprinted with permission from Michael Caruso

Alleged former Bonanno and Luchese soldier James "Froggy" Galione, currently serving time in a federal prison on drug, conspiracy, and murder charges, here in an NYPD photo taken after his 1999 arrest.

From the library of Michele McPhee

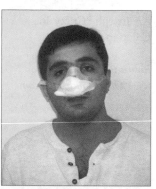

Michael "Mikey Flattop" De Rosa, a Bonanno associate who was arrested days after he had plastic surgery done on his nose. Mikey Flattop is now cooperating with the government.

From the library of Michele McPhee

Madonna, her daughter, Lourdes, and Chris Paciello.

Photo by John Roca

Dennis Rodman and Chris Paciello.

Photo by Seth Browarnik

NYPD narcotics squad sergeant Freddie Santoro outside a Coney Island auto body shop where investigators were digging for Carmine Gargano's remains. Gargano's body has still never been found.

Reprinted with permission of Todd Meisel

Missing Person

MPS no.   99/5381
CIRC no.   2000/018 (1/18)

Subject: **William Cutolo**
Description: Male, White, 50 years of age, 5' 10", 182 lbs., muscular build, medium complexion, gray hair, brown eyes. Scar left forearm & right hand. Missing fingers on right hand.
Clothing & Jewelry: Tan suit jacket, blue shirt, tan pants, brown shoes. Gold Rolex watch, pinky cross ring, gold necklace w/ Saint attached.
Last Seen: On 5/26/99 in the vicinity of 92nd Street & Shore Parkway in Brooklyn within the confines of the 68th Precinct.

ANY INFORMATION: Contact nearest Police Officer, or Missing Persons Squad at:
Tel. # 212-374-6920
Det. H. Gonzalez

Missing under suspicious circumstances

An NYPD missing person card was distributed by the NYPD after Colombo capo William Cutolo vanished in 1999. His body has never been found.

From the library of Michele McPhee

Alleged Colombo crime family boss Alphonse "Allie Boy" Persico.

Reprinted courtesy of www.GangLandNews.com

Top row from left--the investigators: NYPD Intelligence Squad detective Mike Galletta; NYPD Intelligence Squad detective Tommy Dades; Drug Enforcement Agency special agent Tim Foley; NYPD Intelligence Squad lieutenant Kevin O'Brien; and NYPD Intelligence Squad detective Jimmy Harkins. *Bottom row--the prosecutors:* assistant United States attorney with the Eastern District Greg Andres; Kings County assistant district attorney Chris Blank; and assistant United States attorney with the Eastern District Jim Walden. *Photo by Michele McPhee*

Former Madonna galpal and Paciello friend Ingrid Casares outside Brooklyn federal court.

Photo by John Roca

Supermodel Sophia Vergara, who also came to Brooklyn federal court to support Chris during his arraignment.

Photo by John Roca

Federal prosecutor Jim Walden.

Photo by John Roca

Chris Paciello's first taste of freedom as he leaves Brooklyn federal court flanked by his around-the-clock companions, security guards Tom Freeman (left) and Jim Woods, in March 2000, months after the club king's arrest on murder, racketeering, and robbery charges.

Photo by Michele McPhee

shocks me that I have to defend myself against his ridiculous accusations."

Even though Paciello was never charged with Balanca's murder, or even officially named a suspect by detectives, the rumors swirling about his involvement never went away.

He may have seemed a changed man, this new King of South Beach, but the Binger in him still reigned. Especially when it came to defending the honor of one of his women, as was the case when Chris Paciello pummeled Niki Taylor's estranged husband, former arena-football player Matt Martinez. The fight was not over Niki Taylor, even though Paciello was still dating her. The two came to blows over Sofia Vergara.

Martinez had also dated Sofia, and Paciello was convinced the former pro athlete was trying to move in on "his girl." In fact, Martinez later admitted not only had he slept with Sofia, he told her Chris had been cheating on her with a virtual harem of other women. Besides that, Martinez was not exactly thrilled that Paciello was sleeping with his estranged wife and the mother of his two sons. The couple had been talking about a reunion.

On Christmas Eve in 1996, Paciello went with Sofia to Bar None, a South Beach club owned by his pal *Ocean Drive* magazine publisher Jason Binn. As he relaxed in the VIP room, Paciello caught sight of Martinez sitting at a table with a bodyguard and a couple of friends. Martinez was trying to catch Sofia's attention. He met Chris's cold stare instead.

The two eyeballed each other; killer glares Martinez had honed on the football field and intimidating scowls Paciello had picked up from his gangster pals. Before long, Paciello stalked over to the football player's table. "What's your problem?" he asked.

"Hey, fuck you, pal," Martinez fired back. "What are you going to do? Hit me?"

Paciello hauled off and punched the football player in the face. Blood spurted from his forehead. Martinez hit back. Bar None's bouncers broke up the fight, but not before Martinez's face was considerably battered. A *New York Daily News* gossip columnist wrote about the fisticuffs and reported that as Paciello was escorted out of the club, he blew Martinez a kiss. "I'm going to take you out, pal," Paciello said through a smirk.

At first Martinez wrote Paciello off as a big mouth. He was trying to break into the acting business, and was even thinking of suing Paciello because he had to get plastic surgery to fix his face. Then some of the locals informed Matt that Chris was planning to fly some New York City goons down to Florida to make good on his threat.

Martinez got nervous. He called the cops, applied for a gun permit, and hired bodyguards to escort him around, even on the golf course. A police report about the incident reads:

> *Suspect [Chris Paciello] believes victim is seeing his girlfriend. Victim states they are old friends and not seeing each other. Suspect started a fight at above location, causing a cut to the victim's forehead. Suspect is now telling people that is he going to "take the victim out." Suspect comes from New York and flew twenty men from New York to Miami to get victim. Victim is in fear for his life and is now getting a carrying permit.*

Niki Taylor later said that her ex-husband was "egging Christian on" and the club owner had to respond.

"Christian and I were dating and Matthew and I were just going through the divorce and everybody found out that Christian and I were dating. Matthew was just trying to make my life miserable because he didn't want the divorce. Christian hit Matt first, and he also took care of the . . . other guys he was with. Christian just handled all of them by himself and pushed guys into walls and everybody had broken noses or whatever. Christian went back to his club with Sofia and everyone at Bar None was getting stitches."

The brawl was by no means an isolated incident. The King of South Beach felt he could attack anyone he wanted with reckless abandon. That included his own employees, as one of Liquid's managers found out one night in 1996.

Carl B. Dread—whose real name is Carlton Barton—was taking a break without permission as the club wound down for the night around 4:15 A.M. It was another packed Monday night at Liquid for the Fat Black Pussycat party, which was revived from Risk, and Dread was tired. He was stretched out in a back office when Paciello tracked him down.

"What are you doing?" an incensed Paciello seethed.

"I'm relaxing for a minute," Dread answered sarcastically, "if that's all right with you."

No, it wasn't all right at all.

Paciello punched the manager square in the left side of his jaw. Dread stood up, still reeling from the blow, and tried to stumble away. Two bouncers helped him up.

"Take him into the alley," Paciello snarled. "Get this piece of shit out of here."

The club owner gave Dread a kick that propelled him down a flight of stairs, and then followed him. As Dread lost consciousness, Paciello continued to pummel him.

Only when it looked as if his victim was nearly dead did Paciello coolly walk away.

Dread took pictures of his mashed, battered face and called the Miami Beach police. They tracked Paciello down at Liquid and arrested him for battery. The charges were later dropped after Paciello hired Dread back at double pay, and extended a halfhearted apology.

More disturbingly, Chris's flashpoint temper was not limited to employees. He would also attack customers. Lawsuits were frequently filed against Liquid because its owner had gone after them. Paciello's company had settled a civil suit with a group of vacationing Arab Americans from Dearborn, Michigan, who said Chris Paciello had attacked them without provocation. One reveler, Hassan Makled, told detectives Paciello had singled him out—the biggest guy in the group—for a particularly vicious beating. He left the club with blood streaming from his ears.

"He said to me, 'I want to beat the fuck out of him,'" Makled said later. "Those were his exact words. 'I want to show you guys from Michigan, wherever you are from, what everything is about,'" Makled said Paciello screeched in his face.

Scared, Makled's friends tried to calm Paciello down. "Leave us alone. We'll leave."

Paciello had begun to escort the group out of the club when punches were thrown. A melee followed. Makled covered his face as Paciello pummeled away. "My ears were bleeding; my head was bleeding."

Six months later, Paciello picked a fight with a more formidable opponent—Mighty Mike Quinn, a 270-pound bodybuilder and former Mr. Universe.

Quinn never saw the blow coming just before 2 A.M. on June 26, 1996.

He was in the VIP room at Liquid partying with his wife, Denise, and several other couples. They had a few drinks when Paciello walked by their table. Quinn invited him to sit down.

Denise was a cocktail waitress at another club, and Chris had gotten to know her so he sat down and ordered a drink.

Just then, Michael Christian, an African American basketball player who played pro in Venezuela, walked by with a unique-looking baseball cap. Christian shook Paciello's hand. Madonna had introduced the two on an earlier occasion.

"Nice to see you," Paciello said.

"I love that hat," one of Denise's girlfriends told Christian. "I really love that hat."

Quinn piped in. "How much do you want for the hat?"

"It's not for sale," the basketball player answered. It was a treasured playoff hat.

"If you were a real man," another man at the table said, "you'd give my girl your hat. She likes it. If your girlfriend wanted my hat, I'd give it to her off my head. So, Michael, as a nice gesture, take off the hat."

Christian reluctantly obliged. He handed his hat over and walked away. When he was out of earshot, Quinn turned to his wife's friend.

"Give that nigger back his hat," he snarled. "Don't wear no hat from no nigger."

Paciello glared across the table. "I don't think that's right, calling the guy a nigger. I think it was a nice thing he did, giving your girl this hat. Now you're going to call my friend a nigger?"

The bodybuilder stood up. He looked like a six-foot block of solid muscle. His arms alone measured twenty-three inches wide.

"Why don't you shut the fuck up," Quinn said.

"Okay," Paciello answered. "I'll shut up, but I still don't think it's right, your calling the kid a nigger."

"What are you going to do about it?" Quinn yelled.

Chris Paciello stood up, looking for a bouncer to throw Quinn out of the club. He was obviously drunk, so Paciello was willing to give him the benefit of the doubt.

Quinn lunged forward with a glass in his hand. He knocked the table over, sending drinks and champagne bottles to the floor.

Chris sucker punched him straight in the face and the hulking man flew back into the table. Quinn was splattered with his own blood. His wife was screaming. Chris kept punching away until Quinn was knocked out cold. When he awoke, his tree-trunk arms were slung around two security guards' shoulders as they dragged him out onto the sidewalk.

His wife rushed him to South Shore Hospital. Quinn's injuries were serious.

"When I blow my nose, air comes out of my eyes," Quinn told the emergency room doctors. He would need reconstructive surgery on his entire face.

"He didn't look too good," Paciello later admitted.

After he was stitched up and sent home, Quinn called the police. Detectives showed up at Liquid to interview Paciello.

"Hey," he told the investigators. "The guy was out of line with his comment, and I told him so. He came at me aggressively, and I defended myself. End of story."

Paciello then proceeded to hang a picture of his handiwork—a photograph of Mr. Universe's battered, bloody face with broken cheekbones and jawbones—on his office wall at Liquid. An Emergency Medical Technician who had been at the hospital took it for Chris and later mailed it to the club owner.

Quinn was not going to give up, though; he had been

attacked and the club owner was going to pay. He hired a lawyer and filed a civil suit. Then one of his best friends, former professional boxer Vinny Pazienza, got a phone call from Johnny, a New York City nightclub manager. "Why don't you tell Mike to drop the case against these guys?" Johnny said. "They are bad people, Vinny. They told me to get in touch with you because they know I am friends with you and you're good friends with Mike. They wanted me to tell you to tell him to drop the case."

"I'm not going to tell him to drop the case," Vinny said. "I don't know the kid who hit him. From my understanding of the case, he got totally abused."

"You know if he gets the money, he's not going to be able to spend it," John said. "He'll be dead before he has a chance."

The boxer quickly reported the phone call to Quinn, but despite the threat, Mighty Mike Quinn was going to press on with the lawsuit. Chris Paciello would see him in court.

Life was not always about busted knuckles for Chris Paciello. He treated his employees to trips to Key West, and to catered picnics at South Point Park just blocks from Liquid. He was also living the high life. He flew to Los Angeles with Ingrid and Madonna for the Golden Globe and Oscar award ceremonies. His new friend Sean "Puff Daddy" Combs got him into the Billboard Music Awards show. He was a regular in the front row of New York City's trendiest fashion shows. During one spring fashion week in Manhattan, Paciello sat in the front row of Versace's show, flanked by Madonna and actress Julianne Moore. He spent a lot of time traveling to Ibiza, Spain, the nightclub capital of the world, to keep up on the latest disco trends. He attended Sammy Sosa's birthday party in the Dominican Republic and flew to

Colombia with Sofia Vergara on vacation. He attended a millionaire businessman's wedding in Mexico and vacationed all over Europe. He took in Miami Heat games from courtside seats. He was living large.

Then, in June 1997, Paciello's gangster charm and true brutality were merged when he jetted off to Vegas to see Mike Tyson battle Evander Holyfield for the heavyweight belt at the MGM Grand. Chris Paciello could afford ringside seats at the hottest bouts, and often bought tickets in bulk to treat employees or big-spenders at his clubs.

The Tyson-Holyfield match was a perfect fight for a guy like Chris Paciello—who fancied himself as a fairly good boxer. There was bound to be lots of blood, chaos, and even some flying flesh. In the middle of it was Chris Paciello, flanked by Niki Taylor and his close friend, Colombo associate Dominick "Big Dom" Dionisio. Ingrid was seated close by.

In the third round, Mike Tyson bit off a small portion of Evander Holyfield's right ear. Then the former champion marched over and gave his stunned opponent a shove that harked back to Tyson's day as a brawler from Brownsville, Brooklyn. The fight resumed momentarily, until Tyson then bit off a chunk of Holyfield's left ear. Referee Mills Lane called the match off immediately. Tyson was disqualified. Holyfield was rushed to the hospital.

"Look at the bite, I'm missing part of my ear," Holyfield moaned after the fight. "He fouled me in every way. There's no courage there whatsoever. He should put up his gloves, be brave and really want to fight."

Tyson, a convicted rapist who has been called an animal and a derelict, said he "snapped" when Holyfield head-butted him. "He just kept butting me," Tyson said.

"If they didn't stop it, what am I supposed to do? I wanted to fight. He didn't want to fight."

Iron Mike was disqualified and Holyfield was awarded the heavyweight crown. The crowd went crazy. As Tyson was escorted out of the ring to a chorus of catcalls, boxing fans began throwing debris at him. His entourage began throwing objects back at the crowd.

Although Chris Paciello did not know it then, the truncated fight would serve as an omen for his own shortened career. His crimes committed in plain sight would continue for a while longer. But the day was coming when his past in Brooklyn would surface and unseat him from his throne.

11

TAKEDOWN

During the same years Chris Paciello was rising to the top, his former associates were still running amok, engaged in daily criminal activity. They would be arrested in a massive sting and some of them would start to sing about everything they knew. Chris Paciello might not have seen it coming, but his empire was already crumbling under his feet. The beginning of his end started in July 1994, when a young Bay Ridge man went missing, and his family set out to find him.

Carmine Gargano was not a typical street corner thug. The twenty-one-year-old grew up in a sprawling white house on top of a manicured green slope in the high numbers on Ridge Boulevard, a tony address in south Brooklyn. He was enrolled at Pace University in Manhattan, working toward an accounting degree. His parents, Rosa and Carmine Sr., were hardworking Italian immigrants who started a small construction business a few years after they arrived in Brooklyn in the early 1970s. The business grew into a lucrative contracting empire. Their four sons—Carmine Jr., Michael, Gerry, and Vito—joined the operation.

The Garganos led a good life. They had a tight family. And then Carmine Jr. got into a barroom brawl and everything changed.

Some fistfights, especially in Brooklyn, lead to more than a bloody nose. There are reputations to consider as well as mob politics. Was a made guy hit by a "civilian"? Who disrespected whom in front of their friends?

Hitting the wrong guy in Brooklyn can get you killed.

One hot summer night, Carmine Gargano had sparred with "Mikey Flattop" DeRosa, a wannabe mobster aligned to the Luchese family—the same Mikey Flattop who was involved in gunning down Greg Scarpa.

Carmine was said to have hit one of Mikey's friends with a bottle at T-Birds, a popular nightclub on Third Avenue in Bay Ridge, sending him to the hospital. As Mikey Flattop carried his friend out of the club, he looked over his shoulder at Gargano and snarled: "I'm going to kill you. You know that, don't you?"

When a guy like Flattop promises to take a life, it's wise to assume he's serious. Carmine fled the club. To make matters worse, someone at T-Bird's called the cops and fingered Carmine as the injured man's assailant. Now the cops were looking for him, and so were members of Luchese soldier Jimmy Galione's pistol-packing crew.

Carmine soon disappeared.

In late July 1995, detectives Tommy Dades and Mike Galletta were sitting in the squad room at the Sixty-eighth Precinct in Brooklyn poring through their heavy caseload. They got a call from the desk sergeant saying there was a family that wanted to fill out a missing-persons report on one Carmine Gargano Jr.

His parents walked up the concrete steps to the detective squad. Behind them were two of their sons, Gerry and Michael. The Gargano family looked drained, yet jumpy, from too many sleepless nights.

A year had passed since Carmine Jr. had vanished and by then the Garganos feared the worst. They had spent months looking for him, driving around south Brooklyn in separate cars. Cops from the NYPD's warrant squad were also looking for him. He was wanted on assault charges stemming from the T-Birds fight.

As Rosa Gargano tearfully talked, Dades and Galletta realized that the Garganos were telling the truth. They believed their son had been murdered, and as they listed the names of young men their son had been running with, the detectives agreed that murder was a strong possibility.

"Please, please find my son," Rosa Gargano said as she began to cry. "These drug dealers, I think they killed him."

Rosa told the detectives that her son had run out of the house just after waking up on Sunday afternoon, telling her he would be right back. Minutes later his brother Gerry got a phone call from Ronald "Messy Marvin" Moran. "Tell your brother not to go anywhere until I talk to him," Messy Marvin said. Then he hung up.

Of course, it was too late. Carmine Jr. had already driven off in his van. He and the van both disappeared on July 10, 1994.

As the Garganos told them the names of the guys their son had been associated with, Dades and Galletta looked at each other with raised eyebrows and began taking notes. Some of the names were very familiar. They had floated up after small-time crack busts, drug dealer rip-offs, unsolved beatings, and even a few open murder cases. James "Froggy" Galione. Michael "Mikey Flattop" DeRosa. Ronald "Messy Marvin" Moran.

Galletta and Dades were considered to be two of the precinct's toughest detectives. Both were tall, swarthy, and muscular. Both dressed meticulously and, because of their dark European complexions and wavy black hair, they were sometimes mistaken for gangsters themselves when, in the course of an investigation, the duo would knock on a door looking for information. More than once, the precinct had gotten calls asking the detectives' commanding officer to verify they were cops because of their strikingly rugged appearances. Their lieutenant always explained that not only were Dades and Galletta cops, they were some of the best detectives in the city. Each had been awarded more than a dozen medals, including Excellent Police Duty and Meritorious Police Duty honors.

The Sixty-eighth Precinct was in the heart of the organized crime world, and Dades and Galletta had gotten to know the Mafia players in the neighborhood very well. They had witnessed firsthand the unglamorous effect the Mob had on the area's residents. As tough as the two detectives were, they were just as compassionate for the victims of crime. For an NYPD cop, there is no such thing as leaving the job at the office.

Tommy Dades began taking phone calls from Rosa Gargano at home. One of them made him more determined than ever to find Carmine. Someone had pumped bullets into the Garganos' front door as a warning.

"They wanted to scare Rosa, to keep her from talking," Dades said.

Dades and Galletta knew that solving a missing persons case without a body posed a problem. Without evidence that a crime had taken place—blood, a body, or eyewitnesses—they could not even legally question Gargano's friends and associates.

There had to be another way to find out what happened to Carmine Gargano. Cops in the Six-eight knew that Bay Ridge had been flooded with crack cocaine in the early 1990s. And they had heard that Jimmy

"Froggy" Galione, the man who had pumped Gus Farace full of bullets years earlier, was behind its infusion.

They took the case to the very top in the NYPD—Manhattan chief of detectives William Allee. Dades and Galletta told Allee about the murders they might be able to clear if they could take down Galione and his cronies, the very least of which would turn out to be the Gus Farace homicide. The detectives said they would need help from the narcotics division of the NYPD, and they wanted to work with a cop who knew wiseguys: Detective Freddie Santoro.

Santoro was another tough cop who wore leather blazers over silk shirts. He had grown up on the same Brooklyn streets as the crooks he investigated with a vengeance. "The wiseguys of today are parasites," he liked to say.

Allee and the detectives took the case straight to the Police Commissioner himself, Howard Safir. Safir heard them out, nodded, and picked up the phone to call the DEA. The agency was more than willing to get involved. They were already eyeing Galione and his crew.

The two agencies formed a team composed of DEA agents along with cops from the Brooklyn South Narcotics Major Case unit and the Homicide Squad, and Detectives Dades and Galletta from the Sixty-eighth Precinct. Finally the team sat down with two young, dogged prosecutors: assistant United States attorney Jim Walden and assistant district attorney Chris Blank. They agreed to pour federal funding and resources into the investigation. As it turned out, both prosecutors had the mettle and the intuition of much more seasoned lawyers.

Like all major investigations, the case had to have a name. It was quickly dubbed "Operation Little Caesar." The case's moniker came from an obscure reference to its main target, Froggy Galione. Over lunch one afternoon in the early days of the investigation, Detective Freddie Santoro remarked: "Froggy looks just like Edward G. Robinson," the bulging-eyed actor who played Caesar in the famed movie.

To gather intelligence, Detective Santoro went undercover in the south Brooklyn neighborhoods of Bath Beach, Bay Ridge, and Bensonhurst as a drug-crazed crackhead. In the course of his daily interactions with Jimmy Galione's drug crew, detectives and agents came to surmise its lucrative earnings were being funneled to the Mafia's upper echelons of management in the Bonanno and Luchese crime families. This was getting better and better all the time.

Galione, who earned the nickname "Froggy" because of his protruding eyes, was barely a teenager when his father, a respected Gambino hit man, was slain by his own compatriots. Ralph "Ralphie Wigs" Galione was murdered in the early 1970s after he participated in a messy hit along with a young John Gotti, then an up-and-coming gangster. The loss scarred young Jimmy's psyche and would follow him into adulthood.

In 1972, one of Carlo Gambino's nephews, Emanuel "Manny" Gambino, vanished. Right away the family suspected that it was the work of the Westies, a famously deranged gang of violent Irish hoodlums from Manhattan's Hell's Kitchen. Early the next year, the mutilated body of the missing Gambino nephew was discovered. Before long, someone fingered a Westie named James McBratney as the kidnapper.

A contract for his murder was quickly handed to Gambino captain Neil Dellacroce, who passed it along to his underlings: up-and-coming mobster John Gotti and Angelo Ruggiero, Gotti's best friend. Ralphie Wigs was selected as the trigger man.

The hit team planned to lure McBratney out of his favorite Staten Island tavern, Snoope's Bar & Grill, by flashing fake police credentials so they could pretend to arrest him and drag him outside without too much of a commotion.

The plan failed. On May 22, 1973, Ruggiero, Gotti, and Galione rushed into the bar wearing gold detective shields around their neck. McBratney had seen his share of badges and refused to go without a fight. Chaos ensued. So Ralphie Wigs decided to get the job done right there. He'd pulled out a gun and pumped three bullets into the Irish gangster, right in front of a half dozen witnesses.

It was not the kind of clean hit the mob bosses had envisioned. Ralphie Wigs was found dead a few months later. The FBI busted Gotti and Ruggerio. But with the shooter dead, prosecutors did not have much to go on. Both men plead guilty to reduced charges of attempted manslaughter. After serving two years in jail, both came home to Howard Beach, Queens, as heroes, stand-up guys for doing their time without opening their mouths.

After the Farace homicide, the younger Galione had decided he wanted to jump from the Bonanno family to align himself with an old friend, George Conte, a respected and feared captain in the Luchese family. Shifts in allegiances are not uncommon in the underworld, but it takes careful planning. You have to make sure the new captain is more powerful, that he carries more weight.

At that time the Bonanno family, once the most prosperous family making a fortune in gambling, labor racketeering and drug trafficking, was limping toward oblivion. During the 1980s and early 1990s, the family was pushed aside by the other New York mob factions because of its fractious and unreliable members. The family was also denied a seat on the Commission—the corporate board of the underworld—because of its rampant drug dealing.

This was not a new story.

The Bonannos' strength first began to wane in 1957 when its boss Albert Anastasia was gunned down in a barber's chair at Manhattan's Park Central Hotel. Rival wiseguy Crazy Joe Gallo reputedly took credit for the hit, calling himself and his crew the "Barbershop Quintet." By 1975, Carmine Galante had seized the top spot in the family, reviving drug contacts in Sicily and bringing in a notoriously violent group of soldiers from the old country that Italian American mobsters nicknamed "zips." Four years later, Galante was gunned down at a courtyard eatery in Joe & Mary's Restaurant in Brooklyn. One of three masked gunmen opened fire with a double-barrel shotgun just as Galante had stuck a fat stogie in his mouth. He died with the cigar clenched in his teeth, a priceless tabloid snapshot. Rumor had it a salty old NYPD detective stuck the cigar in the corpse's mouth, saying, "Here, Carmine, have a smoke."

Not until a John Gotti ally named Joseph Messina took control of the family in 1993, after serving a ten-year racketeering sentence, was the Bonanno Mob revived a bit. It had again become one of the most potent and dangerous Mafia groups in New York. The Bonannos had regained its seat on the Commission, even as its members continued to pump drugs into the city.

But unlike his good friend Gotti, who wooed the public and the press, Messina was low-key and unassuming. Joe Messina preferred the shadows.

The Luchese members were also disorganized, but its seat on the Commission automatically made it a stronger outfit than the Bonannos. Tough Jimmy Galione had a reputation of being a stand-up guy who was not afraid to do work for the Family. The old-timers remembered his father. After a number of sit-downs the Bonannos agreed to release Jimmy Galione and his close friend and accomplice at the Farace hit, Mario Gallo. They were free to join the Luchese family.

These days, Galione made good money from the drug ring he was convicted of overseeing in South Brooklyn. He got his button under George Conte, the government believes, after he killed rival mobster Richard Taglianetti in July 1992.

As Jimmy Galione gained power and attention from the mob bosses as a good earner, he also caught the eye of the wrong people—the law.

Most days Jimmy Galione sat in his usual red vinyl booth at the Patrina Diner in Bensonhurst. It was his unofficial office. Every morning, fat Messy Marvin Moran piloted his white Cadillac El Dorado to Galione's house. Then the two men drove to the Patrina.

They usually went there to discuss the beeper business. By then, as a Luchese soldier, police believed he oversaw a syndicate of young crack cocaine sellers whose customers beeped them from phone booths and met them all over south Brooklyn. Other dealers paid a street tax to Galione's managers—Messy Marvin, Mikey Flattop, and Mikey Yammine.

Bath Beach was a strange place for a drug consortium. The streets were filled with well-kept apartment buildings and two-family houses decorated with plaster flowerpots and grapevines. The smell of baking bread wafted over the family-owned Italian and Jewish stores. It was a white middle-class, family-oriented neighborhood: not exactly the type of place imagined when a crackhead needed to score a rock.

Crackheads are the worst kind of addicts. They steal

their mothers' jewelry and want their dealers to take it in trade. Home invasions and burglaries had shot up in the precincts where Galione's dealers were plying their wares. Even worse—at least to the older mobsters whose rackets were still loan sharking and numbers running— the dealers were selling poison to Italians, their own people. They were defiling their own neighborhood to make money.

The crew often had to scrape the bottom of the barrel to find dealers to put on the streets. Before long, the pristine avenues of the Italian-dominated neighborhoods— Bay Ridge, Bath Beach, and Bensonhurst—were being patrolled by a macabre assortment of lowlifes.

Investigators bugged one of the dealers' cars and picked up wiretapped conversations about how broke everyone was. Oftentimes, the dealers would call their mothers: "Ma, ya got anything to eat?" Once, detectives overheard a dealer ordering his friend to rob an elderly woman's purse.

The crew went on undeterred. A guy had to earn, and these days the quickest way to earn was through dealing drugs.

Carlo Gambino was right. Law enforcement will tolerate certain crimes like bookmaking and prostitution, but they will never turn their heads to narcotics, Santoro often thought as he watched the spectacle from an undercover NYPD van outside the Patrina Diner. *Drugs are going to be the downfall of the Mob.*

Santoro knew that better than most. During the years he spent on the streets of south Brooklyn as a narcotics cop, he had "flipped" more than a few low-level street hoods caught dealing drugs to get to bigger wiseguys.

"Sometimes it takes a twenty-dollar bag of crack to catch a million-dollar wiseguy," Santoro explained to his colleagues. "The only way to get to Jimmy Galione, and the whole Luchese family, is with the drugs. The drugs are going to sink them."

Santoro did not need to convince anyone.

In the mid-to-late 1990s south Brooklyn neighborhoods fell prone to a rash of break-ins and robberies. In 1996, its residents, who were primarily conservative Italian, Greek, Irish, and Syrian families that voted Republican and sent their children to private schools, could not take it anymore and convened at St. Anselm's Church in Bay Ridge for a town hall meeting with city officials. Among the guests were New York City mayor Rudolph Giuliani and Police Commissioner Howard Safir.

There was a lot of complaining at St. Anselm's Church that night, and a good deal of it came from Rosa Gargano. She wanted the mayor to help find her missing twenty-one-year-old son. "Please, Mr. Mayor," the heartbroken mother pleaded. "Help me find my son. These drug dealers. I know they did something to him."

There was no need for the mayor to get involved. Detectives Dades and Galletta were obsessed with bringing Rosa Gargano peace of mind and a burial for her young son and had already immersed themselves in the case. The slight, dark-haired woman reminded both cops of their own mothers.

Even Carmine Gargano's grief-stricken mother could not have forseen the far-reaching implications that his disappearance would have. Between the cops, the DEA agents, and a pit bull of a prosecutor, Jim Walden, the takedown of the people believed responsible for Gargano's death would snowball into more than two hundred indictments.

Even though his body has still never been found.

* * *

For more than a year, cops and agents quietly flooded Bath Avenue.

They put hidden video cameras on top of two telephone poles near Messy Marvin's home on Bay Seventeenth Street in Bath Beach, and kept track of the stolen cars pulling in and out of the driveway. Another camera monitored the comings and goings across the way at Fabrizio DeFrancisci's house. Detectives even had a camera on top of PS 163—a Bath Beach junior high school on Seventeenth Avenue that had a view of the Pigeon. A live feed from that camera was monitored from the secret Operation Little Caesar's headquarters. They even cloned one of Galione's underlings' beepers so cops could track his every move. Undercover detectives bought drugs directly from Galione's dealers and kept careful records.

Dades and Galletta knocked on doors and put confidential informants onto the streets. Detectives Freddie Santoro and Jack Prunty spent a lot of time in an unmarked van monitoring the comings and goings on Bath Avenue, taking surveillance pictures, scribbling notes on the stolen cars. "I've spent my whole summer in this van," Freddie complained after about three months of the investigation. "I hate this van."

One scorching summer's day, Freddie was sitting in the back of the van taking pictures. It was so hot, he had stripped down to his underpants to stay cool. Then Fabrizio DeFrancisci, by now one of the leaders of the Bath Avenue Crew, spotted him.

Fabrizio stalked over to the van. The detective was frozen. He could not leave the van and give up his cover. He sat still, sweat pouring off his face, as Fabrizio pressed his nose to the window. He tugged on the back doors. Then he tried the front door, but Freddie jumped over and snapped the lock down before Fabrizio could get to it.

Fabrizio would not go away. He shook the van, shoved it. Peered in the windows.

"It was about ninety-eight degrees and we were out there all day, getting pictures, getting video," Freddie told his fellow detectives later. "He was shaking it, and I cracked my head on the roof. I don't want to run out of the van in my Calvin Kleins and give them the satisfaction of knowing I'm in there. But he kept shaking the van, like Magilla Gorilla in a velour jogging suit. I took my Mace out. If anyone got the door open I was going to squirt them right in the face."

Lucky for the detective, Fabrizio had sent his message and walked off.

At three o'clock in the morning on October 1, 1996, Operation Little Caesar investigators were ready. It was time for the takedown. "Okay," NYPD chief of detectives William Allee told the investigators. "Let's go."

More than two dozen NYPD, FBI, and DEA agents fanned out across south Brooklyn armed with arrest and search warrants.

They banged on Froggy Galione's door. He did not want to answer it.

"Open the door, or we'll break it down," yelled detective Mike Galletta.

"All right, all right," Galione finally said. "I'm with my family. Take it easy, I'll be right down."

At Messy Marvin's house, the 300-pound man waddled to the door in his bikini briefs, a sight detectives wished to this day they had never ever seen.

When investigators hit Mikey Flattop's Dyker Heights home, the drama really began. Flattop did not want to come to the door because, just a week earlier, his vanity had gotten the better of him. Wanting to attract the ladies, Flattop—whose squashed head earned him his nickname—had gone to a plastic surgeon to have his hooked nose reduced to a more flattering knob. When the cops busted in, he still had the nose job plaster taped across his face. As the cops cuffed him and threw him onto the front lawn in his pajamas, DeRosa's father collapsed, clutching his hand to his head. He had had a stroke.

Meanwhile, Flattop's mother thought she had a stroke of genius. Panicked that she and her husband might be implicated in her son's crimes, she ran to Flattop's room and grabbed a shoebox full of money that was secreted in his closet. She opened a window and flung all the bills outside.

She did not realize that surrounding her house were NYPD detectives. As $60,000 in ten- and twenty-dollar bills fluttered into the backyard, the money was scooped up and put inside evidence bags. Another $10,000 on top of Flattop's bureau—next to a framed picture of DeRosa as a little kid standing next to Mets player John Franco—was also put into evidence.

In all, thirty-eight suspects were rounded up before dawn. Investigators seized hand-scrawled ledger books, computerized records of drug customers, cash transactions, and even a price list for the drugs. The search warrants netted $290,000 in cash, one-and-a-half kilograms of cocaine, three stolen cars, a slew of stolen car parts, and three guns.

The defendants were transported to an auditorium at the Fort Hamilton army base in Bath Beach. The place was jammed. Drug dogs. Auto crime cops. FBI. DEA. Emergency Services Unit cops. Narcotics detectives. Homicide squad cops.

So many bad guys and investigators were crammed

in the room, investigators had to put luggage tags around the suspects with their names and dates of birth to tell everyone apart.

Not only did the task force just take a giant drug crew off the streets, they also cleared up a slew of unsolved homicides—including the gangland hit of Gus Farace. Galione and Mario Gallo eventually pleaded guilty to whacking Farace.

Now that Messy Marvin and Mikey Flattop were behind bars, they had a lot of time on their hands, so they began sending missives to detectives Tommy Dades and Mike Galletta. The misspelled, inarticulate rants were typed on sheets of paper or scrawled in greeting cards. Some were sent to the Sixty-eighth Precinct. Some were sent to the cops' homes. Nearly every one had a taunt about Carmine Gargano—the missing man whose disappearance sparked the entire takedown.

On Christmas Eve a card arrived at Tommy Dades's home. Along with the holiday greeting was a list of cooperating witnesses being prepped for the Jimmy Galione crew's trial. On the front of the card was a picture of a home decorated for Christmas—along with "Here lies Carmine Gargano," accompanied by a picture of a machine gun and a pistol "that killed [Joe] Randazzo," the man murdered when he accompanied Gregory Scarpa and his son to a shootout at Flattop's house. Inside read:

> To Dades and Galletta. Oh YA, AND RATS.
> May your door get kicked down. Be a
> cheerful welcome home to a home filled with
> bullet holes. Happy Holidays SCUM. Your
> friends at the MDC [The Metropolitan Deten-
> tion Center federal jail].

Dades did not need to recognize Messy Marvin's handwriting. The fat mobster had left his fingerprints all over the letter. He and Mikey Flattop were charged with threatening a police officer, along with a plethora of other crimes of which they were suspected.

After his conviction six months later, Messy Marvin had yet another message for the investigators. This time it was pleading: "Can we make a deal?" Messy Marvin had decided to cooperate with the government. Right behind him came Mikey Flattop DeRosa.

And what they had to say would eventually lead investigators to South Beach.

12

THE EXPANDING EMPIRE

July 1997 found Chris Paciello back in his old stomping grounds. As happens every year, South Beach turns dead in the summer months. The club scene simply withers in the insufferable humidity. For that very reason Chris and Ingrid were discussing opening a Manhattan club. They even bought a condominium on Elizabeth Street in SoHo so they would have a place to stay while they examined their alternatives.

No matter where he went, though, Paciello's penchant for violence reared up and out of control. This time it led to his arrest and a meeting with an old enemy.

Paciello was at a Manhattan nightclub in the company of a former Ms. USSR, Yulia Sukhanova. The tall, blonde, voluptuous beauty was a star in her homeland and thus a constant target of paparazzi. A Russian photographer named Georgi Kandelaki followed Paciello and his date, angling annoyingly for juicy shots. Chris tried to shoo him away, but Kandelaki was not deterred.

A scuffle ensued. In the fight, Kandelaki was stabbed three times in the chest with a fork, either by Chris or one of his goons, the photographer said. As he lay on the floor stunned and in pain, a gold chain was ripped from his neck and pocketed. The NYPD arrived just as

Paciello was pouring himself a glass of Cristal in the nightclub's VIP room.

The police booked Paciello on an attempted murder charge at the Sixth Precinct in Greenwich Village. He was led into the stationhouse with his professionally manicured hands cuffed behind his back.

Detective Danny Massanova eyed him up and down. "That guy looks familiar," he told his partner.

Massanova went over to the arresting officer, Detective Ellen Dickert. "Ellen, what's the guy's name, the guy you just got brought in for assault one?"

"Umm, let's see. Chris Paciello."

The name didn't ring a bell with Massanova. He went back to his desk. The face continued to bother him, though.

Several hours later, Ellen Dickert returned to Massanova after she ran Paciello's prints. "This guy's name isn't Paciello, it's some German name. Ludwigsen."

"Christian Ludwigsen? I know that guy! I locked him up in 1989 for sucker punching me."

Detective Massanova walked over to the cell where Chris Paciello was lounging on a bench in his tailored black Gucci pants. He'd been allowed to make two phone calls. The first was to Ingrid, who was staying at the Elizabeth Street pad. The second was to his Staten Island lawyer, Dennis Peterson. They were both on their way.

"Remember me, pal?" Massanova asked him.

"Yeah, I remember you," the club king sighed. "Still a cop, huh? Still working your ass off for fifty grand a year? You know what? I make fifty grand a week. I have a million-dollar home and a fifty-foot yacht. And I fuck women you only dream about. Who's the asshole now?"

"I don't know," the detective answered. "But you're in there, and I'm out here. Let me think about that one."

Paciello was released from jail after his date bailed

him out. The charges were later dropped. Georgi Kandelaki had somehow changed his mind about pressing charges.

Paciello had less success with his Manhattan nightclub venture. His efforts with Ingrid to open a club in Manhattan were being thwarted at every turn by New York City mayor Rudolph Giuliani. The hardline ex-prosecutor's "zero tolerance" for nightclub policies was changing everything. Strip joints had been swept out of the city leaving Times Square a cavern for high-rise developers. Club owners were being locked up left and right for allowing drugs to be sold and used on their premises.

It was a hard time for anybody to get a lease, and someone with a reputation like Chris Paciello's didn't have a prayer of getting a liquor license.

Paciello would have to give up for the time being and turn his attention back to Miami. South Beach was about to be spotlighted in the national media, and Chris wanted to be a part of the action.

All the glitz-drenched hoopla of South Beach in early 1997 came to a devastating halt when the area's most famous resident, flamboyant Italian fashion designer Gianni Versace, was gunned down outside his Ocean Drive mansion on July 15.

Versace was shot once in the back of the head and once on the right side of his face a few hours after dawn with a stolen .40-caliber pistol. He had been returning home with a stack of magazines from the News Café, just three blocks away from his mansion. His killer was Andrew Cunanan, a handsome young hustler who had gone on a cross-country murdering spree that left five gay men dead.

Seconds after the shooting, Versace's boyfriend Antonio rushed out of the house screaming, "No! No!" He cradled his dying lover in his arms. Strangely, one of the bullets had hit a mourning dove in the eye and the bird lay dead right next to Versace's corpse. The slain dove was spun into some sort of Mafia message and initially spawned rumors that Versace's slaying was a mob hit.

In the hours before the slaying, Cunanan had partied the night away at Liquid, one of Versace's favorite haunts. He had roamed the nightclub for hours, dancing and drinking and trying to pick up hot men. He said that he was a wealthy businessman who lived in a luxury high-rise along the beach. When the club closed down, Cunanan went to the beach to wait for Versace.

News reporters descended from every corner of the earth. *ABC Primetime Live*'s Sam Donaldson interviewed four of South Beach's most prominent citizens about Cunanan's last night at Liquid: *Ocean Drive* magazine publisher Jason Binn, Versace model Naomi Campbell, and Liquid's owners, Ingrid Casares and Chris Paciello.

The killer had tried to pick up one of Liquid's bouncers, Chris Paciello said. "Basically, the guy just walked over to him and started talking to him," he told the national television audience glued to their sets. "He struck up a conversation with him. It's not like he was being low-key. This guy wants to be a part of the scene."

"Creepy," Ingrid added. "Just knowing some guy is running around like that. Trying to be normal, then going ahead and doing something so violent, like an animal, you know?"

Donaldson pointed out that many of Miami's celebrities—Madonna, Sylvester Stallone, Rosie O'Donnell—lived behind tall walls and traveled with bodyguards. Why did Versace feel so free just traipsing down Ocean Drive?

"He was a very modest person," Naomi said of her

friend. "He didn't have to have bodyguards around him because he was very free. He wanted to go around. Taking a walk on the beach or going to get a newspaper is a normal thing everybody does every day."

After killing Versace, Cunanan went into hiding in Miami Beach while the FBI and local cops frantically scoured the city looking for him. Three weeks later, Andrew Cunanan shot himself in the head on a houseboat just as the FBI and Miami Beach detectives were closing in on him.

As South Beach slowly recuperated from the horrible tragedy, Chris Paciello worked hard to maintain the habits of a good businessman. He was in his office at Liquid by 11 A.M. daily, and worked long into the next morning. He was generous and kind-hearted with his employees, treating them to catered cookouts and field trips to Key West. He was also quick to lend money and advice to any one of the hundred employees in his service.

As a result, Liquid's luster had remained undimmed. *South Florida* magazine had named Liquid as the best nightclub in Miami two years in a row, in 1996 and 1997. It also declared the head doorman at the Fat Black Pussycat party at Liquid on Monday nights the most powerful man in the community. That same month, *Elle* magazine called Liquid one of the hottest clubs in the country. "Flooded with nicely tanned models and fish tanks," the item read. "Go for the whacky theme nights and a glimpse of the interior designed by Christopher Ciccone (a.k.a. Madonna's brother)."

Despite the fame, profits were going down, even if the lines continued to snake around the block. Chris was worried. He had taken on the responsibility of caring for his entire family. His mother, Marguerite, and his two brothers George and Keith had all relocated to

Miami Beach. Keith worked as a manager at Liquid. George promoted parties. His mother was enjoying herself, working on her tan.

Maintaining a million-dollar estate wasn't easy. His Flamingo Drive palazzo, all five bedrooms, six-and-a-half baths, and a sprawling living space, was being renovated. The bills never stopped mounting. He was also paying rent on another upscale house while the palazzo was being upgraded. Then there was his yacht—*Liquid*.

It was getting expensive to be Chris Paciello. And he was only twenty-seven years old.

Chris needed to expand his scope. He and Ingrid, along with an Italian expatriate named Nicola Siervo, broadened their business interests with a Tuscan eatery they called Joia on Ocean Drive. Joia was an open-air Mediterranean-style restaurant that catered to sports stars and models. Reservations were hard to come by, and so were parking spaces for the Lincoln Navigators and Rolls Royces in which the wealthy arrived. The menu was expansive, with dishes that harked from both Cuba and Italy and with an exotic wine list. Well-heeled diners nibbled on fresh seafood served on a bed of squid ink linguine, as a sea breeze wafted into the eatery gently blowing the billowy curtains that hung from the ceiling to floor.

Joia made them a great deal of money in the winter of 1999, so Chris and Ingrid then opened a hip upscale lounge a few blocks away from Liquid called Bar Room that catered to a young starlet set. Cameron Diaz was a regular. Gwyneth Paltrow and Madonna often partied there before heading over to the Versace mansion for dinner parties thrown by the slain designer's sister, Donatella. Dennis Rodman stopped by Liquid every time the Chicago Bulls were in town. One night he and

Chris stripped down to only their pants and wrestled shirtless on the floor in front of an audience. Chris was the victor.

One night, Robert De Niro settled in at a VIP table at Bar Room for the night. Even Paciello was awed when the actor walked in, his doorman Gilbert Stafford remembered. "It was the first time I saw Chris a little star-struck."

Still, it wasn't enough. "I don't get to sit back and enjoy what I have," Paciello complained to a business reporter. "I'm always looking for the next project."

To another writer he said, "I'm too busy to go anywhere. My social life led to my business, and now I have no social life."

To the gossip columnists, Paciello's social life was noteworthy enough to chronicle in glossy magazines and newspapers. Weeks after Bar Room opened in early February 1999, Tommy Hilfiger threw a bash there to celebrate a new line of his menswear. The party started at Joia where Hilfiger, k.d. lang, Chris Rock, Ben Stiller, Cameron Diaz, and Ed Norton dined on the five-star Mediterranean cuisine. The celebrity revelers then moved over to Bar Room. Cameron Diaz dirty-danced with Norton on a balcony.

Chris Paciello had his own hands full. He had to divvy up his attention between Fran Drescher, star of TV's *The Nanny,* Daisy Fuentes, and Jennifer Lopez, whom he had lasciviously kissed a month earlier at a New Year's Eve party in the Pelican Hotel on Ocean Drive. Lopez was having such a good time, and gyrating her shapely assets with such abandon, that her tube top fell down. Toward the end of the night, Dennis Rodman showed up at Bar Room with a six-foot-ten drag queen named "Elaine."

"It's always like this," Chris told a reporter during the bash.

Then Paciello got a piece of bad news. He had heard that Steve Lewis—one of the owners of New York's pistol-hot club Life—planned to open a place that winter on South Beach. He had also contacted Ingrid with a deal to reopen Studio 54 in Manhattan. "Ingrid seemed poised to be the next Steve Rubell," Lewis later told a *Vanity Fair* writer. "Ingrid could come in as a partner— she would be the front. The kicker was that Chris could never come to the club."

Lewis did not want to have anything to do with a mobster.

Paciello was livid. Something had to be done. There was no way he was going to let that guy overshadow everything he'd built and steal Ingrid away from him. Paciello called for reinforcements—specifically his old Brooklyn pal, Colombo crime family associate Dominick "Big Dom" Dionisio. An FBI report described Big Dom as a member of a shooter squad that had roamed the streets of Brooklyn during an inner-family Colombo crime family war in the early 1990s.

If anyone could keep Steve Lewis away from Ingrid, it was Big Dom. On December 29, 1997, Chris decided to have a chat with him. Neither realized that federal investigators had put a wiretap on Big Dom's phone and were listening to every bit of the conversation.

"What's wrong?" Dom asked when Paciello called him that morning.

"This Steve Lewis. He keeps trying to get in touch with Ingrid. He wants to meet up with Ingrid."

"Yeah?"

"He wants to open a club down here, with his partner, with Ingrid." And Lewis had told her to keep any conversation secret from Chris. "He said, 'I don't want to meet with Chris. Chris has a temper.'"

"I was thinking," Paciello added. "If I should call

Steven right now and say, 'Steven, do yourself a favor, stay away from her, don't even bother talking to her or . . . I could have you stop by the club to talk to him. Or just leave it alone?"

"Well," Dom said, "it depends."

"They are going to try and pump her up and fucking start offering all kinds of money and no matter what, even if she's loyal and don't leave me or whatever . . . her head gets fucking, like, ya know, right away, she wants everything."

"You know what the problem is?" Dom said. "If I go talk to him, he's scared shit of me. I don't know how you want to handle it. You know what I am saying? I mean I'll go talk to him, but then what happens if they say something to her?"

"I don't care if they say something to her," Paciello said.

"Fucking people," Dom sighed. "That's how people get. And that's the sad part. I'll go to the club tomorrow night. I'll grab him, this Steve Lewis. I'll tell him I want to talk to him. I'll tell him, 'Steve, what are you doing with this Ingrid? Stay away from her.' "

"Then say 'Do yourself a favor, Steve,' " Paciello added.

" 'Don't call Ingrid no more,' " Dom finished. "That's all I'll tell him. I'll tell him, 'Steve, stay away from Ingrid. Don't even bother going to talk to her.' "

"The worst that could happen is he tells me to get outta his club," Dom continued. "I punch him out, then walk out. Might as well poison the meat, before it even gets done."

"Exactly," Paciello said.

Paciello checked on Big Dom's progress after his huge party New Year's Eve at Bar Room. Even though it was a new year, January 1, 1998, it turned out that Big

Dom hadn't been able to get in contact with Lewis because the club owner refused to see him.

"So that cocksucker won't come out?" Paciello said.

"I called, they said he's not available. I left a message on his voicemail. I'm just going to go there tonight," Dom said. "I already left him a message."

"He'll probably think it's about New Year's Eve and you wanna get in [to Life]. That's what he thinks. Believe me. That's all the phone calls I get now. People calling me out of nowhere that I don't even speak to, trying to get into the club."

Paciello brought the conversation back to the business at hand. Even after Big Dom tried to squash Steve Lewis's contact with Ingrid, the club magnate was undeterred. He had called Ingrid again, maligning Chris.

"He told Ingrid, 'Chris, Chris, he has a temper, we're not like children over here. We're businessmen, and I don't want to meet with Chris. He has a temper and we want you. You're the celebrity. You're the one in the paper all the time,'" Paciello told Dom.

"I'll definitely go in there tonight," Dom responded. "I'll definitely go in there and grab him. I'm going to terrorize him a little, too."

Paciello's voice got louder as he talked. "He's a great manipulator. He'll talk her ear off. She'll start believing him. She's fucking stupid. I just gave her a big piece of the club, too. I mean, I just gave her twenty-five percent of it, because I know I'm going to lose her. She's not really making any money, you know what I mean? I got to start taking care of her, or else she's going to fucking leave me. It's my fault. It'd be greedy."

"You get along with her, right?" Dom said.

"Yeah," Paciello said. "She loves me. And that's why she has stuck by me for so long. You know what I mean? But there's only so much."

"Now she starts seeing money," Dom said. "All she starts seeing is money."

"Yeah," Paciello said. "I'm going to hand her a nice stack of money this week. She'll be happy as fuck. Then she'll start seeing money coming through the season."

Chris Paciello ended the conversation describing a fight he was involved in at Liquid the night before, a brawl serious enough that someone called the cops.

"I didn't hit the fucking kid," Paciello said. "I grabbed him by the neck and I flung him, and he slammed the floor, and he just laid there for like ten minutes."

After the replay, Paciello said he had to hang up. "Happy New Year. Careful. I love ya."

Several men approached Lewis a few days later. "Chris was really upset," they told him, Lewis later remembered. "Don't let this happen again."

The deal with Ingrid never came to be.

Nine days after Paciello's phone call to Big Dom, Paciello practiced intimidation in a less businesslike manner. He flew into another one of his rages.

The afternoon of January 9, 1998, was typical of South Beach's busiest season: warm, sunny, festive. Chris Paciello sat inside Joia, readying the place for the tourists who'd be flooding in. But he could not concentrate over the noise of a leaf-blowing machine outside.

Out on Ocean Drive, a landscaper named Anibal Ibanez was busy clearing fallen palm leaves with a gas-powered blower. Chris stepped outside and asked him to quiet down. "Hey," Paciello said. "I'm working in here. I can't hear myself think."

"Leave me alone," Ibanez said. "*I'm* working."

"Listen, you are blowing leaves all over my restaurant." Paciello was steaming now. "I said, turn it off now!"

The heated exchange continued for a few minutes.

Then Paciello could not take it anymore. He went back inside the restaurant and came back out with a two-by-four. The whirling of the leaf blower instantly stopped. The machine's operator was clubbed to the ground. His lip was bleeding and his eye bulged with the beginnings of a shiner.

Bloodied and bruised, Ibanez got up and ran away. When detectives went to him to ask about the incident later, he claimed he "forgot" all about it. He did not want to press charges, and the two-by-four beating was written up as an "intimidation incident."

Still, Chris was not satisfied. He pined to open a club back in New York City, to show anyone who doubted his acumen that he had made it. But his violent history and mob connections proved an impediment in New York.

After a year of searching and two false starts at potential club locations on the West Side of Manhattan, Chris and Ingrid had finally settled on a 200,000-square-foot space at 16 West Twenty-second Street, which was home to another club, Les Poulets. Miami's "It couple" even had a name picked out for their latest endeavor: Liquid Lounge, New York. *New York Magazine* had written about their plans in a glowing feature story welcoming the club impresarios.

By the time they began talking about a deal, the neighborhood had become ultra-trendy. Artists had moved in, opening pricey bistros and posh boutiques. The area's newest residents were wealthy and immediately complained to the neighborhood's Community Board Five about a loud nightclub moving in. They dreaded the traffic and the obnoxious drunken revelers that would no doubt spill into the streets where they owned high-end loft space.

Chris Paciello knew his criminal history would add

to the furor against Liquid Lounge, New York. Ingrid filled out all of the paperwork, listing her father, Raul Casares, as the club's sole shareholder. Chris's name did not appear anywhere, even though he was the face man for the club in negotiations with the space's elderly owner, David Yagoda.

Then, on April 1998, *The Village Voice* newspaper wrote a story that scared Yagoda and helped sour the deal for good. Reporter William Bastone reported that Chris Paciello was really Christian Ludwigsen—a Mafia-associated street thug. His Miami clubs were just fronts for the Mob, the story alleged.

The article, titled "Thug Life," read: "Lurking behind Casares is her Miami Beach partner, a mob-connected thug with a lengthy rap sheet and a history of violence."

Soon after, Yagoda refused to rent the space to the duo, and the city refused to give them a liquor license. Chris was livid. "Just because I grew up in Brooklyn does not mean I'm a gangster," he told the *Daily News*.

He told *Ocean Drive*, "Everybody can talk about my past, and I'm not ashamed of it at all. As a matter of fact, I'm proud of it. To come from where I came from and to do what I am doing now, I can actually pat myself on the back." To *New York Magazine* he said, "It doesn't make me a gangster because I hung out on the corner with people when I was growing up. They're childhood friends, and they will remain friends."

Things only got worse for the king of nightlife after his old partner, Lord Michael Caruso, took the stand in 1998 to testify against another club mogul—his old boss Peter Gatien, who had been arrested on drug and conspiracy charges. Caruso's testimony at the Gatien trial fingered Paciello and his friends in the Bath Avenue Crew as protectors of Limelight nightclub drug dealers, fueling the rumors surrounding Chris.

After that, Chris and Ingrid threw in the towel and abandoned plans for a New York City life. A short time later, Ingrid gave a bitter interview about the yearlong battle to the gay New York magazine *HX*. "They fought me tooth and nail," she complained. "[They] had something against my business partner. You had the landlord, who was in his seventies, who really didn't know what was up. The community board had his ear; and he was listening. He doesn't know me and Chris. We're just some people who own a nightclub in Miami, so who is he going to listen to?

"I had a lot of great people behind me, but it obviously wasn't enough to get an approval. It was a lot of time, and it drained me completely. Drained my business partner even more because he was really exposed."

Ingrid went on. "The whole thing left me with a really bad taste in my mouth. In Miami, we're all fighting for the same people. Here, there's so many from many great walks of life. I'd want to do here what I did in Miami, which is incorporate a glamorous atmosphere where people—gays, straights, drag queens, blacks, whites, whatever—can let themselves go and be a little decadent."

Still, Paciello was a fighter, and he refused to hit the mat. If Yagoda would not help them open a club in New York, he would find someone who could.

In what might have been a last-ditch effort, right after the New Year in 1999, Chris Paciello and Ingrid Casares stopped by an Italian social club in Dyker Heights, Brooklyn, to call on Colombo crime family captain William "Wild Bill" Cutolo. They were hoping the natty union official would be able to help them circumvent the rules. It had worked for Chris before.

The men at the Friendly Bocce Club on Eleventh Avenue were not accustomed to a woman entering their domain, especially not a glamorous, bisexual predator dressed in a tailored men's suit. When the duo walked in, some eyebrows went up. But they were there to discuss a business proposition that could make a lot of people money.

Wild Bill Cutolo had known Chris for years through his close friends, Big Dom Dionisio and Enrico "Rico" Locasio—the aforementioned "Twin Towers."

It would never become clear what was discussed at the Friendly Bocce Club that day because the effort soon turned out to be doomed. On May 26, 1999, Wild Bill vanished. He dropped his Lincoln Navigator off to have its clutch fixed and never came home. Federal investigators believed he was rubbed out in a Colombo power play.

No body has ever been recovered.

13

A FRIEND TO LAW ENFORCEMENT

His efforts in the Big Apple may have proven fruitless, but on South Beach Chris was still a star. Paciello took certain steps to make sure he stayed on top.

Throughout the late 1990s, battles had raged between club owners on South Beach and the city's municipal government. The nightlife industry was a financial and cultural powerhouse, but as the scene gained momentum, armies of rowdy clubbers started causing trouble. Some were even gang members from other parts of Miami who crossed over the causeway to party.

With incidents of disturbing the peace and occasionally serious violence and destruction on the rise, Miami Beach mayor Neisen Kasdin formed a city community board composed of club owners and city officials to ease the tension and to slow down the proliferation of liquor licenses, especially on picturesque Lincoln Road—which, as it happened, was where Bar Room was located.

"What we're looking at is working a transformation," task force member Steve Polisar, an attorney and longtime South Beach investor, told a reporter shortly after the group's foundation in 1999. "Attracting an older, upscale crowd, creating an adult Disney World."

Chris Paciello was immediately one of the most outspoken members on that task force. Paciello—a man who could not even get a liquor license in New York—was now one of the people who could determine if someone else got one. The Colombo family's interests were really protected now. In addition, Paciello wanted the police presence in the club scenes toned down. "Having a bunch of kids on their stomachs in handcuffs on the median outside your club is not an inviting sight to prospective customers," he said.

The community board was especially gracious toward Liquid and Bar Room. All of a sudden, inspectors were rarely hitting Paciello's club even as other packed hot spots were being raided almost nightly.

At the same time, Chris Paciello had cultivated a new friend in law enforcement. In the spring of 1998, Paciello had hired a Miami Beach police detective named Andrew Dohler to work security outside his club when the officer was off-duty. Dohler was on Paciello's payroll partly as hired muscle, but mainly as an in-house security advisor.

Dohler had proven himself trustworthy on a number of occasions. Their unlikely friendship began on July 16, 1998, when Dohler tipped Chris to a raid that Miami Beach cops were planning in order to snag underage drinkers inside the club. Sure enough, later that night a nightclub task force from the Strategic Investigations Unit stormed in, demanding to see IDs.

The next day Paciello called Dohler to thank him. Several days after that, Paciello showed his appreciation by taking the detective out to dinner at Joia. The duo later went to Liquid where they drank together all night, on Paciello.

Then one hot, sunny afternoon late that month, Chris loaded his friends—including Detective Dohler and a group of topless Latina women—aboard *Liquid*, his fifty-foot luxury yacht, steering it north up the Intercoastal Waterway to take in the cool, ocean breezes on Biscayne Bay. The yacht had everything a multi-millionaire club mogul could want: a margarita mixer, busty women sans bikini tops, and great music. Its destination was a waterfront restaurant in Sunny Isles called Shooters.

At some point, one passenger remembered, Paciello noticed they were being followed. He shrugged off the small cutter in close pursuit. All assumed it contained paparazzi working overtime for photographs. "These guys don't give up, huh?" Chris said, smiling.

After he docked, Paciello sat on the sun-splashed deck of the restaurant, flipping through his menu and gazing at the lazy currents of the Intercoastal as his yacht bobbed at its berth in gentle waves.

At another table in the eatery was Alphonse "Allie Boy" Persico, the reputed acting head of the Colombo crime family, son of Carmine "the Snake" Persico. Persico was having lunch at the waterfront eatery with his family when Paciello waved him over to his table. Persico was a frequent VIP at Paciello's clubs, and the two had run into each other a few times back in New York.

Allie Boy Persico was the epitome of Old World gangster. The handsome, college-educated chieftain wore expensive eyeglasses and dressed in stylish, hand-tailored Italian suits. He was a computer whiz and ran legitimate businesses—a bagel store and a limousine shop in suburban Lighthouse Point, Florida, and owned real estate in New York. In addition, the government believes he was the first mob boss who figured out Wall Street was a cash cow, virtually inventing the "pump and dump" stock scam.

New York City prosecutors had alleged that Persico

received a "mob tax" of six cents a share for every bogus stock that was unloaded by unscrupulous brokers for gangland investors. La Cosa Nostra had always been on the fringes of Wall Street, but Persico was the first boss who collected such a huge payday from the market.

As he sat down with Persico for lunch that sunny afternoon, Chris Paciello apparently forgot about his attempt to forge an alliance with another Colombo kingpin, Bill Cutolo—who was considered by mob insiders to be a Persico rival.

The luncheon Paciello and Ingrid Casares had with Wild Bill at the Friendly Bocce Club in Brooklyn months back when they were trying to bring Liquid to New York was moot. Just months after the meeting, Wild Bill disappeared. The reputed Colombo captain who had survived numerous hit attempts during his long stint as a high-ranking mobster dropped from sight just a month before his fiftieth birthday.

The Colombos, one of New York City's powerful crime organizations, had been torn apart by an internal two-year war over control of the family. During the war, twelve gangsters were murdered and about sixty went to jail. Cutolo had been loyal to an insurgent faction of the Colombos led by acting boss Victor Orena, who was at odds with Carmine Persico, Allie Boy's father.

On May 26, 1999, Wild Bill called his wife just after noon and told her, "I love you, and I'll see you later." He had errands to run, among them was having the shift lock fixed on his Lincoln Navigator. At three o'clock, Wild Bill dropped the SUV off at Ralph, John, and Sons Auto Repair on Sixty-fifth Street in Bay Ridge, where the mechanics had been working on his family's vehicles for about five years. Then he asked one of the mechanics to give him a ride down to Ninety-second Street and

Shore Road, a beautiful spot in Bay Ridge with a commanding view of the Verrazano Narrows Bridge.

He was never seen again.

Later that night, after Cutolo did not return home, to the office, or to a meeting at his social club, his family became worried. When he did not show up for work at Local 400 of Production Workers, where he was the head union official, his panicked family filed a missing persons report with the NYPD. It was not until he failed to show up for his weekly haircut at Bruno's barbershop in Bensonhurst that even his crew became worried.

Organized crime detectives and the FBI feared Wild Bill was dead. So did his family, who held a private funeral Mass for him a few weeks after he went missing. To this day, authorities believe it was Allie Boy Persico who made Wild Bill Cutolo disappear.

"If someone did this, it had to be from the past," a Cutolo intimate told detectives from Bruno's barbershop. "Billy did not have an enemy in the world."

In return for all of the free dinners, drinks, and yachting, dirty cop Andy Dohler made sure he made himself available for Chris Paciello many times. On one occasion, someone had stolen Paciello's dog, and he was angry about it. After asking around, he came up with a license plate number of a young man who was in the area before his pup disappeared. He asked Dohler to track down the plate. Dohler called back and said the license plate number was no good. Even so, a few nights later Paciello repaid Dohler's efforts with three VIP passes to an upscale strip club, Miami Gold.

So, Dohler had become as good a friend as any for Chris Paciello to call as he felt his work unraveling.

"Some of my buddies got locked up back in New

York," Paciello told him. "I used to pull a few bank jobs with them, a few robberies. I hope these guys don't start ratting me out. I'm not going down like John Gotti. No way."

Dohler expressed sympathy. Everybody was young and stupid once. "You know Sammy the Bull?" Paciello went on. "They should kill him and his whole family. I know that guy personally, I even knew where he lived while he was ratting out Gotti."

Dohler assured his friend that New York City cops were not smart enough to snag him from so far away. Chris Paciello dropped the subject. It did not come up again.

Instead, Chris focused on getting Dohler to quit the police department and come work for him full time as the manager of Bar Room. Dohler talked him out of the offer, saying he could do more for Paciello from the inside of the Miami Beach police station. Paciello agreed, especially now that he was considering bringing drug dealers into his clubs to peddle the designer drug Ecstasy. For club owners, customers who took Ecstasy were desirable because they danced all night, drank a lot of water and caused little trouble. Selling bottles of water at five dollars each was a great way to increase a nightclub's profits.

Paciello was drawn to Dohler primarily because he was a garrulous New Yorker like himself. He grew up in Queens and spent the first six years of his police career with the NYPD in the Seventy-fifth Precinct. The area covered grimy areas of Jamaica, Queens, and Dohler served through the crack epidemic of the early 1990s. Paciello liked that kind of toughness.

Besides, Dohler was a star athlete in high school. Paciello appreciated athleticism, since years of boxing training had kept his body in impeccable shape.

With Detective Dohler at his side, Paciello seemed to turn over a new leaf. He suddenly became law-abiding. He even asked Dohler to take care of his latest problem in a less vicious fashion than the Binger was accustomed to. He merely wanted justice served.

Gerry Kelly, a famous Irish fashion designer and a sought-after party promoter whom Chris had brought into his fold, had recently quit on him, announcing that he was going to open another club. Kelly had invited Chris and Ingrid into his venture as partners, but they refused. Kelly pressed on, planning to open his club, Level, in a massive space that would directly compete with Liquid.

Kelly put a letter of resignation on his boss's desk, then left town for about a week to let Paciello's legendary temper subside. To Paciello, there was no such thing as forgive and forget. He considered Kelly's leaving the ultimate betrayal, and wanted something done about it. He called Detective Dohler and told him to stop by the office.

"Gerry Kelly has got a bad drug problem," Paciello told him. "I really want to hurt this guy. You get this guy good and I'll take care of you big time."

"Do you know if the guy is into anything heavy or just personal use?" the detective asked.

"I know he has drugs on him all the time," Paciello answered. "People at the club give him drugs, he drives drunk all the time. Every morning you can pull his fucking car over and arrest him. They can pull his liquor license, right? Won't that create a problem with the club?"

As the cop nodded yes, Paciello handed him a piece of paper. On it was Gerry Kelly's address, Social Security number, and phone number. He also scribbled down Kelly's car make and license plate number as an afterthought.

"How about Friday, we follow him around, see what clubs he goes to."

"Where does he go?" Dohler asked.

"He's not going to my place; either Chaos, Living-room. You pull him over after coming out of there and we got him."

"What if he has a little accident?" the detective proposed.

Chris Paciello grinned. "Whatever you want," he said, slapping his cop buddy on the back. "You can have whatever you want if that happens. Friday night, after you get the information, we'll ride by his house, see the car, maybe follow him around, and then Saturday or Sunday we'll see what club he goes into and when he comes out—Boom! You got him."

"Hey, maybe I'll grab him going in," Dohler said. "If he's holding."

"I think he gets it inside. I don't know if he has it walking in."

"We can play around with that," Dohler said, nodding his head. "We can fuck with him."

"I'm telling you," Paciello railed, forgetting his new law-abiding side, "we got to get his head fucking broken in. We got to get him beat up. I got to get him whacked."

After his tirade, Paciello quickly calmed down. "If something happens to this kid now, they are going to be so far up my ass. But not if this happens, it's normal shit. He gets beat up, I'm fucked."

"Just remove yourself."

Paciello sighed. "Yeah," he added. "But even if I'm in my office and somebody walks in and bats him over the head, who are they going to blame? Even if they can't do anything, they can apply pressure."

More than a month after Paciello and Dohler talked,

Kelly was still alive and well. Worse yet, his club was making lots of money.

Chris called Dohler into his cramped office on the second floor of Liquid on the afternoon of Halloween and let out his rage.

"There's fifteen clubs opening," he seethed. "Millions and millions they're putting in all these clubs. Warsaw, Cameo. God, I mean nonstop."

"Hey," Dohler reminded him. "At least you got the restaurant. These clubs come and go."

"That's right. The Bar Room ain't goin' nowhere. Joia's doing well and Liquid's doing all right as long as I can hang in there. It's rough."

"Unless," Dohler said, "you can think of something else to do. We'll do it."

"I wish I knew. I'll tell you the truth, I feel like putting my costume on—going trick-or-treating, you understand?"

"Yeah, I hear ya," the cop said. "I totally understand. There might be a time and place for that; things get bad enough. As long as we do it here, I'll take care of the reports. I hope you still got that costume in your closet," Dohler asked.

"I do."

"You'll have to dust it off."

"Man, I gotta come outta retirement."

"Good," Dohler said, shaking Paciello's hand. "That's what I was waiting to hear."

"I'm telling ya. I've become a big pussy down here. A big sucker."

But Chris didn't know exactly how big a sucker he had become.

Andrew Dohler was wearing a wire, recording every conversation he had with Chris Paciello. The Miami

Beach police had heard enough complaints about Paciello's violent behavior, and had seen enough evidence of Mafia activity, that they had decided to launch an investigation into the charismatic club king.

Andrew Dohler was the perfect mole.

14

IN THE WIND

The Saturday night after Thanksgiving in 1999, Chris Paciello celebrated the opening of his upcoming new club with West Palm Beach's debutante set. Scene queen Lizzie Grubman, the daughter of Madonna's lawyer Allen Grubman, threw the party at the trendy Bice restaurant. Paciello held court in the center of the room. K. C. Johnson, heiress to the Johnson & Johnson empire, was there. Party girl and hotel heir Paris Hilton was there alongside Donald Trump's teenage model daughter, Ivanka. Of course, Ingrid was there. So was Vivianne Duda, a West Palm Beach socialite whose home is around the corner from the Kennedy compound. Some of the guests had arrived in their own private planes.

The party that night had a dual purpose. It celebrated both the opening of a Chanel store in West Palm Beach and it gathered friends of Chris and Ingrid's to hail them as South Beach's reigning "It" nightlife team.

Usually the difficulties presented in opening a nightclub in West Palm Beach thwart even the most aggressive impresarios. Regulations there are enforced to the letter. Fire marshals will appear on crowded nights and literally poke their fingers in the air, counting the heads of patrons to make sure there are no violations.

But somehow Chris and Ingrid slid right in. And their world of friends came with them. Next to the trust fund set—women with perfectly straight hair and simple pearl earrings—sat tanned Brazilian beauties with tight, splashy clothes and spiked heels. Even the men from South Beach looked out of place in the West Palm Beach world: nancy-boys rubbing shoulders with moneyed fraternity members. Chris and Ingrid were about to bring them together. "It was a very funny scene," one socialite later said of the gathering. "It was a confluence of West Palm Beach society and South Beach cheese. It was very funny to watch these tacky girls party alongside these country club kids."

A crew from the syndicated tabloid show *National Enquirer TV* caught up to Chris a few days later. He laughed and chatted and loved every minute of it.

"Yesterday," he told the camera, "Tommy Hilfiger was here. It's everybody. Madonna. Every weekend someone stops by. Dennis Rodman comes every week. It's the music. The image. We're local now and everybody likes us, thank God." He took a slug of Corona. "The new Liquid Room," he continued. "I think it's going to be great. A lot of people are looking forward to it. The place is beautiful."

Despite the boastful optimism, Chris Paciello's usual tough-guy swagger, to some, had noticeably dampened. His olive skin was growing lined with worry. Naturally, he had a lot on his mind with the new club opening. Chris was always a hot-tempered guy, but he was ordinarily levelheaded when it came to business. There was a palpable change in Paciello and it had a lot to do with what was happening back in New York City. Lately he had been flying off the handle, pistol-hot at the slightest provocation.

A famous example of his volatile moods came on

October 21, 1999. Pop superstar Ricky Martin was supposed to show up at Bar Room after his sold out show to kick off his first world tour. Chris Paciello personally extended an invitation to Martin's people and was promised the singer would "shake his bon bon" at Bar Room. Paciello had draped a life-sized poster of the sexy icon and a banner emblazoned with the title of Ricky Martin's famous song, "Livin' La Vida Loca." The visit was supposed to be hush-hush, but Chris Paciello had told a few of his friends, and they had told a few of their friends, and by nine o'clock, the club was jammed. Standing room only.

By 1 A.M.—two hours after Martin's show had ended—it became apparent that Ricky was living the crazy life somewhere else. Chris Paciello was embarrassed. And if there was one thing in the world he hated more than anything else, it was humiliation.

He jumped on top of a table, tore down the poster, and began screeching: "Fuck Ricky Martin! Fuck Ricky Martin!" The party wound down a short time later.

Chris Paciello's friends later gossiped into pink pastel Nokia phones (all the rage on South Beach) about how he was walking around Liquid "like a cat on a hot tin roof" the night before.

"He was very jumpy, very nervous," recalled New York City photographer John Roca. "He's always such a gentleman, such a savvy character. It seemed like he was worried about something."

Paciello had his reasons. Back in Brooklyn his friends were being indicted at a rapid-fire clip. In May some of his old compatriots in crime had been locked up for murder, racketeering, conspiracy, drug dealing. He knew it was only a matter of time until his name came up.

Worst of all, word on the street in New York was that Mikey Yammine and Jimmy Calandra, two of the participants in the Judy Shemtov homicide, along with Willie "Applehead" Galloway, had vanished. Their cohorts were afraid they were singing to the government. Chris Paciello was worried all right.

Luchese associate Mikey Yammine had been picked up for selling drugs as part of the Jimmy Galione crack cocaine crew. He had pleaded guilty and was going into the third year of his seven-year sentence when he heard of another upcoming racketeering and robbery indictment. This time it would snare Bonanno crime family associates, his close friends in the Bath Avenue Crew. And Mikey Yammine's name was among those on the Bath Avenue Crew indictment.

Shortly after he was sentenced, the anxiety of his ordeal had caused him to start wetting the bed and sucking his thumb. As a result, he was jailed in a federal unit for the criminally insane at the Burner Correctional Facility in North Carolina. Sure enough, Yammine was contacted at the Burner and told he had been indicted again. A few weeks after that indictment was unsealed, Yammine had enough and called his lawyer. "If I don't give certain things up," Yammine told the attorney, "someone else will."

Yammine's lawyer called the Brooklyn federal prosecutors office and asked to speak to assistant United States attorney Jim Walden. "I think my guy has something you'll be interested in. An old murder," the lawyer said. "It was a woman."

Walden flew to the jail immediately to meet with Mikey Yammine, an awkward-looking man with a slight hunchback and buckteeth. As Yammine recounted the night of February 18, 1993, the seasoned prosecutor, who had heard about countless murders and shoot-outs during his long career, must have felt queasy. The victim's husband had been home. Her young daughter cradled her dying body. It had to have been a horrific scene, if what Yammine was telling him turned out to be true. Walden came back to New York and called Staten Island homicide squad commanding officer Deputy Inspector Charlie Wells.

"Do you have an open murder from 1993, a white female?" Walden asked. Yammine did not know the victim's name.

Wells said he would check into it and call him back. Then he pulled the file on Judy Shemtov. He dialed Walden's number. "Judy Shemtov. She was shot dead while she was making a cup of tea for her husband."

One problem prosecutors had was that Yammine did not know getaway driver Chris Paciello's real name. He knew him only as Chris Binger. He did know Tommy Reynolds's name, though, and quickly gave him up along with Jimmy Calandra.

Both of them knew the Binger's real name, and in a matter of months, so would Jim Walden.

Yammine was put into protective custody. From behind bars he began a letter-writing campaign requesting to be relocated in the Southwest in the federal Witness Protection program. "Jim, do me a solid please," Yammine wrote in one postcard to Walden. "Send me to Arizona. I heard there are no setup artists or piezano [sic]. I'm not asking but begging."

In the years after the Shemtov murder James "Jimmy Gap" Calandra had been stricken with panic attacks. His mother, Madeline—a born-again Christian—had to calm him down almost daily as heart palpitations and nausea washed over him. It did not stop his bank-robbing sprees, though. He spent the next few years in and out of jail.

Then in May 1999, Jimmy Gap was indicted again.

So were his childhood pals in the Bath Avenue Crew. Fabrizio "the Herder" DeFrancisci. Tommy "TK" Reynolds. Joey Calco. Charlie Calco. Little Joey Deliatore. Anthony "Gonzo" Gonzales. Old man Joe Benanti. And the boss himself, Anthony Spero.

Mikey Yammine gave everyone up. They all knew it was coming. But there was no real way to be prepared.

It was a Bath Avenue Crew reunion at the Metropolitan Detention Center federal lockup in Brooklyn. Everyone was there but Christian Ludwigsen. He was still busy in South Beach being Chris Paciello, the handsome young lord of Miami nightlife. No one in law enforcement knew he was the Binger—yet.

Then on November 6, 1999, Jimmy "Gap" Calandra had had enough. It was his twenty-ninth birthday, and he decided he did not want to spend his thirtieth in jail. He told his lawyer to call Jim Walden and set something up. He would spill the beans.

In the middle of the night a few days later, corrections officers snuck him out of the cell. As he walked past Fabrizio, his good friend woke up.

"Where ya going, Jimmy?" Fabrizio said menacingly.

"Uh, I made bail."

"Really, Jim?" Fabrizio snarled. "You got bail?"

Jimmy Gap was not shifted to another jail. He was just moved to solitary confinement so his Bath Avenue Crew cronies could not get to him. His family packed up their Gravesend home and got out of town in a hurry. And Jimmy began retelling the story of the Shemtov homicide.

"That kid the Binger is big-time," Jimmy said. "He's got all that money and all those clubs down in Florida. And he knows a lot of people, big-time people."

Jimmy had Chris Paciello's Miami Beach phone

number scrawled in his Bath Avenue Crew phonebook. But the cops already knew it.

Andrew Dohler, the Miami Beach detective posing as a crooked cop, also had a fat file on Paciello. In a short time Florida law enforcement officials would be making their own move against the club king.

Chris Paciello's disco ball was about to stop spinning.

The sun shone brightly on the first day of December 1999, two days before the West Palm Beach Liquid Room's grand opening party.

Chris Paciello worked out. He jumped rope, pummeled a heavy bag in his garage. He ran. He did stomach crunches.

Then he showered and slipped on a pair of Adidas running pants. He jumped in the Range Rover and drove seventy miles to the West Palm Beach Liquid Room, listening to mixes by DJ and techno mix master Junior Vasquez. Sometime earlier, he had introduced Vasquez to Madonna, and the two had collaborated on the pop queen's latest album.

He drove down palm-lined Clematis Street toward the club. When he pulled up, he did not notice the burgundy Cadillac and the red Grand Am idling outside.

Inside that Cadillac sat Drug Enforcement special agent Timmy Foley and his supervisor, Jamie Hunt. The Grand Am carried four FBI guys, including Bonanno Crime Family Squad agent Wayne McGrew. Their target was Chris Paciello.

When Paciello strode into his newest club that afternoon, the agents noted that he looked exactly as he'd been described: six-foot-one, 210 pounds, built like a prizefighter and swathed in expensive couture with slicked-back hair, a disarming smile, and cold eyes.

The agents knew they had to be careful. They knew Paciello's reputation for throwing punches first and asking questions later.

Paciello swaggered into the club like he strutted around the rest of his properties—shoulders back, chin up, jaw clenched, arms flexed. The New York City street kid shuffle. After a few minutes, Chris Paciello emerged again. He pulled a briefcase out of a colleague's car and looked around.

Paciello was running on instincts. He grew up in a neighborhood where someone was always under surveillance. Something about the two cars outside did not look right.

The agents watched Paciello stroll back inside the club nonchalantly, like he had not a care in the world. His dark eyes did not even look their way.

Paciello slipped out the back door. The next sound the agents heard was the squeal of tires.

"We've been made," an agent yelled into his radio. "The suspect is in the wind! Repeat. The suspect is in the wind!"

The agents went inside the club to make sure. They checked the bathrooms, searched the back offices. The club's manager looked at them and said, "He's gone," and then gave Chris's cell phone number to DEA agent Hunt.

Paciello picked it up on the first ring. Agent Hunt introduced himself. "Mr. Christian Ludwigsen? My name is Special Agent Jamie Hunt with the Drug Enforcement Agency," he said.

Paciello sucked in a breath of air and said in a calm, steady voice: "I'm driving to my lawyer's office. I'll talk to you from there."

Paciello surrendered to authorities at four o'clock sharp on December 1, 1999, at the United States Marshals building in downtown Miami. His celebrity lawyer, Roy Black, was at his side.

"I'm sure you've been expecting us," DEA agent Tim Foley told Paciello as he patted him down for weapons and cuffed his hands behind his back. Foley was a Chicago detective before he joined the DEA and moved to New York.

"Nope," Paciello replied.

After his rights were read and he was processed on federal charges of felony murder and robbery, Paciello politely answered Foley's questions.

Name?

"Chris Paciello. I mean, Chris Ludwigsen. Paciello is my stage name. My mother's maiden name."

Date of birth?

"September 7, 1971."

Nationality?

"German."

On December 4, the night that should have been the West Palm Beach Liquid Room's maiden gala, Chris Paciello sat in a windowless cell at the Miami Federal Detention Center in prison blues and plastic flip-flops. Agents had clipped a strand of his hair to submit as DNA evidence. They also took his Gucci leather belt to make sure he would not fashion it into a noose.

After all of the paperwork was taken care of and the sullen club mogul was escorted to a cell, prison guards allowed him to make one collect phone call.

That call was made to his old lover, supermodel Niki Taylor. The lithe blonde beauty was on the cover of *Self* in the months after Paciello was arrested.

It's unclear what Paciello told the supermodel. Maybe he knew federal agents would be knocking on her door sooner rather than later to ask about a bundle of money she brought to New York City for him on a recent trip. But maybe he just wanted to say he was sorry. Sorry that his life was in shambles and it could never work between them. Sorry that he had to call her collect from a pay phone in a federal jail.

The grand opening gala at the West Palm Beach Liquid Room had to be postponed. A $300-a-head millennium bash that Paciello had planned for the chic Ice Palace in downtown Miami on New Year's Eve also went on without him.

For months, it had been billed as the hottest millennium party in town with a host of superstar disc jockeys, live video feeds, and a drag queen show. But after Paciello was arrested, the soiree's producer, Susanne Bartsch, disassociated herself from the event. The Ice Palace affair went ice cold. Only two thousand of the expected five thousand showed up.

And Chris Paciello kicked off the twenty-first century in a federal jail cell.

15

A RAIN OF INDICTMENTS

As Chris Paciello cooled his heels in jail, Detective Andrew Dohler entered a private room at his police station. Dohler's commanding officers, Captain James Mazer and Major Chuck Press, sat with Chris Paciello's indictment in front of him. Jim Walden, the feared and intense-looking prosecutor from New York, was by his side. Walden had just set into final motion what Dohler had plotted for almost two years—the takedown of the club king.

Jim Walden had already done his homework on the Bath Avenue Crew case. The thirty-four-year-old federal prosecutor worked late every night and was at his desk just after sunrise. His energy was almost manic, in the courtroom and out of it. He had been known to personally accompany cops and agents in neighborhoods with mob strongholds to conduct interviews, a dedication that had earned him a rather derogatory nickname from defense attorneys: "Tiger Boy." When not on trial, Walden had a certain waggishness that charmed even the toughest of detectives. "Jim Walden is the best mob prosecutor out there," NYPD organized crime cop Freddie Santoro often said. "He's a pit bull."

The walls of Walden's offices were festooned with

awards and citations from various law-enforcement agencies. Standing out among the nondescript plaques is a large poster of Clint Eastwood, not as the avenging Dirty Harry, but as the Outlaw Josey Wales. It hangs on the wall as a reminder, explained Walden, of what happens when government and prosecutors don't abide by the law.

One of Walden's proudest moments came when an elderly resident of an Italian stronghold in Brooklyn sent him a note that thanked him for locking up some of the wiseguys who oversaw a brutal narcotics ring in his neighborhood. The streets had been cleared of drugs and destruction, the letter said, and the man felt safe leaving his home for the first time in a decade.

Walden grew up in a blue-collar Pennsylvania mill town with his parents, two sisters, and grandparents. He idolized his grandfather Vernon Strandgard, a steel worker who helped put Walden through college. He was the first in his family to get his bachelor's degree and the only one to get through law school. He was the product of working-class roots and became successful, which is one of the reasons he reserves such a fury for organized crime figures.

"There's a myth in the popular media, especially in Hollywood, that mobsters are men of honor who keep their neighborhoods safe," Walden said. "That's a lot of rubbish. The Mob shakes down honest businesses. Mobsters rob and steal. They murder. And most of them had a choice, a chance to make it in the world. For all their antigovernment talk, they believe in rules and laws—just their own. They're despots who love to use their power.

"There are people in this world who have nothing. No money, no resources, no family. Many people in organized crime have strong families. They have legitimate ways to make money by legitimate means. But they choose to put money over family."

Walden had tried for years to become a federal prosecutor. When the offer finally came, Walden had already signed on with a private firm that gave him a $10,000 signing bonus. He took out a loan to pay back the bonus and quit to take the prosecutor's job at half his salary. "It's a dream job," Walden often said.

Andrew Dohler had heard of Walden's reputation before he arrived. He reached out and grabbed the prosecutor's hand. "Nice to meet you."

"Great work," Walden responded, referring to Dohler's undercover surveillance of Paciello. "I'm very impressed."

The Miami Beach Police Department's investigation into Liquid was sparked when Dohler was standing at the door of Liquid night after night as a steady parade of organized crime figures made their way inside. He mentioned the mobsters to his boss, and, after consulting with the FBI, Miami Beach Police brass quietly decided to look into Paciello by having Dohler wear a wire. It was a daring operation. As Paciello came to consider Dohler a confidant, there were plenty of close calls when the club owner patted him on the back or even embraced him, nearly finding the hidden tape recorder.

During the investigation, Detective Dohler was the center of a task force made up of agents from the FBI, IRS, and Florida Department of Law Enforcement. He was specially recruited for the job based upon "his prior law enforcement experience with the City of New York Police Department, his intelligence, communications skills, and high level of motivation," his superiors said.

The plan was to have Dohler work a sanctioned off-duty detail at Liquid and become friendly with its owner to try to uncover his organized crime connections. Over time, Dohler presented himself as a dirty cop open to committing criminal acts at his bequest, and now his work had paid off. Chris's braggadocio and threats were crucial evidence that could be used against him.

Dohler had been wearing a wire most of the time. When he wasn't he had a memory tight as a mousetrap. For almost two years Dohler had kept his eyes open and his mouth shut. He gained intimate knowledge of Chris's business and his personal property holdings. He was so deep undercover, fellow officers began calling Internal Affairs to complain about Dohler. Also, there was a concern that Dohler's double-dealing would make it back to the ears of Paciello himself, so they debriefed the detective in a secret location and did not tell any other cop in the department what his assignment was.

"It was one of the most dangerous undertakings we have done in the history of this department. It was something we have never done before," said Miami Beach Police major Chuck Press. "Every day his life was in danger. Mr. Paciello has an extremely violent nature and [is] the type of guy who took things into his own hands. He had very dark friends with connections to organized crime. He was also a very high-profile person in South Beach.

"It takes a special kind of undercover cop to be able to create a rapport with a figure in the community like this, develop a trust, and then be able to take that individual down," Press said. "Not every cop is made to do that."

Even in November—when Dohler had been alerted that the federal authorities in New York had developed a case against his target for murder, racketeering, and robbery under the RICO statutes—he kept tight-lipped for more than a month until Paciello could be arrested. Dohler was the one who told his fellow investigators that Paciello would be in West Palm Beach on December 1, 1999, the day of his arrest.

Maybe if Paciello had become a celebrity without the fisticuffs, two-by-four beatings, bottle breaking, and car thieving, Miami's law enforcement community would have let him be yet another shiny character among its veneer-coated throngs. He paid his taxes. He raised money for charity. He was beloved up and down the beach. He had clout. The mayor of Miami Beach himself considered Chris Paciello a friend.

His lawyers insisted in the national press that their client was a changed man. But Chris Paciello had not changed. He was no longer a two-bit hood with a violent streak; he was a quasi-legitimate businessman with a violent streak.

Dohler's secretly recorded tapes proved Paciello had not changed very much. He was still the Binger, only swathed in expensive couture.

Jim Walden had flown to Miami to personally debrief, and to thank, Detective Dohler. Later that month, Dohler was honored with the Miami Beach Police Officer of the Year Award for his "bravery, dedication, and investigative expertise." They also bestowed upon him the Officer of the Month and Outstanding Service honors.

"Detective Dohler put himself at great personal risk during this operation, and his safety will continue to be in jeopardy due to the dangerous nature of the criminals targeted for investigation," his supervisors wrote in a letter of commendation.

"This very complex, highly sensitive operation was done secretly and required Detective Dohler to perform his primary duties as a patrol officer, and his undercover duties without raising the suspicions of the criminals under investigation, his peers, or his supervisors. He was able to do this in an outstanding fashion. Detective Dohler's efforts greatly contributed to the arrest of a high-profile criminal, actively operating under the guise of a legitimate South Beach club owner," wrote his supervisors.

"His arrest should send a message that this community will not tolerate organized criminal activity and will go to great lengths to investigate and arrest criminals such as Chris Paciello."

Chris Paciello's much publicized arrest hit South Beach like a bomb. No one wanted to believe that there was much more to Paciello than the image that Miami's mon-eyed and beautiful had embraced. No one really believed he was guilty, at first. After the initial astonishment, they became convinced that even if he had done what the government said he did, he successfully managed to put his past behind him.

"He's innocent," insisted Ingrid Casares.

"From what the prosecutors are saying, there is the Chris that South Beach knows," said Paciello's business partner in Joia, Nicola Siervo, "and the Chris from New York that none of us know. We know a very different Chris."

Even the mayor of Miami Beach defended him. "A lot of people have rough pasts," Neisen Kasdin declared. "Chris was a friend." Kasdin had a vested interest in Paciello's innocence. He had hired the mobbed-up club owner to host his reelection party at Bar Room just a month earlier. It was a grand affair with free drinks and a lavish spread and it did not cost the mayor a penny. He had written the party off as a campaign contribution. In fact, just weeks after the party, Kasdin had awarded Paciello with a key to the city, telling the club king he had been instrumental in reviving South Beach into the booming tourist destination it had become.

Two weeks after Paciello's arrest, he was brought to Miami's federal court for a bail hearing. The normally quiet courtroom swarmed with a crowd to rival Liquid on a Saturday night. Limousine after limousine disgorged south Florida's wealthiest businessmen and society mavens. Among them was real-estate developer Gerry Robbins, as well as *Ocean Drive* and *Hamptons* magazine publisher Jason Binn. Paciello's face had been featured on the thick glossy pages of Binn's magazines many times. Ingrid was there, flanked by her billionaire father, Raul Casares. Sofia Vergara made an entrance in a low-cut shirt and tight jeans, and sat close to Chris's mother, Marguerite.

Even Paciello's lawyer, Roy Black, had celebrity status. He was the man who had successfully defended William Kennedy Smith on rape charges; and his face had appeared on TV every day during the trial of sportscaster Marv Albert, who stood accused of biting a longtime lover. Albert later pleaded guilty to assault charges.

There were audible gasps as Paciello was escorted, handcuffed, in front of United States magistrate Ted E. Bandstra. Two weeks in the slammer had dimmed the club king's tan. Even his muscles sagged. Paciello had been deprived of his daily dose of steroids.

As Paciello was led in, he blew kisses to his supporters as Walden watched him with disgust. Walden had heard his name for years. It kept coming up in connection with other cases. But this was the first time the wiry, energetic prosecutor would lay eyes on Paciello, whom he had come to know by his street name, the Binger.

Walden had reviewed a series of mug shots and rap sheets: Chris at sixteen, after he was arrested for stealing car radios. Chris at seventeen, arrested for criminal mischief. Chris at eighteen, collared after he punched an off-duty New York City policeman in the face. Chris at twenty, pinched for driving without a license. Another shot of twenty-year-old Chris, busted for causing a ruckus outside a Staten Island barroom. Chris at twenty-one, arrested for being aboard a stolen boat.

The list went on and on. Chris at twenty-one again, collared for assault and harassment. Chris at twenty-two, arrested for robbery and assault after he and some pals used sticks and bats to steal a set of car keys from a young acquaintance. Chris at twenty-three, arrested for assault again. Chris at twenty-four, busted for getting into a gunfight. Chris at twenty-seven, charged with stabbing a Russian photographer in a Manhattan hotspot.

Finally, there was the U.S. marshal's mug shot of Chris at twenty-eight taken after he was charged with racketeering and murder on December 1, 1999.

Walden had seen his share of up-and-coming mobsters during his long career of prosecuting organized crime cases. Most of them had sported the same arrogant grin Paciello was flashing now. Almost all of the young thugs like the Binger were cocky enough to think they could beat the charges in the same manner they solved all their disputes: with threats, intimidation, and even murder. Walden saw it in their swagger.

By then, Jim Walden had heard plenty of stories about the Binger. He would retell some of the best of them now in front of Paciello's high society friends.

Roy Black had elected to skip the bail hearing, and handed the reins to his associate, Howard Srebnick, who was also one of Chris's close friends. Srebnick approached the judge first.

"Your Honor. Seventy people have come for this hearing on behalf of Mr. Ludwigsen, and they cannot all fit in the courtroom, and we don't intend to have everybody come in, but there are several witnesses who will be here on the issue of lack of danger to the community, lack of risk of flight, who I would like to present to the Court and have them address the Court at the appropriate time."

He waved his arms toward the beautiful people that crowded the room. It looked more like a society ball than a criminal bail hearing. "It's much like Mr. Ludwigsen's clubs—standing room only," Srebnick added as he handed the judge a list of Miami's A-list in attendance.

The list would be stamped and entered into evidence. But the dozens of people that signed their names on the yellow legal pad, proving their allegiance to Chris, were not the friends who got Paciello into the mess he was in to begin with.

Then Walden presented his case.

"Taken together," Walden said, "the evidence will show that for a lengthy period of time, dating from approximately 1987 through 1993, Mr. Ludwigsen was involved in a series of other robberies and burglaries in the Brooklyn and Staten Island areas, including burglaries and robberies of commercial establishments such as a pet food store, a hardware store, a pharmacy, multiple video stores, and an armed robbery of drug dealers in Staten Island.

"The Staten Island drug dealer robbery, Your Honor, is particularly strong in the sense that there were six cooperating witnesses who have evidence concerning Mr. Ludwigsen's role, mostly because he boasted about his role in that robbery to several other individuals," Walden said.

"Mr. Ludwigsen planned the robbery with others, robbed a large quantity of marijuana, broke it up into portions, resold it to another individual, and then stole it back."

Walden began outlining Paciello's affiliation with a brutal gang of mob wannabes and made members of the Mafia in a group that called themselves the Bath

Avenue Crew. The members of the Bath Avenue Crew
ran a crack cocaine ring in south Brooklyn and murdered anyone who came between them and their profits. The crew reported to Bonanno elder statesman
Anthony Spero, a Mafia boss who had been indicted
along with the Binger. Seven of the crew members had
tiny numbers etched into their right ankles. The tattoos,
dubbed "shooter ink," signified their willingness to
take on any task for the Bonannos—including murder.

"Mr. Ludwigsen is an affiliate of a particularly violent crew within the Bonanno organized crime family.
Other codefendants in the case include the former boss
of the Bonanno family [Spero], soldiers within the family, and violent associates of the family, who are together charged with multiple murders, drug trafficking,
extortion, and armed robbery," Walden said, looking
straight at Paciello as he outlined the charges.

Paciello's supporters shook their heads in disbelief.
At least one person tittered nervously.

"The case against Mr. Ludwigsen is particularly
strong," Walden went on. "The case will include testimony from five accomplice witnesses. Some of the best
evidence comes from the mouth of the defendant himself." Walden shook a pile of wiretapped conversations
between Paciello and Dominick "Big Dom" Dionisio.

Then Walden dropped a bombshell.

"We have substantial, credible evidence that Mr.
Ludwigsen . . . attempted to import organized crime tactics from New York to control legitimate business deal-
ings here in the Miami area.

"These tactics, Judge, are the same tactics that members and associates of organized crime and La Cosa
Nostra have used time and time again to control the
sanitation industry and labor unions in New York,"
Walden said. "We have clear and compelling evidence

that Mr. Ludwigsen was attempting to do the same thing here in Miami."

Walden outlined charges that Paciello asked "Big Dom" Dionisio to threaten a business rival who was trying to lure Ingrid Casares into opening a club without him. Walden said Paciello bribed an undercover cop in an attempt to have another business rival, Gerry Kelly, arrested. He stole a car in Miami and was arrested a half dozen times for assault. He threatened to "baseball bat" someone in the head. He was also accused of threatening a government witness.

Howard Srebnick rebutted those charges, saying the case was merely a result of Chris's jealous former friends and overzealous prosecutors trying to use Paciello's celebrity to forward their own careers. "The government's theory is that Mr. Ludwigsen was in a car, or so the confidential witnesses will say, when these confidential witnesses committed these acts of violence as alleged in the indictment, and that as the confidential witnesses will now say, conveniently, with no corroboration, he's in a car when we did all of these things," Srebnick said.

"So let's hold him liable!" Srebnick yelled. "The popular guy down in South Beach. Let's get him!"

Besides all that, Paciello's lawyer went on, Chris did not even know the "so-called acting boss" of the Bonanno crime family, his codefendant, Anthony Spero. "And, I should say, when you run a nightclub in South Beach, given the nature of the beast, episodes like that happen from time to time," the lawyer proclaimed.

"He's twenty-eight years old. I daresay there's nobody else who's invested more money, more time, more effort, more dedication to our community than Mr. Christian Ludwigsen.

"We're talking about danger to the community and risk of flight. His face has been publicized in every single magazine in South Florida. He's been seen in *Ocean Drive*, *People* magazine, *Details*, *Hamptons* magazine, and *The Wall Street Journal*. Where can he hide?"

Srebnick reserved a special disgust for Detective Andy Dohler. "And when this off-duty police officer, who tried to chew Mr. Ludwigsen's ear and pose as somebody who could help him out—to try and set him up, of course, because for the last five years, everybody's trying to do something to set Chris Ludwigsen up." Srebnick trailed off.

"Nobody likes to see a guy his age achieve the success he's achieved." Srebnick shrugged. Then he shook his head sadly. "Chris didn't choose to grow up where he grew up. By the same token, he hasn't turned his back on the people he grew up with, nor has he committed any crimes with them."

At least one prominent businessman was not deterred by Paciello's background. Raul Casares took the stand, painfully describing how Chris helped his daughter kick a cocaine habit. "Ingrid was a total disaster for many years," he said in a heavy Cuban accent, tinged with tears. "Until she met Chris. And our family thinks Chris was the one responsible for stopping her to taking drugs. Okay?

"Our family is a very united family. We're a very religious family, especially my wife. We sent Ingrid to several different places for therapy, et cetera," he said. "As far as the Casares family is concerned, Ingrid has abandoned drugging because of Chris."

One by one, Paciello's supporters took the stand with stories about his achievements. The way he gave money to charity. Held fund-raisers. One employee, doorman Gilbert Stafford, said Paciello had "saved his life." Stafford had been seriously ill, and so sickly he was contemplating taking his own life when his boss stepped in and held a huge fund-raiser on his behalf. The party had raised $10,000, cash that was bundled and placed in a plastic shopping bag before Paciello handed it to his doorman.

When Srebnick was through detailing the attributes of his client, Walden argued that Paciello should be detained without bail because he had enough money— from both his clubs and his crimes—to flee the country. Besides all that, he had a penchant for intimidating witnesses, the government alleged.

As word of the coming indictment was circulating through Paciello's criminal circle back in Brooklyn, Chris had mailed Tommy Reynolds's father Andrew an envelope stuffed with $5,000 in cash. Reynolds, the gunman in the Judy Shemtov murder, had already been arrested on other crimes. It later became clear that Paciello gave Andrew Reynolds the money for lawyers' fees. But at the time, Walden believed it was a payoff.

Sometime after Reynolds received the money, prosecutors said, the girlfriend of one of the government's cooperating witnesses was returning to her Brooklyn home when another car sped alongside her.

"If he testifies," someone yelled out the window, "your entire family is dead."

After both Walden and Srebnick presented their arguments, Judge Bandstra admitted to being confused by both. The dizzying laundry list of crimes, and the defendant's two different names, had left him bewildered. He thought the lawyers were arguing over two separate defendants. In a way, they were. Christian Ludwigsen was a low-life wannabe mobster from Staten Island with a trail of crimes and a dead body littering his past. Chris

Paciello was a hardworking celebrity businessman on South Beach who had support from dozens of prominent South Floridians.

When Judge Bandstra ruled to release Paciello on a $3 million bond, Walden immediately announced he would appeal it. It was finally agreed Paciello would remain in custody until after an appeal could be heard back in Brooklyn, in front of a federal judge in the Eastern District, the federal division that had built the case.

When the hearing was over, a handcuffed and shackled Paciello was led past the glitterati that had crowded into the court. As he shuffled by them, wearing a navy blazer, white dress shirt, gray slacks and loafers, handcuffed to a half-dozen other inmates in olive-tan prison jumpsuits and plastic sandals, the crowd applauded him.

"We love ya, man!"

"They ain't got nuthin'."

"Hang in there!"

Paciello curled his puffy lower lip and blew his audience kisses. Ingrid Casares, her tears shielded by a massive pair of dark sunglasses, made a statement to the press. "He's innocent, and everyone here today knows it."

Walden was stunned. *Be careful who you step on on your way to the top,* came to his mind, as he thought of the people Paciello had crossed and robbed and hurt back in New York, people who were ready to testify against their former friends, *because those are the same people you meet on your way back down.*

About a month after that hearing, Roy Black and Jim Walden squared off again at Brooklyn federal court for the second bail hearing in front of federal Judge Edward Korman, who sits in the Eastern District Federal Court. Chris Paciello stayed behind in a Miami federal cell.

Walden continued his argument that the South Beach

club king was a violent thug. Black insisted his client was a changed man with a shaky past.

"Since 1987 and continuing into the month before his arrest," Walden testified, "Mr. Ludwigsen was involved in extremely violent criminal activity. More than ten individuals have given statements to police officers, indicating Mr. Ludwigsen assaulted them in some manner.

"He's used three different dates of birth. He's used two different social security numbers, including a social security number that was issued in Ohio before Mr. Ludwigsen was even born.

"Mr. Ludwigsen has become high-profile and is now attempting to capitalize on his celebrity. Mr. Ludwigsen now knows what the taste of prison is like, and at the time he surrendered, he had no idea of the gravity of the charges," Walden went on. "Because of his celebrity, Mr. Ludwigsen has left the country five different times, including a trip to Colombia, a trip to the Dominican Republic, and trips to Mexico. He's a risk of flight and a danger to the community.

"Besides that," Walden added. "It is a character trait of Mr. Paciello's to resort to violent activity."

Then it was Roy Black's turn. He outlined Chris Paciello's ties to his four businesses. He had Liquid. Bar Room. West Palm Beach Liquid Room. Joia. All with employees to pay, bills to maintain. Paciello needed bail, Black argued, and deserved it because of his extensive ties to the South Beach community.

"He's made a remarkable turnaround," Black told the judge. "He has become a remarkable success. This is a man who not only is a success in business, but is an enormous success in the cultural affairs of the city of Miami. That's why so many people showed up at his hearing earlier in the month in Miami.

"Chris traveled out of the country, for example, to

the Dominican Republic, for Sammy Sosa's birthday party and there were five presidents of five different countries present at that. He went to Mexico for a wedding. To somehow say that proves that this man is unreliable is totally unfair.

"Who is going to run every one of these clubs and restaurants? What is going to happen? Without him there, it's all going to fall apart. This man has worked five years to build this," Black said. "Also, this is a young man who grew up on Staten Island, who originally was from Brooklyn. And sure, he knew some people in those times that perhaps are somewhat unsavory, but we will explain those kinds of relationships and he does not have those kinds of relationships now. He has legitimate businesses with legitimate people.

"Nobody wants to spend Christmas in jail."

But that's exactly where Chris Paciello was on Christmas Day.

16

NO PLACE LIKE HOME

The sun beamed bright and balmy on Miami Beach as federal U.S. marshals escorted a handcuffed and shackled Chris Paciello—inmate number 61500004—onto an airplane for extradition back to New York City. None of Miami's glitterati that crammed the courtroom just weeks earlier came to see him off, and the plane ride would be a far cry from the first-class accommodations Paciello had grown accustomed to.

Paciello would fly on a government-owned 707 used to transport federal prisoners to court appearances in other parts of the country, nicknamed "Con Air" by law enforcement authorities. It was a hot day when Paciello boarded, but he was destined for a colder climate: New York City, to be exact.

The U.S. marshals pushed their prisoner into a row of seats that sat three across. He was sandwiched between two alleged Colombian drug dealers. Other travelers included an accused Nigerian credit card swindler, a couple of reputed mobsters from the Southeast, an alleged Mexican drug mule, and a hulking dreadlocked Jamaican hit man charged with murdering his probation officer.

It was going to be a long flight.

The plane stopped in Oklahoma City to refuel, and its passengers passed the hours at a local federal jail. The next morning, it took to the skies again, bound for New York. Egg salad sandwiches on white bread and boxed juice comprised the on-flight meal.

After a number of stops at small airports along the East Coast to pick up prisoners, the plane landed at a remote upstate New York airstrip, where the prisoners were taken off the plane and marched past all manner of armed agents of the law: U.S. marshals, guards from Bureau of Prisons, state troopers, and local police.

An unmarked white van pulled onto the tarmac to pick up the human cargo. The U.S. marshals, responsible for their prisoners during the flight, signed a "body receipt" for each suspect. Paciello's next stop was New York City's largest federal jail, the Metropolitan Detention Center (MDC), located near the Brooklyn neighborhoods where Chris made his bones as an associate in the mob.

The roundabout flight and overnight stay in a packed federal holding cell had taken a toll on him. His handsome face was unshaven and sweaty, his hazel eyes red-rimmed from sleeplessness. His hair, usually slicked back with expensive pomade, flopped in disarray. Thinning strands formed an untidy widow's peak on his wide forehead. The tan he sported year-round had faded. He could use a good shower, or better still, an afternoon in his Jacuzzi and sauna.

The MDC is a mammoth, ugly, sandstone facility and houses three thousand federal prisoners at full capacity. It is located on the waterfront in an industrial stretch of car repair shops and warehouses in Brooklyn's Sunset Park, and is surrounded by strip joints and dilapidated warehouses.

If Paciello was self-conscious about his own smell, it

was soon dwarfed by the overpowering stench that greeted the prisoners once they disembarked from the van. The inhuman stew of rotting garbage and sewage clung to the clothes of anyone who passed by.

"Welcome to the MDC," a smiling corrections officer told Paciello. He snapped a picture of the club king, which would be entered into a national database of federal prisoners.

"Have you taken any drugs today, sir?"

Paciello shook his head no.

"Are you infected with the AIDS virus?"

No.

"Tuberculosis?"

No again.

"Hepatitis?"

No.

"Are you on any medication?"

No.

"Enjoy your stay."

Officers led Paciello to a first-floor processing room. He was strip-searched and given a pair of stiff khaki cotton pants and a matching shirt.

If the prison had windows, its inmates might have enjoyed commanding views of Manhattan and the Statue of Liberty. Of course, there were no windows. Just long dorms crammed with bunk beds lined with thin, lumpy mattresses. If Paciello could have looked north he might have been able to spot the tidy row houses in Borough Park. His childhood apartment building was only twenty or so blocks from the cell Paciello would now call home for the next eighty-five days.

The MDC was a long way from Miami Beach, but it was not the worst place for Chris Paciello. The prison, opened by the federal government in the early 1990s, boasts a "Mafia wing" that has housed such famous thugs as Colombo family boss Victor Orena, Luchese acting boss Anthony "Gaspipe" Casso, and Carmine Agnello, John Gotti's son-in-law. Michael Swango, the doctor who murdered dozens of his patients, was also jailed there for a time. So was celebrity stockbroker Dana Giacchetto, who was arrested for swindling famous clients like Leonardo DiCaprio, Matt Damon, and Ben Affleck out of millions.

In the mid-1990s, the MDC's corrections officers had a reputation for being fascinated by the Mafiosi under their auspices. For years, the mobsters at the MDC could buy just about anything but freedom by bribing the low-paid guards. Wiseguys kicked back with imported cigars, smuggled Italian cold cuts like sopressata, fresh provolone, and long sticks of pepperoni. Anything was obtainable: a vat of mixed Sicilian olives, veal cutlets, fresh eggplant, even steroids, cocaine, and gallons of vodka—all courtesy of the guards, who arrived for work looking like "Santa Claus carrying a sackful of presents on their backs," according to one inmate.

Some guards urinated into specimen bottles for narcotics-abusing inmates scheduled for court-ordered drug tests. The most helpful were kept on weekly $500 retainers. One Luchese crime family *capo,* George "Georgie Neck" Zappola, even got his sperm to the outside while awaiting trial for murder, attempted murder, extortion, labor union payoffs, and racketeering. The married mobster smuggled his seed to a Manhattan fertility clinic so he could impregnate his longtime *goomada* (mistress).

The woman, unnamed in court records but code-named "Connie" by prosecutors, "agreed that she [and Georgie Neck] wanted to have a child together." Connie was the daughter of a slain Colombo crime family boss.

The fertility clinic gave her two plastic medical vials for her donor to fill. She and Georgie Neck then bribed prison counselor and guard Derryl Strong to smuggle the vials in and out of jail in exchange for a $1,000 shopping spree at a Bay Ridge clothing store, Gentleman's Quarters—whose inventory catered to flashy Brooklyn men with its imported Italian shoes and hand-tailored silk shirts.

The smuggling scheme unraveled when Strong's fellow guards noticed he was wearing "alligator-type" shoes and other expensive clothes to work, and told the warden.

There were already rumors of wrongdoings by the guards, and the government got interested. After federal investigators paid her a visit, Connie decided that not only did she not want to have her boyfriend's baby, especially if he was going to serve twenty-two years for murder and racketeering, she did not want to go to jail herself.

Connie played ball with investigators, and Derryl Strong became one of eleven MDC corrections officers charged with bribery during an investigation into the Mafia wing dubbed "Operation Badfellas."

When Paciello arrived, the prison was crowded with his former Bath Avenue Crew cohorts. DEA and FBI special agents started locking them up in May 1999 on federal charges ranging from murder to racketeering to burglary. A few of them had been doing time since 1996, after they were busted for participating in a crack ring run by Luchese mobster Jimmy Galione.

Paciello took his cell in the Mafia wing and became reacquainted with some of his old *paesans*. During the week, the inmates would play cards and call the women in their lives collect from the pay phone. The ladies always accepted the charges. On Saturdays they would sit at long metal tables griping to family or lawyers or both.

Sundays were the best. During the week many of the Bath Avenue Crew defendants were separated. But no one could stop them from going to church. On Sundays, Paciello and his buddies would huddle in the back pews of the jail's tiny Catholic church discussing strategies, trying to track down cooperating witnesses, and plotting their defense. Sunday Mass became the de facto Pigeon Club while the crew was behind bars.

In the meantime, Jim Walden wrangled with Paciello's team of lawyers over the unprecedented bail he was proposing. Walden, of course, wanted Paciello held behind bars until his trial started, but if the federal magistrate decided the club king was entitled to bail, Walden was going to make sure it cost him. Paciello's wealthy friends and family members would have to put up $15 million, an exceptionally high number. The bail seemed even more extraordinary because Paciello was not even a made member of the Mob. He was not even a true associate. He was *il malandrini,* the old Italian guys might say, a wannabe. Even Gambino top boss John Gotti had been released for $10 million.

Still, Walden wanted him closely monitored as he prepared his witnesses—those cooperating accomplice witnesses that had given up Paciello in the first place.

Defense attorneys wanted Paciello to be allowed to live in his mother's Staten Island townhouse, a narrow gray structure on the edge of the nation's largest dump, the Fresh Kills Landfill, with two around-the-clock security guards watching his every move inside the house.

It would be a far cry from Paciello's posh Miami Beach estate.

* * *

At 9 A.M. sharp on January 7, 2000, U.S. marshals brought Paciello through the back door of Brooklyn's federal courthouse. Out front, New York's party scene publicist Lizzie Grubman grimaced at the press assembled at the entranceway. She linked arms with Ingrid Casares. The two high-heel-clad women sashayed past a row of news cameras in Gucci wraparound sunglasses.

Minutes later Sofia Vergara stepped out of a white stretch limousine and marched defiantly past the press. Paciello's aunts, Barbara Tafuri and Bernadette Zdanowicz, arrived in an older car along with their father and Chris's grandfather, Louis Paciello.

In the courtroom Ingrid sat on a mahogany bench in the second row of U.S. magistrate Joan Azrack's small courtroom. Casares and her father had put up more than a million dollars in cash and property as part of Paciello's bail. While the national media disseminated Paciello's criminal past, three of Paciello's aunts signed away their homes and pledged to keep an eye on him while he was under house arrest, as did his grandfather.

Actor Mickey Rourke, a longtime mob aficionado who was among the spectators at John Gotti's trial, coaxed his mother, Annette Rourke, into signing over her Miami estate. Paciello's grandfather Louis, a trim, fit older man who came dressed for court like he was going to a funeral, with a dark suit and black turtleneck, also signed over his life savings, but not before he stared straight at prosecutor Jim Walden and mumbled, "Son of a bitch," under his breath. Paciello had put up $100,000 of his own money and pledged the assets of Liquid.

The jury box was filled with the detectives and agents who had gathered the evidence that led to the Bath Avenue Crew's indictment. Staten Island Homicide Squad sergeant Bobby Losada and detective Bobby Walsh sat with their commanding officer, Inspector Charlie Wells.

DEA agent Tim Foley and NYPD Intel detectives Mike
Galletta, Tommy Dades, Jimmy Harkins, and Lieutenant Kevin O'Brien—the investigators who had rounded
up Paciello's cohorts in predawn raids weeks earlier—
were also there, eager to see their work culminated with
the club king's arrival.

After a two-hour procession of drug dealers, wife
beaters, and bail jumpers, Paciello entered. A collec-
tive gasp sounded. The King of South Beach was no
more. His muscular frame sagged under a rumpled
blue smock and wrinkled prison pants. He smiled
weakly at his friends and family, then faced the judge
and whispered to his lawyers, Roy Black and Howard
Srebnick.

The judge reviewed the government's bond package
terms and called Paciello's supporters to the bench.
When Sofia approached Paciello's side, he touched her
arm and blinked hard, as if he was trying to stop himself from crying. He clasped his hands behind his back
and stared straight ahead at the judge as his aunts wiped
at their own tears.

"I understand that all of you have now signed this
bond," Azrack told the group. "I just want to make sure
that you understand if Mr. Ludwigsen does not come
back to court, not only will you lose whatever property
that's posted, but each of you will have a legally binding
judgment against you in the amount of fifteen million
dollars. According to this bond, you agree that a violation of any provision of his bond will give rise to forfei-
ture of the bond. So you're liable not only if he flees and
doesn't come back to court; you're liable if he violates a
term of the bond. In this case it could be something as
simple as contacting somebody, a witness in the case,
and trying to have a communication, an unauthorized

communication with him, or going outside his electronic monitoring. Do you all understand that?" she asked.

"So you should not agree to sign this bond unless you have every confidence that not only is he coming back to court, but that he is going to abide by every one of these conditions," Azrack said. "There are more conditions on this bond than I think I have ever seen. Do you understand that, Ms. Casares?"

"Yes."

"Mr. Paciello, do you understand?"

"I understand."

"Ms. Tafuri?"

"Yes."

"Ms. Vergara?"

"Yes."

"Mr. and Mrs. Zdanowitz?"

"We understand."

Under the conditions of the bond, Paciello's every move would be tracked by video surveillance, and he would wear an electronic bracelet. He would be allowed outside only with an approved escort for court appearances. He couldn't be near a computer, cell phone, or pager, or have visitors or any contact with his codefendants. He agreed to have his phone monitored, to hire two twenty-four-hour security guards to live with him, and to permit investigators to conduct random searches. Still the fight was not over. The government had to carefully peruse the package, making sure none of the money being used for bail was tainted by the Mob.

After the January 7, 2000, bail hearing, Paciello was brought to another courtroom upstairs to face United States district judge Edward Korman. The judge had scheduled a status conference hearing involving all of the indicted defendants facing charges. This was the first time Paciello met a few of his codefendants face-to-face, but for most of the other Bath Avenue Crew members, it was like a reunion.

Joseph "Little Joey" Dellatorre, a pudgy drug dealer who apparently earned his nickname from his short stature, was also there, along with the crew's mentor, Joe Benanti, who for years had been begging all of the younger Bonanno guys to "get out of this rotten, stinking life."

Paciello's old pal Tommy Reynolds had his brown hair shaved around his ears and on the back of his neck, making his dark eyes all the more menacing. Prosecutors had kept him in the "box," or solitary confinement, for more than a month, and he had left there looking skinny and pasty. On his ankle remained the number 3 tattoo.

Fabrizio "the Herder" DeFrancisci, who had become a "made man" in the Bonanno family, was also present. The Herder had a most contradictory nature. His longtime girlfriend, Mary, was a schoolteacher, and when he was working as a plumber, the couple seemed the epitome of a workaday family. But the Herder was too tangled up in "The Life" to ever break free.

Also in the courtroom that day was Anthony "Gonzo" Gonzales, a burly drug dealer whose pounded face looked like a lumpy mattress. Gonzo's husky body was scrawled with tattoos; a Grim Reaper on his right forearm, a rose on his left arm, and inked on his stretch-mark infused stomach was a permanent apology for his bloody lifestyle: "Forgive Me Mother."

Crazy Joe Calco, a killer for the Bonanno family, was also there. He had fled to Italy five years earlier, but was caught as he tried to sneak back into New York from Canada. Crazy Joe was the first Bonanno associate to realize the "shooter tattoos" Paulie Gulino had wanted the Bath Avenue Crew to ink on their ankles were now being used as evidence against them. Enraged, Crazy Joe took a knife to his ankle and carved off the top layers of his skin to hide the number 7 tattoo from federal agents. It didn't work.

DEA agent Tim Foley, the lead investigator on the Bath Avenue Crew case, filed for a court-ordered search warrant that would let a plastic surgeon examine Crazy Joe's bloody scab for sign of tattoo ink, writing: "The tattoos signified the defendants' commitment and ability to undertake murder as part of their criminal endeavors." The request was granted.

Anthony Spero had been indicted alongside the young members of the Bath Avenue Crew, but he was not in court that day. He was already under house arrest at his Staten Island estate.

A number of the Bath Avenue Crew's finest, though, were conspicuous by their absence in the courtroom alongside Chris Paciello.

Where was Willie "Applehead" Galloway? Mikey Yammine? Jimmy Calandra? Every one of them should have been indicted, and a couple of them were named on the latest indictment. But now Paciello's old cohorts had somehow vanished.

The answer was simple: within hours of the arrests, the detectives and agents had wooed the low-level mobsters into cooperating, trading information on their cohorts and in some cases, their closest friends and relatives, in exchange for reduced sentences.

Without the informants, Chris Paciello might have remained nobody in the eyes of law enforcement. "Six months ago, I never even heard of this guy," legendary cop Inspector Charlie Wells stated before the hearing. "Now his name is everywhere. Chris Paciello, the guy who dated Madonna. Chris Paciello, the guy who owns all the clubs in Miami. He's a big star. To us he was just another thief, another bank robber, another kid who thinks he's a bad guy. Another name that just came up."

The last thing the Bonanno crime family needed was Paciello's celebrity. His name was attracting the national media. Notoriously private crime bosses' mug shots and details of their bloody crimes were being splashed across the country and on nightly gossip news shows.

As the lawyers tried to set a trial date for the Bath Avenue Crew case, Tommy Reynolds focused his attention on Staten Island homicide detective Bobby Walsh. Walsh, a tall, gray-haired, twenty-five-year veteran of the NYPD, was known throughout the department for having a sense of humor as large as the soft girth that earned him the nickname "Big Boy." Walsh had become the lead detective on the Shemtov homicide and had attempted to process the murder suspects in a holding cell minutes before the court hearing.

"Hey, Tommy, we need some fingerprints," Walsh had said.

"Why don't you get my fingerprints off your mother's ass?" Reynolds fired back. "Who are you anyway?"

"Staten Island homicide," Walsh responded. "And watch your mouth."

"I'm not talking to you," Reynolds spat at the cop. "Go fuck yourself."

"You can talk to me now, or you can talk to me later," said Walsh. "But one way or another, you're gonna talk to me."

During the court proceeding Tommy was spotted mouthing, "Fuck you, cocksucker," at Detective Walsh when the judge and the prosecutors were not looking.

* * *

As he sat in court alongside his Bath Avenue Crew cronies, Paciello seemed unfazed by the serious charges against him and the rock-solid case the prosecution claimed it had against him. To have so many cooperating witnesses—already six people had signed up to testify against him—was an extraordinary coup for the government.

Paciello made kissy faces at Ingrid and Sofia and bantered with his codefendants. He made fun of Jim Walden's off-the-rack suit. It was like a get-together of old friends. The courtroom was filled with big-hair molls and Mafia moms wearing diamond-studded gold crosses. The women waved at their sons and husbands and leaned forward to listen intently to the expensive-suited lawyers.

Anthony Spero's lawyer, Gerald Shargel, was considered a renowned New York City Mob attorney. He had represented John "the Dapper Don" Gotti. Roy Black was there in a Florida summer suit, his trademark long gray hair and glasses in place. Vincent Romano, a tough Brooklyn lawyer, represented Fabrizio. Tommy Reynolds, and most of the other defendants, had court-appointed attorneys.

Maryanne Reynolds closed her eyes after the hearing was over as her handcuffed son was led back to his jail cell. After he was out of sight, she stalked up to Ingrid Casares and said, "These boys are innocent. Just because they grew up together, they are being blamed for everything that went wrong on Staten Island."

Ingrid, who looked out of place in her pricey black suit and expensive sunglasses, nodded in startled agreement.

When the hearing was finished, Sergeant Bobby Losada of the Staten Island Homicide Squad brought

Paciello downstairs to the U.S. marshals' processing room to take fingerprints of the club king.

Paciello decided to try a new ploy. He pretended he had no idea who his defendants were and struck up a conversation with Losada. "You know, last week I was on my yacht. It's a $550,000 yacht. Now look where I am. Look at these mutts," Paciello said, swinging his muscled arms toward the cells where the rest of the Bath Avenue Crew was caged until the bus ride back to the MDC. "I've never seen any of these guys before in my life. I don't know how they know me."

Then he and Losada made small talk. The two had grown up blocks away from each other on Thirteenth Avenue and attended the same high school, Franklin Delano Roosevelt. The men chatted about the old neighborhood as Losada took a print of Paciello's entire palm. During the fingerprinting, Paciello's wrist was limp, his fingers flexible—he knew the drill.

"Listen, guy, I'm sorry I smell," Paciello confided.

"These guys, they took me on a plane for two days, to Atlanta, Virginia, I didn't know where I was. I haven't showered. Listen, does my lawyer know about this? This type of fingerprinting? I guess it's all right, as long as my lawyer knows."

Paciello's usually gruff Brooklyn accent was smoothed out by three years of Miami beachfront life. "I have no idea what this is about," Paciello said. "Do you have any idea?"

Then the chatter turned to expensive boats and Brooklyn restaurants and Cuban nationals. "You're Cuban? All my friends are Cuban," Paciello told the cop. "Everyone in Miami is Cuban."

Paciello was so persuasive, Losada, a hard-bitten detective who has heard his share of stories from suspects trying to beat a rap, was nearly won over. He even escorted Paciello to the bathroom and gave him a chance to freshen up before he was brought back to the MDC.

"He was slick," Losada told his boss after the hearing. "He was classy and soft spoken, so different from the other idiots in the room. Reynolds was telling Bobby Walsh to 'go fuck yourself,' the other guys were laughing it up. Ludwigsen was just polite. He was so slick he almost convinced me he had no idea what he was in there for. I almost believed him. I half wanted to let him go."

Still, Losada had a job to do, get a fingerprint that may link Paciello to the unsolved murder of Albanian drug dealer Ilber "Billy" Balanca. His body had been discovered frozen solid in the trunk of his father's car four years earlier. Paciello's name was still being floated as a possible suspect in the homicide.

After the fingerprinting, Paciello went back to his cell at the MDC.

Out front, Ingrid Casares stood in front next to Lizzie Grubman as the publicist read from a prepared statement. "Ingrid stands behind Chris one hundred percent."

Roy Black told the media that his client had been targeted by the government, and by the rats, because of his celebrity. The informants were motivated by their jealousy over the fact that Paciello had catapulted himself into a very different world than the one he left behind in Staten Island. Black also promised that Paciello would make bail and be allowed to move back to his Miami Beach home by the spring.

"He's one of the best-known people in the South Beach area," Black gushed to the TV and print reporters. "He's the leader of a real Renaissance there. He really helped put South Beach on the map. Unfortunately, the way our society is, anybody who becomes a success in this country becomes a target."

As Black boo-hooed the charges against Miami's

club king, the judge signed off on a $15 million bail package, secured with $2.8 million in property that would let Paciello out of jail and be placed under house arrest. It would take months before the bond could be set into place. The condominium Sofia Vergara put up as part of his bail package was worth much less than what she estimated. Ingrid Casares pulled out of one of the Miami properties she initially signed away and gave only $50,000 in cash, half of what she had promised. Even Paciello's business partner in the West Palm Beach Liquid Room balked at using his share of the nightclub for the Binger's bail.

There would be no move back to South Florida either. The judge ruled that if Paciello wanted to be under house arrest, it would be in the eastern district of New York City. He would live around the clock in a humble vinyl-sided townhouse owned by his mother on Staten Island.

Paciello had to bide his time in the MDC until March 29, 2000, when he walked out of Federal District Court in Brooklyn, flanked by two men who would become his constant companions. They were Jim Woods and Tom Freeman, a pair of $25-an-hour security guards. Both were retired lawmen. Woods was a former FBI agent. Freeman was a retired California cop.

"You can characterize us more as jailers," Freeman said, sucking on the nonfiltered end of a Camel. "We're not used to babysitting mobsters. Mostly, we get the Fortune 500 types."

Woods and Freeman would be responsible for picking up groceries until visits from Paciello's mother and aunts were approved. The guards warned that until the homemade meals showed up, Paciello would have to get used to cop food. "I hope that boy has a likin' for chili dogs," Freeman said. Paciello's own brothers were kept off of the tightly monitored visitors list because they both had criminal records. The only women allowed in were his mother, his aunts, and Sofia Vergara.

Paciello also had to submit a list of his assets to the court. It read in tiny scrawled letters:

My name is Christian Ludwigsen. I presently reside at 93 Simmons Lane, Staten Island, under house arrest pursuant to court order. In addition to the assets identified in my previous affidavit, I also own the following assets.

A) $200,000 cash
B) Household furniture which is in storage
C) Jewelry, to wit, two watches, a Patek Phillipe and a Cartier watch
D) Wardrobe
E) Artwork on consignment at Bal Harbor Shops.

Finally, late that spring afternoon, a pale, haggard-looking Paciello pushed past a crush of media waiting for his release, wearing a prison blue smock. There was no Ingrid. No A-list socialites. No celebrities as he jumped into a Lincoln Town Car ready to whisk him to Staten Island. When he climbed into the back seat, there was only one problem: that car was there to pick up a different reputed wiseguy—Gambino associate Joseph "Jumbo" Berger.

"Chris, wrong car!" Woods yelled.

"You said a black car." Paciello shrugged.

"That one," Woods said, pointing to another black Lincoln at the curb.

Before climbing in, Paciello turned to the reporters,

and flashed his trademark charismatic smile. "I'm happy to be out," he said. "I'm happy to be seeing my family. It's in God's hands now."

Even Ingrid released a press statement through her spokeswoman. "It will be easier for Ingrid to conduct business now that Chris is under house arrest. I continue to support him one hundred percent."

The black Lincoln sped off to 93 Simmons Lane. Security cameras were trained on the garage door, on the front door, and on the back terrace. His phones were tapped, and an upstairs bedroom was fitted with an electronic monitoring system. When he opened his windows, the house smelled just like the MDC. The Binger's bedroom window looked out onto the Fresh Kills Landfill, the city's largest dump.

The first week, Paciello spent most of his time in the garage, pummeling a punching bag. Then, in late March, pre-trial services officers conducted a full search of the townhouse, from top to bottom. They emptied drawers, lifted ceiling tiles, swept through closets. One of the officers flipped a mattress in the upstairs bedroom and discovered items that could have sent Paciello right back to the MDC.

Stuffed under the bed was a small bag of stale pot and a rolled joint. There were also naked pictures of a woman and a half-empty box of .40-caliber bullets. Paciello's brother Keith swore that the items belonged to him and had been left there at least five years before when he was just a teen. Still, prosecutors moved to remand him, saying they were alarmed because Paciello had displayed a nasty temper when talking with his brothers on the phone.

The judge was unmoved. "That just makes him human," Judge Azrack snapped. She ruled that Paciello could remain under house arrest. But that did not cool his temper. After the ruling, he called his attorney Howard Srebnick. "You fucking idiot," he screamed. "You told me everything was all set in here. You're fired. I'm hiring Ben Brafman. I should have hired him to begin with."

Brafman was a former Manhattan assistant district attorney who had become experienced in representing alleged mob clients, like Salvatore "Sammy the Bull" Gravano. Strangely enough, after the Bull cooperated, Brafman became the attorney for John Gotti's son-in-law Carmine Agnello. Brafman was charismatic and scholarly about the law. Besides all that, he successfully defended Peter Gatien, New York's high-profile club tycoon, against federal drug charges and he also represented rap mogul Sean "Puff Daddy" Combs during his trial for a nightclub shooting. (Combs was later acquitted on those charges.)

Chris Paciello was the perfect client for Brafman: an accused wiseguy who was also a celebrity. Before long, Paciello dumped his Miami legal dream team and hired Brafman.

Brafman immediately filed a motion that his client should be tried separately from the Bath Avenue Crew members, saying Paciello was just "an associate of an associate." He also said the joint trial would be "particularly prejudicial" to Paciello because the media had already written about the case extensively. "He already is on trial in the court of public opinion, and the media attention will likely increase as the trial progresses," Brafman wrote in a legal brief. "The best and most compelling defense available to him is to distance himself from the many crimes alleged in this indictment that he had nothing to do with." Maybe so. But that did not change the fact that Paciello was indicted alongside one of the Bonanno family's prominent elder statesmen: Anthony Spero.

The first order of business for the lawyers protecting Paciello's future was to learn everything they could about the Bonanno crime family's past.

Paciello's new lawyers began reading the discovery material sent to them by prosecutors detailing the murders and shakedowns and crack deals and shootings and armed robberies that the Bonanno crime family had carried out over the past decade. It was a bloody, violent history, and Chris Paciello would have to make himself very familiar with it. A jury would hear it all.

And, if prosecutors had their way, Chris Paciello would be sitting next to Spero at the defendants' table as the gory crimes were detailed one by one.

17

A GOOD PIECE OF WORK

One of the crimes Anthony Spero was accused of was the conspiracy to murder both Gus Farace, and then, in a strange twist of Mafia drama, Farace's killer, Louis Tuzzio. In typical gangland drama, mobsters lamented how the Gus Farace slaying should have been a job well done, a good piece of work.

And Louis Tuzzio was threatening to ruin it all. When he shot Joey Sclafani that night, he set off a chain of events that caused a great deal of problems for the Bonanno family.

The Sclafani shooting was not sanctioned, and Bonanno elders were invited to numerous heated sit-downs with Gambino crime family head John Gotti. It helped, a little, that the acting boss of the Bonanno family—Anthony Spero—and Gotti were friendly. Spero had been a guest at John "Junior" Gotti III's April 30, 1991, wedding at the majestic Helmsley Palace Hotel in Manhattan. The FBI later seized the guest list for the matrimonial ceremony, and it provided a Who's Who of the city's Mafia. Spero's name was on it.

He was there as a representative of the Bonanno crime family, which at that time was moving toward extinction. The family's 120 or so made members were considered Mob outlaws. The family did not have a seat on the Mafia's fabled Commission, the governing group started by Lucky Luciano that oversees the city's five crime families. The Bonannos were booted off the board because of their rampant drug dealing, and because of an internal war that left four high-ranking mobsters dead.

"This is no good, that Sclafani kid got hurt. John is not happy about it," a Gambino associate said. "Something has got to be done about it."

To make matters worse, Louis Tuzzio would not keep his mouth shut about the hit. He bragged about whacking Farace to his friends and even had the audacity to approach Anthony Spero and ask when he would be proposed for official membership. "He was so thirsty to get his button," his brother Nicky Tuzzio later remembered. "Anthony Spero just gave him this shocked look." The Bonannos decided to get rid of Louis Tuzzio before his big mouth brought everybody down. Besides that, he would be a sacrifice to the Gambino family to appease them for the Sclafani shooting.

Later that week, Bonanno higher-ups called Louis Tuzzio to the Pigeon. "Kid, put on your best suit. The books just opened. You're going to get your button."

Christmas was coming and Louis Tuzzio was in the mood to celebrate. He'd been invited to the annual Bonanno crime family Christmas party at Hollywood Terrace, a fancy catering hall in Bensonhurst. The yearly holiday bash gave top bosses and their underlings a chance to socialize with each other without the pressure of business. Envelopes stuffed with cash would be passed around, with the fattest going to the top bosses. It was seasonal gift giving, Mafia style.

It was a nice affair, a sit-down dinner with tuxedoed

waiters and white tablecloths. Tuzzio was impressed. A DJ played a combination of big band-era favorites like Tony Bennett and Frank Sinatra, and old doo-wop tunes from the Platters.

This year Tuzzio sat at a table with made guys. After a few drinks, Louis sat back in his chair and stretched his legs. He looked around at the revelry and smiled. This was it. He had made it. He deserved his place among the old men he had respected his entire life. But what Louis didn't know was even as the old men were shaking his hand, they were quietly shaking their heads, knowing the ink had dried on Louis Tuzzio's mob career.

As the party died down toward midnight, Tuzzio and some of the younger associates made their way to Pastels, a disco popular with wiseguys in Bay Ridge, Brooklyn. Disco might have been dead in the rest of the country, but in Bay Ridge, butterfly-collar shirts and Donna Summer still ruled the night. Near-naked women gyrated on Pastels's dance floor as Tuzzio pressed flesh with friends who congratulated him for doing a good piece of work. People in the know discreetly raised their champagne glasses in his direction.

For all the seemingly good feelings, though, Tuzzio knew something was amiss. Someone had to pay for the Sclafani shooting. Deep down he knew that it might be him.

The Mother Cabrini social club on Avenue U was a well-protected place on January 3, 1990. It was located in the memorably named neighborhood of Gravesend, another corner of Brooklyn infiltrated by organized crime. New members of the Bonanno family would be initiated that night. The new wiseguys would take the vow of *omerta*, which roughly translates into death before revealing the secrets of the Mafia. Louis Tuzzio had been given a false promise that he would be among those initiated that night.

The ceremony is the most secret and protected bastion of all Mafia activities, because men actually are "baptized" into a family. To become "made" is a hallowed goal to any mob hanger-on who had the good fortune of being born a full-blooded Italian. Usually, a ceremony like the one slated to be held at the Mother Cabrini opens with a speech given by the family's boss, or the host of the service. He introduces himself and all of the captains present to the new members of the family. Then he explains its history and the rules they are expected to live by. The newly made men are also warned that if the rules are broken, the punishment is usually death.

In October 1989, the FBI penetrated the secrecy of the Mafia initiation, after they bugged a house in Medford, Massachusetts, with the help of a government co-operator who was going to "get his badge" at a ceremony there.

In that case, one of the bosses of the Boston-based family told his new underlings: "You can never say anything to anybody about this organization. There is no such thing as resigning." Then the inducted swore in Italian to enter alive into this organization and leave it dead: *"Did non en, did entro vivo, esco morto."* The speech at every induction ceremony may be different, but the principle is the same. Once you're in, you can never get out.

Louis Tuzzio knew all that as he got ready at his mother's house that night. After the ceremony he would forever be introduced as "a friend of *ours*," rather than as "a friend of mine." He looked in the mirror and commented to himself: "I'm either going to get made tonight, or I'm going to get whacked."

His brother Nicky overheard the comment and told him, "Come on, Louie. Don't go, please, just don't go. It's not worth it. At least bring a gun, something."

Going to another gangster's club with a gun was a sign of disrespect. Even if Louis had a feeling he might not leave the Mother Cabrini alive, he still believed in the Old World rules that governed the secret society. "Nah, it will be all right," Louis told him. "Don't worry."

He pulled on his black leather coat and zipped it up to the top of his tight black silk T-shirt. Then Louis gently pulled his mother, Antoinette, into the kitchen by her hand. He kissed her neck and whispered in her ear. "I'm either going to get my wings," he told her, pointing an index finger to his temple, simulating a gun to his head, "or I'm going to get my button," pointing to his lapel. Then he asked his terrified mother to make him one promise.

"If I get killed tonight, I want to be buried in a brass coffin with my gray shoes and gray slacks."

Louis climbed into his midnight blue Camaro with tinted windows and drove off.

Nicky and Mario Gallo, who had been at the Tuzzios' apartment to wish Louis well, waited until the Camaro turned the corner and then began to follow it. Nicky had a shotgun strapped under his jacket, and Mario carried a .38 in the waistband of his jeans. "I can't let them whack my brother," Nicky repeated over and over as they followed the Camaro. "I can't let them whack my brother."

A mile away, Louis spotted them in the rearview mirror. He pulled over on Avenue U and West Sixth Street. "Get out of here, you idiots!"

But Nicky and Mario refused to listen. They followed

Louis all the way to the Mother Cabrini. They watched as Louis embraced someone outside. Then Nicky and Mario reluctantly drove off.

They would never see Louis alive again.

Louis's body was pulled from his Camaro early the next morning. He had been shot eight times in the head, neck, and back at the corner of Avenue L and East Fourth Street in the Jewish neighborhood of Midwood. His car was parked on the wrong side of the street behind a navy blue pickup truck alongside Friends Football Field. The Camaro's headlights were still on. Louis's foot was on the brake and the car was in drive.

There was a bullet hole through Louis's left arm and left elbow, as if he saw the bullets coming and tried to block them. There were rope burns around his chin and cheeks. His black leather jacket was splattered with blood. So were his favorite gray slacks and Italian leather shoes. He had a clump of dark hair grasped in his fist. Detectives were amazed at what a fight he must have put up.

The Tuzzio family granted his last wish and buried him in a brass coffin. But he was not wearing his gray shoes. Louis had them on the night he was killed, and his family could not get the bloodstains out of the soft leather.

After his brother's death, Nicky Tuzzio spent most of his adult life behind bars.

Ten years after he buried his brother in a brass coffin, Nicky Tuzzio was still incarcerated at the Metropolitan Detention Center, finishing off his fifteen-year sentence on drug charges, when a handsome, muscular new inmate swaggered into the recreation room. The rookie prisoner reminded Tuzzio of some of the guys from the old neighborhood, like his slain brother. He soon found out the new guy was Chris Paciello, the club king from Miami who was in all the newspapers practically every day.

Paciello may have been arrested more than a dozen times, but he had not spent more than a few nights in jail. Nicky Tuzzio knew the system. He had jailhouse status. Paciello saw a friend in him.

They started hanging together. They played handball against the Mexicans for MDC commissary stamps, and usually lost. They played cards at night. They gossiped about girlfriends. Chris Paciello grew to trust Nicky Tuzzio.

He shouldn't have.

Tuzzio turned on him. Even as Paciello forked over Tuzzio's share of commissary stamps after a handball loss, his newfound prison buddy was busy repeating Paciello's every jailhouse word, every threat, every late-night confession, to investigators in an eastern district's prosecutor's office a few miles away from the jail.

Nicky Tuzzio had decided that the Mafia had killed his brother. Cooperating with the government would be his final revenge and giving up Chris Paciello was part of the process.

18

FALLING LIKE DOMINOES

If Chris Paciello broke the conditions of his bond and landed himself back in the MDC, he would be there among plenty of familiar faces. His friends were being taken down in sweeping indictments at a rapid-fire pace. After the Feds tore apart the Bath Avenue Crew, they went to work on the New Springville Boys. As each aspiring mobster and Mafia associate was charged, there was also pressure for the mobsters to "flip" or cooperate against their cohorts in exchange for lighter sentences.

By the time Paciello was arrested and indicted, the government had secured more than a half dozen cooperators. One of them was Dean "Caesar" Benasillo, the effeminate one-time club kid who promoted parties at the Tunnel nightclub. Like Paciello, Benasillo jumped from crew to crew. He was close with guys who aligned themselves in either the Bath Avenue Crew or the New Springville Boys. He was not a violent thug, but a small-time drug dealer and aspiring wiseguy with a college degree.

Benasillo was picked up in the first Bonanno family takedown in October 1999, months before Chris Paciello was arrested. He was placed in a holding cell at the Drug Enforcement Agency building in midtown Manhattan, charged with racketeering and narcotics trafficking. Former Bonanno boss Anthony Spero and soldier Fabrizio DeFrancisci—the very men who could have helped him reach his goal of becoming a made mobster—were silent. Not talking to him. Not talking to each other.

The silence made Benasillo very nervous. He began to sweat and pant in anxiety. Fabrizio tried to calm him down. "They don't have anything," he said. "Don't worry, Dean. We'll be fine. We'll all stick together." But after a few minutes, Dean panicked. He began banging on the door, yelling: "I'll tell you anything you want to know. Just get me out of here! These guys will kill me in here." Then he looked over his shoulder and said, "I'm not going to jail for the rest of my life for you guys." After that, Benasillo's rat name became "Eight Is Enough" because it only took him eight minutes to flip.

Benasillo was not the only former friend ready to testify against Chris Paciello and the rest of the Bonanno clan. Mikey Yammine and Jimmy Gap sang about the Judy Shemtov murder. Crazy Joe and his cousin Charles gave up the Bath Avenue Crew's many murders. Then a New Springville Boy named Rob cooperated, too, largely because he owed the unofficial leader of that crew, Lee D'Vanzo, more than $100,000 in shylock loans.

Among Chris Paciello's old bank robbery cohorts, one group was especially rampant. They were Danny Costanza, Lee D'Vanzo, Joey "Gams" Gambino, Beck "Castro" Fisheku, and Ned "the Head" Bilali. The government believed the crew worked for an alleged Bonanno captain, Anthony Graziano, and had close ties to the Bath Avenue Crew.

During a spree in December and January 1998, the crew robbed a half-dozen night deposit boxes in Seattle, Washington, using the smash-and-grab technique. They also robbed banks in Florida, the Carolinas, and New Jersey. The New Springville Boys were a traveling crime wave.

One of their biggest scores came in early 1999, when they arranged to score 450 pounds of pot from a dealer in Arizona at a low price to smuggle back to New York City. Beck Fisheku got his uncle to rent him a long RV with beds and a kitchen for the cross-country trip. Everything went according to plan. They picked up the marijuana, shrink-wrapped it, jammed it into coolers, and stashed the bales under one of the RV's beds. Then they rented a blue Lincoln Continental to use as a "crash car" in case anyone tried to pull over the trailer with the drugs.

On February 9, 1999, a sharp-eyed Nebraska state trooper, Christopher Bigsbey, spotted the RV rambling along the interstate in Lincoln. Something about the driver did not look right. He seemed nervous. Not only that, he looked out of place wearing a shiny Yankees jacket and a backward Yankees baseball cap.

The driver was Ned "the Head" Bilali.

The trooper slowed down alongside the RV to take a closer look. Next thing he knew, the Lincoln blew past him, speeding. He threw on his lights and pulled the car over. Ned the Head and the RV full of pot roared along. A video camera mounted on the trooper's dash recorded the chase.

But Bigsbey knew something was amiss. The men in the Lincoln—Costanza, D'Vanzo, and Fisheku—were being evasive. He radioed ahead to the next town, Illinois.

"There's a suspicious-looking RV, white, coming your way."

Ned the Head was pulled over, and they were all arrested. Fisheku's uncle had put both vehicles in his name, a dead giveaway that the foursome was working together.

Later, when the crew was indicted on federal charges, NYPD detective Jimmy Harkins and DEA agent Rob Roth burst out laughing as they watched the tape of the New Springville Boys arrest. "These guys looked like they were on their way out to hang under the El on Eighteenth Avenue, and here they were in the middle of cowboy country," Harkins said.

The New Springville Boys were not the only ones taken down.

Some of the Bath Avenue Crew guys and their friends were also re-indicted—Fabrizo DeFrancisci, Tommy Reynolds, and Skeevy Bellafurie—for robbing banks up and down the East Coast. Thirteen were indicted for robbery and drug trafficking.

Investigators believe they struck dozens of times. Armed with crowbars, hammers, police scanners, and walkie-talkies, the crew had robbed more than $1.3 million from thirty banks over a seven-year period. Most of the money was used to fund a lucrative marijuana trafficking business.

In January 2000, the FBI grabbed Skeevy in Florida, where he was working as a DJ at South Beach hot-spots. Tommy and Fabrizio were already in the MDC. Ten others were rousted from their homes.

The last to be arrested was George Ludwigsen, Chris Paciello's older brother.

Chris saw his *paesans,* and his blood, falling like dominoes. The pressure was on. Every time someone got arrested, the likelihood increased that someone would turn on him.

By then, his South Beach world had fallen apart. Paciello's gated million-dollar estate had become an eyesore after months of neglect. Windows were boarded up. Weeds were knee-high. Stray cats roamed in and out. There was a FOR SALE sign in the front yard offering to sell the house for $1.7 million. There were no immediate takers.

The Bar Room was sold to one of Paciello's old partners—Michael Capponi—who pulled the disco ball down and planned to reinvent the club under the name 320. "I've taken away the icons, the chandeliers—everything that would remind you of Bar Room," Capponi said over the wail of power tools as he rebuilt the club. Liquid's business had dwindled considerably. The club started hosting teenage dance parties for the underage crowd. The club's manager, Paul Thieleck, tried to keep the club afloat, but he was having a hard time. "Ever since the indictment, the cops and fire department have been harassing us. Now the connections we had no longer work for us," he said. "Chris's presence is ninety percent of the business. Since he's been gone, we've been trying to fill his shoes, but they are very big shoes to fill."

Before long, the club died altogether and it was reported that Paciello sold his share of Liquid to the model Tyson Beckford.

Meanwhile, another model in Chris Paciello's life, Niki Taylor, was livid that his arrest had turned her own life upside down. After Paciello's arrest, she had been subpoenaed to testify in front of the grand jury about a pile of money she had transported from Miami to New York City for him in 1996.

Taylor told the grand jury that Paciello had called her cell phone and asked her to pick up a package from his secretary, Janet Navarro, Mickey Rourke's sister-in-law. The supermodel was going to Manhattan the following morning for a photo shoot, so she agreed. She picked up the envelope at the China Grill and dropped it off to Paciello in his room at Manhattan's posh Royalton Hotel.

"He asked me to bring it because he needed cash," Taylor later testified during Paciello's civil trial stemming from the fight with Mighty Mike Quinn. "He was staying in New York longer than he thought, and he didn't pack clothes. He spent the money on four Prada suits."

But prosecutors now wondered if the cash was some sort of Mafia payoff and wanted to question Taylor about it. Her grand jury involvement quickly became fodder for gossip columnists, and her lawyers released a statement to the press. "It is our hope that we can avoid her further involvement in this investigation."

Even Ingrid had distanced herself from Chris Paciello. She was facing her own legal problems brought on by his arrest. Weeks after Paciello turned himself in, Ingrid had met with him and one of Liquid's corporate attorneys at the Florida federal pen where he was locked up. The meeting was held in a small private attorney room at the jail. Ingrid was nervous. She did not need these kinds of headaches. She had a reputation to maintain, a fledgling business to run.

"They sent me a subpoena," Ingrid told them. She was being summoned by the government to appear in front of a grand jury. She allegedly had never paid taxes on the cash Chris had paid her for more than two-and-a-half years.

For years, Ingrid had presented herself as an owner of Liquid. The truth was, she was a paid employee. Chris was essentially renting her name, paying her for her contacts. For the better part of two years, she had received upward of $5,000 a month for the privilege. Chris had paid her with $100 bills stuffed in sealed envelopes.

Of course, it was income Ingrid had failed to mention to the Internal Revenue Service.

Prosecutors filed a request for a warrant to search

Ingrid's South Point Drive apartment in Miami Beach. It was granted.

On March 3, 2000, FBI agent Michael Leveroc was sent into Ingrid's luxury high-rise to look for "$50,000 located within a shoebox, which she had secreted inside her home." The shoebox full of money was more evidence Walden could use to prove Paciello was skimming cash from Liquid's revenues.

While going through Ingrid's belongings, the FBI agent became one of the first people—aside from Madonna—to discover the thirty-four-year-old Cuban princess was pregnant. Along with the shoebox full of money, the agent found that the apartment was littered with baby books: natural childbirth, infant names, healthy eating for expecting moms.

The agent reasoned the books could have been Madonna's. She was pregnant with her son, and the expectant mom had been the subject of more than a few newscasts and gossipy items in the paper. But nearly a month after Ingrid's apartment was searched, her spokeswoman made an announcement on her behalf. "Ingrid is pregnant."

The father was a twenty-five-year-old Danish model, Dennis Schaller, whom Casares had been dating for about six months. By this time, Ingrid was out of the news as the business partner of a jailed reputed mobster and suspected murderer. Instead she was photographed going to a Manhattan obstetrician with Madonna, and riding on a motor scooter with her protruding belly resting against television host Rosie O'Donnell's back on Miami Beach.

Casares was forced to testify in front of a grand jury. Her testimony remained secret. For some reason her tax problems vanished. Ingrid was never charged. She had apparently gotten away with a crime. And South

Beach observers keeping tabs on Paciello's case assumed it meant nothing more than the fact that Ingrid was going to help the government by giving up information on her partner, or turning over the clubs' books.

Whatever was going on, Ingrid refused to talk about it. So did her attorney, Bruce Maffeo. "I have no comment," he said, "other than to observe that Ms. Casares has not been charged."

By 2001, Ingrid was hiding behind her publicist when asked about her good friend. "Chris is still very dear to her," Lizzie Grubman insisted. "She's too busy focused on her pregnancy right now."

That August, Fabrizio DeFrancisci, Tommy Reynolds, Joe Benanti, and Chris Paciello sat around a table on the first floor of the MDC. It was a codefendants' meeting, and everyone at the table—except Paciello and the lawyers—wore khaki prison pants and khaki buttondowns over white T-shirts.

Both Fabrizio and Tommy had recently spent time in the "box," solitary confinement in a pitch-dark cell. Fabrizio's parents, elderly Italian immigrants, were heartbroken that their son was behind bars. So was his girlfriend, Mary, a leggy blonde schoolteacher who had been with him since they were teens.

Reynolds's parents, Andrew and Maryanne, were also standing by their son, and insisted that he was a different man than the murderous aspiring mobster he was in his younger days. Reynolds had a six-year-old daughter he wanted to go home to while "he still had some life left in him."

All that ran through the inmates' minds as they faced one another at the table. "Must be real nice being on the outside, no?" Tommy asked Paciello, eyeballing his old pal.

"Yeah, real nice. Locked up in my own house with a guard twenty-four hours a day. No one to talk to but my lawyers. My mother's the only one on the list now," Paciello said. "And my aunts."

Vincent Romano, Fabrizio's attorney, brought the discussion back to the business at hand: a global plea. Fabrizio would accept twenty-four years for his role in two murder conspiracies, drug trafficking, and racketeering. Tommy Reynolds would get thirty-six years for the role he played in four homicides—including the shooting of Judy Shemtov. Joe Benanti, charged with ordering a hit on a burglar who had robbed the wrong gangster's daughter, Jill Spero, would receive fifteen years. And Chris Paciello would get fourteen years.

Romano, a thickset lawyer with slicked raven black hair and monogrammed shirts, grew up in Bay Ridge and the suspected mobsters he represented trusted him. He was young, only 35, but he knew the neighborhood, he knew the players, and he knew the law both in court, and on the streets. He had represented Jimmy Galione and a host of other accused wiseguys. Romano knew how important it was to make sure that every defendant took the global offer so that his client—and Fabrizio's codefendants—would see the outside of a federal jail before they were old men.

Every defendant at the table already in jail wanted to take the global plea offer. They were trying to convince Paciello it was the only way. The government had them nailed. The witnesses, the rats, were lined up ready to testify about every detail of their crimes.

Paciello was the holdout. He was the only guy at the table who could afford a high-priced lawyer to defend him at a trial in the first place. He was making Tommy Reynolds furious. Fabrizio was also enraged. Old man

Benanti, always the peacemaker, tried to calm them down.

"So, what are you going to do? You don't like fourteen, go back and try to get a couple less. Tommy and I will both eat a couple of extra years," Fabrizio told Paciello.

"I'll think about it," Paciello answered. "But whatever I do, I have to ask my mother."

"Your mother!" Whatever composure Fabrizio was trying to maintain had disappeared. "What about my mother? Huh?"

The discussions were on the verge of escalating into fisticuffs. But Paciello stood firm. "I want to go to trial," he told them over and over. "I'm going to beat this case."

Without Paciello aboard there was no deal. Either everybody signed up, or the global offer was no good. The discussion quickly got out of hand.

"I heard you've been calling me a pussy," Paciello said to Reynolds.

"Yeah," Reynolds responded. "And? What do you think? You're going to be a selfish fuck, and we're going to get life, and we're all going to sit around in jail watching you on some talk show holding hands with your whore girlfriends?"

The prison guards peered into the room to make sure no blows were about to be exchanged. The lawyers desperately tried to calm the defendants down. There could not be animosity between the cohorts. Every person at that table needed one another.

"You know, half the guys from the old neighborhood are in here," Tommy told Paciello.

"Yeah, I heard," Paciello said. Then he stood up and walked out of the meeting without saying a word.

Everyone Paciello had been tight with since his teens

was now either angry with him, or cooperating against him. They had vacationed together, hung out together, committed crimes together. And now it was all over.

An old photograph of Chris Paciello was entered into evidence after the New Springville Boys were arrested. It showed Paciello and three other young guns with their arms slung around each other with their girlfriends. In the photograph was Lee D'Vanzo snuggling with Karen Gravano. Jennifer Graziano, the daughter of an alleged Bonanno soldier, sat on Paciello's lap, kissing his ear. Danny Costanza was in the picture, too, with a pretty brunette. The picture was taken years earlier when the group had gone on spring vacation together in Mexico after a score.

Those days were long gone.

As were the days of the infamous Bath Avenue Crew. Weeks after the jailhouse meeting, Tommy Reynolds, Joe Benanti, and Fabrizio DeFrancisci pleaded guilty—to life sentences. It was an emotional hearing. Judy Shemtov's children were in the small courtroom and their sobs punctuated the defendants' every word. Arlyn, a beautiful redhead who had cradled her mother's dying body, looked as if she would collapse with grief. Her sister, April, a petite pretty blonde, spent the hearing alternately crying and glaring at the back of Tommy Reynolds's head.

Joe Benanti's health was failing. As he admitted his role in a host of crimes, he looked like a mere shadow of the muscled rough-and-tumble wiseguy he was in his youth. He even paused in his confession to ask the court if he could take his high-blood-pressure medication. Then he took a deep breath as he accepted responsibility for his role in the slaying of a burglar who had broken into the boss's daughter's home.

"I said it was okay, but I didn't pull the trigger," Benanti muttered.

As Benanti was handcuffed by U.S. marshals and escorted out of the courtroom and back to a cell at the MDC where he would likely spend the rest of his life, the balding gangster looked intensely at his wife, Marguerite, a striking Ava Gardner look-alike who had a teenager's figure and gray shoulder-length hair. He shrugged his shoulders before blowing her a kiss. Marguerite Benanti, who had been dabbing at tears with a white handkerchief, smiled back at him.

The Benantis were an unlikely Mafia couple. Marguerite collected modern art and antiques. She wore stylish eyeglasses, and little makeup. Her husband spent much of his time in jail reading highbrow books from the *New York Times* bestseller list—such as Joe Eszterhas's critically acclaimed *American Rhapsody,* a parody of President Bill Clinton's affair with White House intern Monica Lewinsky. Marguerite often carried a picture of her husband talking to Fabrizio—whom he loved like a son—in the couple's Staten Island kitchen. On the photograph she had cut out a line from one of her literature magazines and taped it above their heads. "*Sometimes people need to be forgiven, Jim muses sadly, and sometimes they need to go to jail.*"

The day he went to jail, Benanti may not have been the rugged, rowdy hellion of his youth, but he was a man who was ready to accept his fate. That fact did not make it any easier for his wife.

"This is a hard day for me," Marguerite said as Joe was led away. "This is a hard damn day."

Her friend Maryanne Reynolds, Tommy's mother, had gone into the courtroom's hallway and ran smack into Judy Shemtov's daughter April. Not knowing what to say to the family of her son's accidental victim, Maryanne looked at her intently.

April stared back. "You have the nerve to look at me?"

Maryanne then reached out to put a hand on April's shoulder and began to say she was sorry. But before she could open her mouth, April flung her hand away.

"Don't put your hands on me," April screamed. "Your son killed my mother. There is no forgiveness here."

Taken aback, Maryanne cursed under her breath as she hurried down the hall with her brother-in-law, Thomas Reynolds, her son's namesake.

"He hasn't been convicted yet, just remember that," Maryanne yelled over her shoulder. She was thinking of the Tommy she knew. That Tommy was a hardworking, successful Teamster, a loving son and father. He may have admitted to being a killer, but the drugs had made him do it. And he was sorry. So was she.

April screamed back: "You deserve the son you got!"

The argument was not over. Tommy Reynolds's uncle—still wearing his laborer's bright orange construction vest—stopped in his tracks, looked back at the Shemtov family and the cops that surrounded them, and yelled: "You're all a bunch of jerk-offs! That's right, jerk-offs. Now, who wants to do something about that?"

DEA agent Tim Foley and NYPD detective Mike Galletta quickly intervened and escorted the Shemtov family back to their cars.

"Let's get out of here," Foley assured them. "Everyone is upset. Let's not let it escalate."

"This isn't over," Arlyn said under her breath. "I want these people to know what they did. I want them all to admit what they did."

On October 13, almost seven years after she buried her mother, Arlyn Kidan's wish came true. All four of the men involved in the robbery that left her mother dead pleaded guilty. Two of them—Jimmy Calandra and Michael Yammine—were government witnesses ready to testify against Chris Paciello.

But there would be no need. Chris Paciello was about to confess himself.

Chris Paciello decided to cop a plea on October 13, 2000—Friday the 13th.

Murder. Robbery. Racketeering.

Guilty. Guilty. Guilty.

The plea came just four days before prosecutors would question potential jurors, responsible citizens who'd have had to be sequestered to avoid jury tampering and the daily stories that were sure to have played out in the media. It was less than a week before his lawyer Benjamin Brafman would have argued that Paciello was a victim of jealous former cohorts and overzealous prosecutors. It was just two days after Brafman said the government's case was "razor thin."

The surprise plea also came merely a day after assistant U.S. attorney Jim Walden revealed the conversations between Paciello and Dohler where the club impresario had vowed to an undercover investigator he would "not go down like John Gotti," and snarled that Sammy the Bull Gravano—whose daughter Karen was a close friend of his—should be murdered along with his entire family for betraying the Dapper Don.

By noon, the U.S. Department of Justice issued a press release, faxed to the major news organizations along with the headline: "Ludwigsen scheduled to plead guilty in racketeering case." Unfortunately for the prosecutors who worked long, hard hours proving that the South Beach celebrity was really a hardened criminal, most New Yorkers had bigger things to worry about than a small-time hood copping to a life of crime.

For the first time in forty-four years, both New York baseball teams—the Yankees and the Mets—would battle for the World Series Championship. Subway Series fever swept the city, sick days soared, and even the presidential debates between the two candidates, Republican governor George W. Bush and Democratic vice president Al Gore, were met with indifference.

Then a suicide bomber in the Middle East plowed a small boat crammed with explosives into a navy ship, the *USS Cole*, killing seventeen American sailors aboard. It was a busy news day, and, for the first time since his arrest, there was not a swarm of television cameras outside ready to record Paciello's forlorn shuffle into the Brooklyn federal courthouse.

Even if his face was not plastered on the six o'clock news that night, word of Chris Paciello's plea spread in the Metropolitan Detention Center, where the Binger himself was likely to be shipped, once again, after his sentencing. He would have plenty of company there. For the most part, the white guys at the MDC stuck together, and when Paciello was indicted, so were many other Italians.

Carmine Agnello—John Gotti's son-in-law—had been locked up without bail there for threatening a rival scrap metal business. His competitors were, in reality, a sting operation composed of undercover cops from the NYPD's Auto Crime Unit. To make matters worse, his wife, Victoria Gotti, filed for divorce when the government played her some secretly recorded wiretapped conversations Agnello had with his reputed *goomada,* or mistress, a secretary for his debris business. For Victoria, a gorgeous blonde and successful novelist who had grown up with Carmine in Howard Beach and had dated him against her father's wishes (at one point, John Gotti tried to steer Agnello away from his daughter with a baseball bat beating), an affair was the last straw.

Agnello and Paciello had more in common than mob connections—both shared the same lawyer, Benjamin Brafman.

Ironically, the reason Chris Paciello had hired Brafman was because he had gotten Peter Gatien, owner of two of Manhattan's best nightclubs, the Tunnel and the Limelight, off on federal drug charges. But to get Gatien off, Brafman had had to malign Chris Paciello.

Brafman had described Paciello as a "gangster and a thug" and joined the ranks of those fingering the club owner as the killer of Billy Balanca, the man whose dead body was found frozen solid in the trunk of his father's car on Staten Island.

At the 1998 trial, just two years before Paciello would hire him, Brafman cross-examined Lord Michael Caruso, who had been ensnared in the drug charges that had brought Gatien to trial and had agreed to testify against his boss.

"Tell me about Chris Ludwigsen. He was your partner?" Brafman asked. "Chris Ludwigsen put a gun to your face and threatened to kill you."

"Yes," answered Caruso.

"You know that you identified him to be a tough guy," Brafman said.

"Yes."

"You mean a gangster?" Brafman barked.

"He's a tough guy."

"Do you know he administered beatings? You know that, you were there," Brafman asked.

"I seen him have fights and beat people up."

"I'm not talking about a fight," Brafman said. "I'm talking about beating someone."

"Yes."

"You went down to work for this tough guy in Florida?" Brafman asked.

"Yes."

"You invested money with this tough guy, didn't you?" Brafman said.

"Yes, I did."

"Tell us," Brafman asked, "how does that rumor circulate that you are talking about with the government, that Ludwigsen whacked Billy Balanca?"

"It was a street rumor."

As the testimony went on, Brafman described Chris Paciello as hired muscle for Caruso. "Chris's position," Brafman said, "if you will, in Michael Caruso's life was the gun-toting hit man-type guy that is going to protect you from people who made threats against you?"

"There were threats made and he stuck up for me, and he did it more than once," Caruso answered.

Brafman then assailed Caruso for investing in the Florida nightclub with someone who was rumored to be a gangster. "But it's Chris who you know to be a connected guy who is bringing you down there to invest, right?" Brafman yelled at Caruso. "When you went down, you knew Chris was a guy who ran with gangsters, right? That Chris was a stone killer?"

"Nobody ever said Chris is a stone killer," Caruso said. "Nobody. He's tough, yeah. If you get into a fight with him, you're going to lose. Definitely going to lose and get a beating. No one ever said that Chris was a stone killer."

What a difference two years makes.

The day Chris Paciello admitted to being a thug and a gangster, Brafman would describe him as an upstanding citizen who was targeted by the government only because of his celebrity. For months Brafman had said his client was a "businessman," not a Bonanno associate.

"He's not even an associate of an associate," Brafman had said after every one of Paciello's pre-trial hear-
ings. "To me," Brafman said, "he's a guy from Brooklyn
who has come a long way."

Chris Paciello might have come a long way, but he
was about to go back to where he came from: Brooklyn. If prosecutors were right, he would spend at least
thirty-three years in a federal jail cell.

Chris Paciello's plea would unfold in front of U.S. magistrate Joan Azrack, the same judge who had approved
the Binger's bail package earlier in the year. The courtroom had six small benches for spectators positioned
only a few feet from the judge's chair. Two mahogany
tables were placed on either side of the judge, one for
the defendant and his lawyers, the other for the law enforcement team that had arrested him.

By 3:30 P.M., the time Paciello was slated to arrive,
Courtroom 340 was crowded with agents, police officers, and reporters awaiting his arrival. Among them
was NYPD inspector Charlie Wells, who had been promoted to a job at police headquarters as the commanding
officer of the Special Investigations Division. Detective
Mike Galletta, the cop who had first met Paciello more
than a decade earlier when he arrested the sixteen-year-
old punk with stolen car radios, was there. So was Detective Jimmy Harkins, the cop who began locking up
Paciello's Staten Island friends for bank robberies. FBI
special agent Wayne McGrew was also there. The only
investigator on the Bath Avenue Crew team missing was
DEA special agent Timmy Foley. His grandmother had
passed away and Foley was attending her funeral in
Chicago.

At the prosecutors' table, they were smiling all around.
Assistant U.S. attorneys Jim Walden and Greg Andres

stood alongside Kings County assistant district attorney Chris Blank. The men were too excited to sit down. Every defendant on the Bath Avenue Crew indictment save one—Anthony Spero—had pleaded guilty. The prosecution had a right to be ecstatic. They had sacrificed weekends and vacations, holidays and dinners with their families over the past year working on Paciello's case. Watching him admit his guilt was a sweet reward.

By 3:45 P.M., those in the courtroom were stirring, looking at their watches. Paciello was fifteen minutes late. It was to be expected. A man who knows he's eligible under federal sentencing guidelines to be locked up in a federal jail for twenty-eight to thirty-three years is probably not in a tremendous hurry.

He was facing more time in jail than he had even been alive.

Finally, at 3:48, he showed. Paciello walked through a metal detector with a U.S. marshal in close pursuit. He took his time, his Italian leather shoes clicking on the gray marble floor, down the narrow corridor, past a jury room, the clerk's office, and a bank of phone booths until he reached the four gleaming steel doors of the elevator that would take him to the third floor. When he stepped out of the elevator, he nodded toward a guard who pointed him to Judge Azrack's chambers.

Numerous high-profile criminals and terrorists and gangsters have made their way through the hallways of the Eastern District's federal courthouse, but celebrities were few. By then the building's court officers had become accustomed to the swarm of reporters that followed Paciello's movements.

Paciello was dressed sharply, in a neat black suit set off with a red silk tie. His hair was close-cut and slicked back with gel. His fingernails were manicured and shined with a coat of clear nail polish.

After months of house arrest, his complexion was sallow. He looked lanky and underfed. His expensive suit had been fitted in better days to hug his muscular frame. Now it hung baggy on him. He looked like a teenager who had borrowed a suit from his dad.

The beaten-down man who stood in front of the judge and became the twentieth member of the Bath Avenue Crew to plead guilty to racketeering was no longer Chris Paciello, King of South Beach. He was once again Christian Ludwigsen—the Binger.

At 3:49 P.M., Chris Paciello faced the judge. He also faced up to his past.

He raised his right hand and swore to tell the truth, the whole truth, and nothing but the truth. Judge Azrack stared at the defendant. "Are you ready to plead?"

"Yes."

"How do you plead?"

"Guilty, your honor."

Benjamin Brafman handed his client a yellow legal pad, which had a scribbled statement. Paciello took a breath, and as he let it out, his shoulders sank. Looking at the pad, he read in a voice barely audible to those in the small courtroom:

"I agreed with others to participate in a racketeering conspiracy," he stammered. "I knew that these were part of a larger criminal enterprise. In furtherance of this agreement, I participated in the robbery of a Chemical Bank at the Staten Island Mall in December of 1992.

"And I participated in the attempted robbery of the Shemtov home on Staten Island in February of 1993."

He paused. His faced turned the color of his crimson tie. Flustered, he stared at his attorney.

"Judge," Walden said, annoyed that Paciello left out the most brutal aspect of his crimes. "The Government's evidence would show—"

Paciello glowered at Walden and coughed out his next words like they were chicken bones snared in his throat.

"Which resulted in the death of Ms. Shemtov."

Walden was not satisfied. He had worked a long time to hear a jury read back a guilty conviction. Paciello pleading guilty was not nearly as satisfying, and he was going to make sure Paciello admitted every detail of his crime.

"Mr. Ludwigsen, is it fair to say in December of 1992 you went to Chemical Bank in the Staten Island Mall?"

"Yes, it is."

"And what was your role on that day?"

"My role was to let others know when the money was being removed from the safe inside the bank."

"Did you perform that role?"

"Yes, I did."

Walden asked if there was a device Paciello used to communicate with his co-conspirators.

"Yes, I did. I used a walkie-talkie radio."

"As a result of that robbery, did you receive a share of the proceeds from the bank?"

"Yes, I did."

Then Walden asked about that cold February night Paciello had been trying to forget for more than seven years.

"My role was to drive the getaway car after the robbery was to occur."

"Did you take the conspirators to the house knowing they were going to rob the house?"

"Yes, I did."

"Was one or more of the conspirators armed with a weapon?"

"Yes, they were."

"Did you understand that they would have to use that weapon?"

"Yes, I did."

"And," Walden asked, "did one of those conspirators shoot Mrs. Shemtov?"

"Yes, he did."

"Did you then drive them away from the scene?"

"Yes, I did."

In addition to jail time, Paciello would have to pay the United States of America $400,000 in restitution for his crimes. Azrack slammed her gavel down. The plea was entered. Chris Paciello's bail was extended for thirty days, or until Jim Walden decided to revoke it.

Chris Paciello had nothing to say to the reporters who swarmed around him as he walked out of the courthouse. Ben Brafman handed out a prepared statement to be issued on behalf of "Christian Ludwigsen-Paciello."

"The decision to enter a plea of guilty is a courageous and honorable effort by him to accept responsibility for the criminal acts he committed many years ago, which he deeply regrets," the statement read. "His decision to plead guilty and bring closure to that part of his life will allow him to, hopefully, one day begin life anew without any involvement whatsoever in the criminal justice system."

Ingrid Casares was still standing by her man, despite everything. She quickly released her own statement. "I love Chris and I always will."

Chris was given thirty days to take care of his personal life before he was remanded to jail. The route his driver took to bring him back to the Staten Island townhouse took Paciello past a gigantic billboard that sported a mammoth image of his busty girlfriend, Sofia Vergara, who used her ample bosom to advertise a

Spanish TV show, *La Bomba*. "Make a date with So-phia at Club *La Bomba*," screamed the ad for Vergara's Latin music-oriented, weekly TV show on cable's Metro channel. By then gossip columnists in Miami had linked Sofia to Tim Allen, the star of the television show *Home Improvement*. The two were shooting a movie together in Miami called *Big Trouble*.

Funny, because that's exactly what Chris Paciello was in. Big trouble.

Couldn't anyone see he was a different person now? Maybe, but no one saw the injustice of this changed man going to jail except for Ben Brafman.

"It was an agonizing process for him," Brafman said as he climbed into his chauffeur-driven Mercedes after the hearing. "This brings closure to that part of Chris's life. It gives him a degree of comfort in the knowledge that he will take responsibility for his crimes. It takes a great deal of courage to do what Chris did. He's man enough to step up. He's very sad about this.

"The saddest thing about this case," Brafman added, "is that the Chris Paciello that is going to be sentenced is a far different person than the one who committed these crimes ten years ago. This is the only homicide Chris Paciello has ever been linked to, and her death was an accidental discharge. Chris is not now, nor ever has been, a murderer. He has regretted for every minute of every day that Ms. Shemtov died. He's a fundamentally decent person.

"He employed four hundred and fifty people," Braf-man went on. "He had the hottest clubs and restaurants on South Beach. For me, it's very sad to see this story end this way."

But Jim Walden, who later heard about Brafman's comments, quickly added: "No, the saddest part of this case is that there are three children who have no mother because of the action of these thugs."

As he talked about those men he had just jailed for life, Walden unwrapped a package that was sitting on his desk with a return address from the MDC. Inside were twenty cans of dried cuttlefish, a squidlike creature that when disturbed ejects a dark ink that shields them from predators. There was one can of cuttlefish for every Bath Avenue Crew member who pleaded guilty.

19

KING RAT

On November 8, 2000, nearly a month after Paciello pleaded guilty to murder, racketeering, and robbery, he violated an unnamed condition of his bond, and assistant United States attorney Jim Walden moved to remand him back to the MDC. This trip would not merely be a pass through. It would be a long, long stretch. Paciello's only time outside of the prison for at least two decades, in fact, would be to court the day he was sentenced for his conviction.

Ben Brafman, Paciello's attorney, scheduled a hearing in front of U.S. magistrate Joan Azrack to argue that Chris's bail should be extended to the agreed-upon date of November 13, 2000.

Five days of freedom means a lot to a man facing thirty-three years behind bars.

But at 3:30 P.M., the time the hearing was to take place, Chris did not appear at the federal courthouse. Nor was there any sign of the prosecutors, or any other lawyers for Chris. Or even the judge, for that matter. The only person around was the judge's clerk. At 4 P.M. Walden announced to the press corps waiting for Paciello's arrival that the hearing was canceled. No explanation was given.

Just before dawn the following morning, a handful of Chris's paid security guards, including the ones who had lived with him for the last nine months, raced into the garage of his Staten Island home. Paciello's possessions were hurriedly swept into cardboard boxes. Whatever could fit into the trunk of a sedan would be part of his new life. Everything else would be left behind until U.S. marshals could arrange for movers.

Paciello was quickly moved to "an undisclosed location." Officially, his name was placed on an inmate list at the MDC to throw off his former cohorts. He was actually placed in protective custody in a jail somewhere within driving distance of New York City.

His mother and brother Keith told friends in Florida they were going to New York to visit Chris. They were actually relocated somewhere in the United States. His brother George, still facing his own trial on federal charges on burglary and conspiracy charges, was also put into protective custody.

Paciello had become a gem in the government's crown: the federal Witness Protection Program. Christian Ludwigsen, Chris Paciello, even the Binger would cease to exist. Everyone he had ever met was now a bargaining chip he could trade for his own freedom—every made man and bubblegum gangster right on down to the small-time crooks, car thieves, burglars, and dope peddlers.

Now, like Henry Hill, the turncoat crook immortalized in Nicholas Pileggi's book *Wiseguy* and the Martin Scorsese film *Goodfellas*, Chris Paciello would live out the rest of his life "like a schnook."

The government has always argued that the means justify the ends in regards to using criminal informants. Coupled with wiretaps, the use of cooperators had slain much of the dragon that had been La Cosa Nostra.

"Without informants, we're nothing," FBI director Clarence M. Kelley declared in 1972 after he was inaugurated into the role following J. Edgar Hoover's death.

Chris Paciello was by no means the first Bath Avenue Crew hanger-on to give up his cohorts. Mikey Yammine and Jimmy "Gap" Calandra had gone first. Then Dean Benasillo. Crazy Joe Calco was next—the same Crazy Joe who once killed a guy just for thinking he was a rat—was next, followed by his cousin Charles. Of course, without the cooperators from the Froggy Galione case, "Mikey Flattop" DeRosa and Ronald "Messy Marvin" Moran—two other self-confessed rat haters—there would not have been a Bath Avenue Crew indictment in the first place.

No, Paciello was not the first. He was merely joining the rat parade.

His friends back on South Beach did not want to believe there was yet another flaw in the character they had grown to love. Paciello's fall from romantic gangster to low-life goon was a sudden one, too sudden for some of his old pals.

"He's not going to squeal out people, no way," insisted one friend who did not want to be named. "He's very strong on that, and I believe him. The women, the money, the cars, the boat, he told me he thinks it's all bullshit now. He doesn't want that life anymore. He said to me, 'There is more to life than walking around with a six-foot blonde.'

"Okay, yeah, by nature he's a thug. You can't take that out of him. It was camouflaged in Miami, but everyone still knew he was connected. All he hung around with is his guido friends, all these tough guys. But he would never, ever be a rat. No way."

Chris Paciello had them all fooled.

* * *

The government is extremely closemouthed in the handling of its witnesses. Only a few agents are briefed in order to prevent leaks. Only top-level intelligence NYPD detectives know any details. Secrecy is a priority, and the new informant is referred to as a "source" or "liaison."

But when a guy supposedly under twenty-four-hour house arrest is suddenly not home, it clearly sends a signal to the criminal world. Of course, there were already rumors that Paciello had "gone bad," Mafia street lingo for flipping from the Mob's side to the government's. What kind of person turns down a fourteen-year bid, then pleads guilty when the offer on the table is thirty-three years? The kind that has decided to save his own behind, his old friends had determined from their dorms at the MDC.

The question was not whether Paciello had flipped. Now it was: *Who was he going to give up?* Would the Witness Protection Program get its money's worth from a small-time wannabe gangster like Chris Paciello?

The Shemtov homicide was no good to the government. The prosecution already had a guilty plea from the gunman, Tommy Reynolds. In fact, all three of the other participants in the murder were cooperating. The government also did not need Chris Paciello to clear up old bank robberies, unsolved burglaries, or home invasions. These were too insignificant.

For Chris Paciello to have any leverage at all, he had to have good information on some big-league gangsters. In all likelihood, Paciello had been privy to enough conversations amongst high-ranking crime figures that he would be a worthwhile source.

Intense pressure and endless investigations had broken the spine of the Old World La Cosa Nostra. Top-echelon mobsters had pinned their hopes on business-savvy young men to maneuver their interests into new areas—the clubs, the stock market, and the Internet.

Chris Paciello had looked like the future of the Mob and had probably learned more than a few Mafia secrets.

In all likelihood, the government was interested in reputed Colombo boss Alphonse "Allie Boy" Persico. The government had obtained information that Chris had introduced the mob boss to a bevy of his celebrity pals. Was Allie Boy involved in Miami's burgeoning nightclub business? Did Paciello know what happened to Wild Bill Cutolo, Allie Boy's archrival, who vanished in May 1999? Was Wild Bill's disappearance, and apparent death, a sanctioned hit to help the Colombos gain its seat back on the Mafia's Commission? Did Chris even know? Who killed Billy Balanca, the kid in the trunk on Staten Island? Besides all that, the Mob does not let guys like Paciello into their ranks for any other reason than money. There was probably a money trail, and the government would want Paciello to help them uncover it.

The questions would go on and on and on.

New indictments would be drawn up within a matter of months.

As Paciello was grilled, his childhood friends from New Springville had become increasingly nervous. On November 14, 2000, a week after Chris vanished, two of his close friends were in the courthouse. Two alleged Bonanno gangsters, Lee D'Vanzo and Danny Costanza, pleaded guilty to drug distribution charges. They each faced upward of fifteen years.

After Paciello exhausted his knowledge about others' indiscretions, he would have to come clean about his own crimes. All of them. It would be a lengthy list. But if prosecutors had any plans to put him on the stand, they had to know more about his rap sheet than any defense attorney would.

Chris Paciello had become everything he had railed against just months earlier, when he ranted that Sammy the Bull and his family should be killed. Perhaps he had forgotten about his own self-proclaimed important virtue: loyalty. Or maybe his allegiances had changed.

Paciello had once given a word association interview for a Miami magazine, *D'Vox*, in which he claimed that loyalty was a human being's most important attribute. An excerpt reads:

Chris Paciello: "Myself."
A Virtue: "Loyalty."
A Hero: "My mom."
Models: "Delicious."
Family: "Forever."
A Film: "*King of New York.*"
Something That Worries You: "Everything."
A Defect: "Temper."
Violence: "NO more! Lost TOO much!"
Now Chris Paciello would lose himself.

Of course, Chris never took a vow of *omerta*, the Mafia code of silence, so, technically, he could not be expected to honor one.

His German blood would have banned him from the official books even if a Mafia chieftain had proposed him for a button. Besides all that, Chris Paciello was a hanger-on, a jumper. He never aligned himself to any one family. When Wild Bill was going to help him open a Liquid in New York, he was his man. He liked Allie Boy, a gentleman like himself, because he wanted to stay close to his friends associated with the Colombo family like Big Dom Dionisio and Rico Locasio.

When he worked with the Bath Avenue Crew faction of the Bonanno family, it was only because he needed muscle from Tommy Reynolds. He was closer to his friends in the New Springville Boys, a crew that also aligned itself to the Bonannos. Still, he had even angered that gang. When his pal Beck Fisheku, a New Springville guy, was in jail, Paciello was spotted squiring his voluptuous girlfriend around South Beach.

Paciello's objective was to make money. He kept a tight hand on his pockets once he had it. And his commitment went to whoever was going to help him make it at any given moment. Cooperating with the government would not be the first time Chris screwed over people he considered friends. He had a history of burglarizing his pals' homes and casing his dates' apartments. This would also not likely be the last time Paciello turned on those close to him.

On the other hand, maybe cooperating was Chris Paciello's way of saying he was sorry for his crime sprees, sorry that Judy Shemtov was dead and her family was blown apart. Perhaps taking gangsters off the street, helping the government plug the flood of the Mob, was Chris Paciello's way of making amends to his family, and making peace with God.

Even after he went into "the program," the letters from his South Beach supporters kept pouring into Ben Brafman's office. There were hundreds of testimonies about Paciello's good side, his charitable acts, and his helpful nature. In his own way, Chris Paciello had always wanted to assuage his dark past and start anew. South Beach was that fresh start. When his new life soured, Paciello felt he had no choice but to go bad, and help the feds, he had told his friends. It was over.

One close friend, who, like most of Chris's intimates, asked that they be kept anonymous, put it this way: "He tried to hang tough," said the friend, a prominent Miami businessman. "But the feds had over seventeen witnesses. Everybody was working with prosecutors. No one is his friend. I think he finally said, 'What's the point?'

"Chris blew up in a whole new way down here in Miami," he added. "It was something that I have never seen before. I've seen people blow up, then shrivel up and blow out of town. Chris blew up, and kept blowing up. He was unstoppable. Chris got bigger and bigger and bigger and bigger.

"He told me, more than once, since he was busted, if he had to live his life all over again, he never would have done what he did. He looks back at his life, and he's embarrassed at himself. When you get put in the slammer, you are reading a Bible every day. He's become spiritual since he got busted. I truly, truly believe that he will become a changed man."

Other friends believed Chris's motive for cooperating was simple: revenge on the people who tried to use him. It was payback time for the people who wanted his hard work and financial success to become theirs. "You have to remember," Ben Brafman once said about his client, "everybody wanted a piece of Chris Paciello. Everyone was trying to use him, to take a piece of his pie."

It may be a flaw of American society that everyone loves a stand-up villain, a guy who is just as willing to do the time as he was to commit the crime. But cooperate with the government? Give up your friend? Put your family in danger? That was abhorrent. Yet more and more mobsters were doing just that.

Just prior to Chris Paciello's witness protection deal, a *capo* in the New Jersey DeCavalcante mob family flipped as well. Vincent "Vinny Ocean" Palermo, who had been recorded on government wiretaps boasting that his crew was the basis for the popular HBO series *The Sopranos*, delivered twelve other DeCavalcante members to the feds. They were indicted on charges that included five murders and six murder conspiracies. Palermo himself pleaded guilty to orchestrating a racketeering conspiracy that included three hits, extortion, loan-sharking, and gambling charges. It was still unclear if Palermo would do any time in jail at all.

But sometimes giving notorious criminals protection backfired.

One glaring example is Sammy "the Bull" Gravano, the famous Gambino hit man who had killed nineteen people but served only four years in jail after his testimony put away thirty-seven top-level mobsters. It also put a $1 million Mafia bounty on his head. In fact, rumor had it that one Gambino associate offered Paciello that contract to take Sammy the Bull out in the mid-1990s.

When the Bull decided to cooperate, he was transported under heavy guard to the FBI's training academy at the U.S. Marine base in Quantico, Virginia, to iron out a deal with prosecutors. When he vanished, Gravano's lawyer, Ben Brafman, immediately dropped him as a client. In Gravano's autobiography *Underboss*, he wrote that after his discharge, Brafman immediately forwarded a request to the judge. Brafman wanted everyone to know that he had nothing to do with Gravano's decision to become a cooperator.

The Witness Protection Program paid for Gravano to get plastic surgery and set him up with a new life in Phoenix, Arizona. He became Jimmy Moran, a simple man who owned a bagel store . . . for a while.

When Sammy the Bull gave up the Gambino crime family, he signed a plea agreement that stated that he "must not commit, or attempt to commit, any further crimes whatsoever." The contract also promised that if he "violates these conditions," he should be "thereafter subject to prosecution for any federal criminal violations he committed in the past," such as nineteen murders.

In February 2000, Sammy humiliated the government when he was arrested in Phoenix as the mastermind of a drug conspiracy that flooded Arizona with Ecstasy. Cops also arrested his wife, Debra; his son, Gerard; his daughter, Karen; and her fiancé, David Seabrook.

Chris Paciello was no Sammy the Bull, but his cooperation earned him nearly as many headlines. A month after Paciello disappeared, *Daily News* columnists George Rush and Joanna Malloy wrote an item reading, "Club King May Be Set to Sing." A few days later, *Florida Sun Sentinel* gossip Jose Lambiet wrote, "Paciello Disappears; Is He Headed to Witness Protection?" The *Miami New Times* devoted a full page to "the snitch," reading, "South Beach clubland tough guy Chris Paciello may soon show himself to be not so tough after all." And a *New York Post* headline blared, "Paciello to Rat on Colombo Kingpin."

According to the U.S. Marshals Service, nearly seven thousand criminal informants are hidden throughout the United States as participants in the federal Witness Protection Program. With family members, the number balloons to sixteen thousand.

If any of those thousands could successfully alter his persona enough to blend in to his surroundings, it would be Chris Paciello. He had already reinvented himself more than once. He changed from a blue-collar street kid to a hardcore street thug who was not beyond using whatever violent means necessary for his shot at the good life. Then, after Christian Ludwigsen became an accessory to murder when one of those crimes went terribly wrong, he shed that skin too and transformed himself into Chris Paciello, King of South Beach. He was the handsome and good-natured gentleman who charmed all comers with his sexy, rough-around-the-edges life aura.

Now Chris Paciello would have to change once again. His celebrity pals had moved on. His clubs had closed down. Paciello's glory days on South Beach were over.

Ingrid got out of the nightclub business after the birth of her son, Nico, and began throwing parties along with her publicist, Lizzie Grubman. Madonna gave birth to her son, Rocco, and moved to London to live with her husband and the baby's father, British film director Guy Ritchie. Sofia Vergara was on her way to movie stardom. Niki Taylor was rumored to be back together with her former husband, Matt Martinez. Months after her old flame Paciello went into the Witness Protection Program, Taylor was critically wounded in a car crash in Atlanta, grinding her career to a halt. Jennifer Lopez would date Sean "Puffy" Combs and then marry her choreographer. And Chris Paciello would soon be living in the comfort of his "undisclosed location."

Some of Paciello's friends would be easier to find, such as Tommy Reynolds. He had been offered a cooperation agreement before anyone else, but he had politely turned the detectives down before they even finished asking him.

Before any of the indictments had been unsealed, Reynolds had been in a Brooklyn court facing charges of borrowing a friend's car without permission when NYPD detectives Tommy Dades and Mike Galletta approached him, along with DEA agent Tim Foley.

"Something big is going down soon," Detective Dades told him. "Come along with us. We'll give you a new house, a new start. You have a little girl. You should think about this."

"Let me stop you right there," Reynolds responded. "I

think I know where you are going with this. That's not the way I go. The way I see it, you take responsibility for what you did without bringing other people down."

Reynolds was the only participant in the Judy Shemtov homicide who saw it that way. Chris Paciello, of course, would be forced to do some time behind bars. Mikey Yammine and Jimmy Gap Calandra had been jailed in federal cells designed especially for government witnesses.

But Reynolds would be the only person who was facing a life sentence for the murder of Judy Shemtov. "I don't care whether his name is Binger, Chris Paciello, Chris Ludwigsen, whatever," Tommy Reynolds said after news that Paciello had flipped. "He's a rat. That's it. A rat."

Reynolds sucked in a breath to calm himself. "One of the things I do feel bad about," he said, "is that lady. She was an innocent person. Honestly, I'm sorry. Those people are still going to live without their mother forever. I think about that a lot. It was wrong."

There was no question Reynolds was genuinely remorseful about Judy Shemtov's murder. Surely, though, when Reynolds's head hit the hard mattress in the dark of his MDC dorm, his mind raced back to that freezing February night and nagged him with an even bigger regret.

When Reynolds pressed the cold barrel of his .45 to Chris Paciello's head in a fit of fury on February 18, 1993, he must have wished he had squeezed the trigger.

20

THE AFTERMATH

On the last day of Chris Paciello's existence as he knew it, he was escorted into an unmarked car that would take him to federal prison somewhere in New York State, where he would be under around-the-clock protection under an assumed name. The next time he would likely see the streets of Brooklyn would be when he was transported to federal court to testify against his former friends.

As the former club impresario turned to say goodbye to his five-hundred-dollar-an-hour attorney for what may have been the last time, he dug his hands into his pockets and pulled out $1.75. It was all the money he had to his name. "You might as well take it all," Chris said, as he handed Ben Brafman the wrinkled dollar bill and pocket change.

By then, his entire empire had collapsed. It had been a year since his arrest. Liquid had been sold to another nightclub mogul, Shawn Lewis, who owned five other hotspots on the beach. By January 2001, Lewis had begun to rehab the space to open his own vision, a new club he would call Spin. Lewis—already courted as "the new Chris" by South Beach's clubbing denizens—had hired Ingrid Casares to be Spin's publicist, paying her a half-million dollars a year in increments of $8,000 a week to bring some of Liquid's old magic to his new venture. The supermodel Tyson Beckford was also reportedly in on the deal, making plans to open his own lounge in a rented section of the massive club.

Paciello's share of Joia had been sold to a French restaurateur, who was grateful that even without its celebrity owner, the eatery still did a booming business. Bar Room was nothing but a memory, and in its place, Paciello's old pal Michael Capponi had opened 320, a classy lounge and disco. Four local businessmen had purchased West Palm Beach Liquid Room, and were pleased by its success.

A year after his arrest, Paciello's waterfront palazzo was in complete disrepair. Overgrown palm trees and weeds littered the lawn. The structure itself looked weak enough to topple in a bad tropical storm. A deal with new owners had apparently fallen through. The government might even seize the mansion at some point.

Even South Beach's crowd had changed considerably since Chris's departure. Some said his arrest sparked the end of a decadent nightclub era. "Paciello's wild, seamy clubs were to Miami in the nineties what Studio 54 was to New York in the seventies," said paparazzi photographer Seth Browarnik, who complained there was nothing but "trash" coming to the clubs now. No celebrities. No models. No A-list.

"It's changed for the worst since he's been gone," he said. "To tell you the truth, it will probably never be the same."

When Chris Paciello entered the Witness Protection Program he came in with two sponsors, an assistant United States attorney and a federal agent. In his case, it was probably prosecutor Jim Walden and the lead investigator on his case, and DEA agent Tim Foley.

Walden and Foley had to fill out an application listing the reasons why someone like Paciello was any good to the government at all, how he had information that they could not obtain any other way. The paperwork would then be forwarded to the Department of Justice in Washington to determine if the witness was "workable or unworkable." The DOJ would review the application, then hand it over to a witness security inspector for the U.S. marshals.

Throughout the process, Paciello would have been hidden in a safe spot. Finally, the witness security inspector would bring Paciello in for an interview.

"This is the reality check for the witness," said a high-ranking official in the Witness Protection Program, who asked to remain anonymous. "The witness is told this is a real sacrifice. They cannot go back to the danger zone, contact their friends or family. All ties to their old life have to be severed. School-work, jobs, projects. We do things so they can live a normal life, but it can never be the same."

The next step was the actual move. A snitch could be moved anywhere in the United States, or even the world, for that matter, depending on how much danger their testimony could put them in.

Before a witness is settled into a new location, he and his family are brought to the top secret Witness Orientation Center in the Washington, D.C., metropolitan area. They fill out a twenty-two-page agreement, complying with the conditions of the Witness Protection Program, including a vow that any and all criminal activities will be discontinued. The witness is given a legal name change, and documents to back the name up. U.S. marshals make sure witnesses—and the family members that come into the program with them—clear up any outstanding debt, and sell off their belongings.

Then the marshals pick a place for the witness to live, usually a small house or good-sized condominium where their mail is forwarded, and a special phone service is installed so calls cannot be traced. No one gets the witness's new location, not even the prosecutors and agents on his case.

Along with free housing, witnesses are given a monthly stipend, a new car, and access to doctors. Then the program helps them find employment, even footing the bill for special training—chef school, truck driving classes, anything that can lead to a new career.

Even rich witnesses like Chris Paciello are entitled to all of the program's benefits, courtesy of the tax-paying public. Any money not seized by the government to pay for fines and fees Paciello is allowed to keep, even if he does not have to spend very much of it.

"It's the lesser of two evils," said the source in the Witness Protection Program. "He'll probably be effective in taking a lot of bad guys off the streets. Anyway, he's a young, handsome guy. He probably won't last in the program very long. Those guys never do."

The government is hoping Paciello lasts long enough to follow through with their plan to have him testify against his acquaintances in the Colombo crime family, old pals like Alphonse "Allie Boy" Persico, the reputed boss.

In early February 2001, on the very day Persico would have been released from a Florida jail after serving time for gun charges, he was re-indicted for racketeering and money laundering. The star witness against him was expected to be Chris Paciello.

Persico's attorney, Barry Levin, began to assail Paciello's character immediately after his client's arraignment. "Chris Paciello is a human pile of garbage," Levin said. "He's nothing but a playboy who will say anything to get himself out of trouble. Allie did not even really know Chris. That day he had lunch with him in Miami, Allie was with his family and Chris caused this whole commotion by pulling up to Shooters with a boatful of topless women. Allie was with his wife, but Chris waved him over to say hello. That was it. There was no meeting."

There were two other familiar names charged with racketeering along with Persico. They were Paciello's childhood friends, the "Twin Towers" Rico Locasio and Big Dom Dionisio. Both men were already jailed on an unrelated stock fraud case and were now facing even longer stints. "He wants to take everyone down with him," Levin said. "Even his friends."

Paciello was not the only one lined up to testify against Persico. Missing Colombo mobster William "Wild Bill" Cutolo's only son, William Jr., had decided to seek revenge for his father's disappearance by agreeing to be one of the witnesses that would testify at Persico's trial. Cutolo had worn a wire for a year to gather information on his father's old friends. Then Cutolo's mother, wife, and young son vanished, too, only they were removed very much alive to "undisclosed locations" by the government.

The New York City mob would be decimated from within.

On a frigid day in late February 2001, Tommy Reynolds and Fabrizio DeFrancisci appeared before Judge Edward Korman to be sentenced. The courtroom was packed. On one side, directly behind the prosecutors, sat the family of Judy Shemtov, the Staten Island woman murdered eight years earlier. Adam Kidan sat between his two sisters, Arlyn and April, flanked by two bodyguards and a spokesman for the family. Next to the Kidans was the family of young Bath Beach teen

Jack Cherin, who was gunned down years earlier when he was only nineteen because the Crew suspected, erroneously, that he was cooperating with law enforcement against the Bonanno family.

Behind the defense attorneys, the rows were filled with family members of both men. DeFrancisici's elderly, Italian-speaking parents were there along with his brothers and his fiancée, Mary. Next to the DeFranciscis was Maryanne Reynolds, Tommy's mother, and a host of his aunts and uncles. There was also a contingent of young Bath Avenue up-and-comers, twenty-something Italian Americans dressed in velour running suits already filling the spots left by the crew members behind bars.

Reynolds's attorney, Jason Solotaroff, argued that his client deserved a break for pleading guilty and saving the government a lengthy, costly trial. He also maligned Chris Paciello for refusing to accept the global plea agreement that would have guaranteed him and his codefendants lesser sentences.

"Mr. Paciello could not have damaged Mr. Reynolds any more than he did by refusing to take the global," the attorney said. "Now Mr. Paciello—who planned the robbery at the victim's house—is not going to be looking at thirty-eight years, forty-eight years, like Mr. Reynolds. Mr. Paciello is reportedly cooperating and looking at a significantly lower sentence.

"What Tom Reynolds is asking for is hope. Hope that he can come out of jail as an old man. He has a daughter and has been a model father. He has spent all but nine months of the last six or seven years behind bars, but he has no self-pity," the attorney continued.

Then Reynolds faced the judge. In a voice barely above a whisper he apologized for the toll his violent impulses had taken on his family. "This is not a happy

day for anybody. I'm really sorry for what my actions
have caused people—especially the families who were
not involved in 'This Life.' " Reynolds's family sobbed.
But Judy Shemtov's three adult children simply glared
at him. When Reynolds was finished talking, Adam
Kidan faced the judge.

"The other day we tried to remember my mother's
voice. We couldn't," Kidan said through tears as his
sisters Arlyn and April wept openly behind him. "There
were so many times of joy he has taken away. This is not
something that can be wiped away as years go by. She
was forty-six years old. She had a hard life as a single
mother.

"We're not here to incarcerate a defendant. We're
here to sentence an animal," he continued. "He walked
into a person's home and shot her at point-blank range.
He killed my mother!"

Judge Korman was so moved by Kidan, his own eyes
welled with tears. He ordered a short recess, then re-
treated to his chambers for twenty minutes and returned
to the bench looking frazzled and pale. Citing Tommy
Reynolds's extensive criminal record, he shook his head
sadly and declared that his was "not the appropriate
case for downward departure" from federal sentencing
guidelines.

Then he consigned Reynolds to serve a life sentence
with no possibility of parole.

As the news sank in Maryanne Reynolds began to
wail. "No! No! My son! My son!" She collapsed into her
brother's arms and had to be carried out of the courthouse by relatives, her grief resonating throughout the
halls of the courthouse. Maryanne Reynolds's screams
were so heart wrenching, a court officer began to cry
himself.

By then, Fabrizio DeFrancisci's loved ones were panicked that he would face a similar sentence. The blood drained from their faces. He faced the judge, flanked by his attorney, Vincent Romano. Romano immediately argued that his client was a changed man who deserved a chance to start a new life. He, too, maligned Paciello for hurting his codefendants with his refusal to plead guilty until it was too late.

"He wants to be married, have a job," Romano said, describing how DeFrancisci struggled with dyslexia his entire life and had problems at school that forced him to make poor choices in life. DeFrancisci himself expressed his remorse, saying, "I would like to apologize to my family for putting them through this. I would like to apologize to God Almighty. If you give me another chance, I will change."

But Korman was unmoved. He looked squarely at DeFrancisci and sentenced him to fifty years in a maximum-security federal jail.

"Fifty years?" Fabrizio yelled. "Did he say fifty years?"

Romano, also stunned by the sentence, simply nodded. Fabrizio's fiancée, Mary, began to yell at the cops and agents in the courthouse. "I hope you're proud of yourselves. He is a good man."

As the youngsters from Bath Avenue Crew left the courthouse in a rage, they began cursing Chris Paciello in high-pitched screeches to anyone who would listen.

On March 7, 2001, two weeks after DeFrancisci and Reynolds were sentenced, Anthony Spero's trial on murder conspiracy, gambling, and racketeering charges began in Brooklyn federal court. Spero had been under house arrest for more than a year on $13.5 million bail, less than Paciello's bond package. The seventy-two-year-old *consigliere* bided his time well in the year he spent at his Staten Island estate. He looked trim in a worsted suit, with his white hair neatly cropped close to his head. Behind him in the courthouse was his longtime girlfriend, Louise Rizzuto, a shapely blonde who was flanked by his daughters, Diane Clemente and Jill Spero, and his brother, Sal.

Courtroom spectators spent most of their time craning their necks at a celebrity who was sitting next to Spero's girlfriend, with his arm draped over her slender shoulders. He was Dan Grimaldi, the actor who plays Patsy Parisi—one of Tony Soprano's mobsters from the hit HBO series *The Sopranos*. The night before, Grimaldi's character exacted revenge on Tony Soprano by urinating in his pool in the debut of the series' third season, a performance that most of the courtroom observers had apparently seen. "I'm here to lend support to Mr. Spero and my sister," Grimaldi said, shrugging off a reporter's question about the irony of an actor who plays a mobster being linked to a real-life crime boss. "It's just a coincidence."

Another Spero pal, boxing promoter Teddy Atlas, was also present. He sat in the back row, nodding hello to the elderly gangster's family and friends who filled the pews behind defense attorney Gerald Shargel. Television and newspaper reporters, along with NYPD detectives, DEA agents, and the FBI, spread out in the rows behind prosecutors Jim Walden, Chris Blank, and Greg Andres.

Prosecutors wasted no time letting the anonymous jury know they had the evidence to prove that Spero ordered the murders of Vincent Bickelman, Paulie Gulino, and Louis Tuzzio along with a hodgepodge of other crimes like owning illegal "Joker Poker" video games and collecting kickbacks from drug dealers working for the Bonanno family. Brooklyn assistant district attorney

Chris Blank depicted Spero as a calculating and feared Mafia boss who killed the three men in twisted acts of "mob justice."

And prosecutors had a parade of government informants ready to testify against him—including once loyal underlings, *il malandrini*, like Crazy Joe Calco, Jimmy Calandra, and Mikey Yammine. Chris Paciello did not know enough about the Bonanno family's *consigliere* to be of any help.

The month-long trial relied largely on circumstantial evidence. There were no wiretapped conversations commanding the troops to murder. No physical evidence linking him to the crime scenes. And only three of the government's ten informants had ever heard Spero give an order to kill. One of those informants was Crazy Joe Calco, who was chagrined as he admitted he was violating one of La Cosa Nostra's most fundamental tenets: never be a rat. "It means what I'm doing right now, testifying against, you know, my friends." Calco also admitted that in the years following Paulie Gulino's murder he had fled to Italy to escape the law and become a part of the Sicilian Mafia, helping a crime family there extort construction companies. "I was the one setting up the gas bombs at all these locations to threaten the owners that if they wouldn't pay, their place would be blown up," he said. Calco also testified that upon his return to New York, he immediately took up with the Bath Avenue Crew again.

Spero refused to glare at the nervous witnesses as they took the stand. Instead he looked at his hands, or watched his lawyers, as the government's informants recounted mob secrets. He looked as if he were merely listening to the clatter of his pigeons on a rooftop. Unlike his close friend John Gotti, Spero possessed none of the smug showmanship that the Dapper Don became infamous for. Spero was a throwback to La Cosa Nostra's less spectacular days, an era before the excesses of young underlings brought unwanted attention to the Mob. During trial breaks, Spero ignored the reporters who gathered in the courthouse every day, and sat quietly in the hallways of the courthouse eating sandwiches from a deli tray his brother brought in daily.

After a month-long trial, the anonymous jury decided that the prosecutors had proven what the Bath Avenue Crew members had testified to: Anthony Spero had ordered the murders of three young men and run a lucrative loan-sharking and gambling operation. Jurors may have been swayed by scores of undercover surveillance photographs surreptitiously taken of Spero during his rise in the Mafia. Spero at Victoria Gotti's lavish wedding. Spero at John Gotti's father's funeral. Spero attending the funeral of an elderly Bonanno gangster. Spero and Joe Benanti holding court outside the Pigeon. Spero engaging in "walk talks" with his underlings.

It had the effect of a La Cosa Nostra family album.

As the forewoman of the jury uttered "guilty" five times, Spero merely nodded his head stoically as his daughters and girlfriend screeched and doubled over in pain. "What trial were those jurors attending?" sobbed Louise Rizzuto. "Where's the evidence? They were not at the same trial I've been sitting at every day." Spero's brother, Sal, began to shake and weep. "I can't believe it," he said, tears streaming down his face. "I just can't believe it."

Shargel said he was stunned and vowed to appeal the verdict. "I am left to believe that the presumption of innocence is just words on a piece of paper. The jurors were blinded by the Mafia image, and it allowed them to ignore the inconsistencies in the evidence. This was a trial where the majority of the evidence and testimony was about what the witnesses themselves did."

Walden defended the government's case, as he hugged co-workers and shook hands with the agents and detectives who had successfully taken down one of the city's most powerful Mafia kingpins. "It was a powerful circumstantial case," he said. "I think the jury saw the realistic face that the Mafia is very good at hiding its operations, and Spero in particular was a master at that."

Judge Korman immediately remanded Spero. Without saying a word, Spero handed a set of house keys and a money clip to his girlfriend. Then he was handcuffed and led out of the room by U.S. marshals. Within a few hours, Spero had arrived at the MDC and was placed in the same segregated wing as Fabrizio De-Francisci and Tommy Reynolds. Like the two Bath Avenue Crew underlings, Spero was immediately placed under suicide watch—the longstanding custom at the federal prison for convicts facing life sentences.

Chris Paciello's friends and former cohorts were falling down around him. He had taken down members of the Colombo family. He had helped send guys from the Bonanno family away for life. His old friends were gunning for him. His new friends were not really friends at all. They were prosecutors, agents, and detectives wearing government-issued suits and clothing that in sunnier days might have made him laugh.

Life as Paciello knew it was over. At least for now.

In a system where Sammy Gravano could go from the trenches of Brooklyn to the tree-lined streets of Arizona, and publish a bestselling tell-all on the way, why not Chris Paciello? In a country where every week millions tune in to the learn the gruesome family secrets of the Soprano clan, who's to say that Chris Paciello couldn't someday make a living peddling family secrets that have the added bonus of being true?

After Paciello testifies at a number of mob trials and serves time for the murder of Judy Shemtov and his other crimes, he could once again resurface—this time with a new name, a new face, and a new future. The government gave him the choice of undergoing plastic surgery because that handsome mug of his would always be hard to forget. But, in the end, many of us forget. Especially if the façade looks different, only the inside staying the same.

"It's not impossible that someday he could open a nightclub in Tel Aviv or Brazil," said one law enforcement source, "or hook up with a model in Casablanca or start a business in Phoenix, Arizona. Nothing is impossible."

Not for the Binger.

EPILOGUE

A few years ago, the *New York Post* Page Six folks asked this question of Chris Paciello: " 'Does jail time hurt a man's reputation—or enhance it?' The answer for Paciello would be the latter.

It didn't take long, either. Fresh from a stint in federal prison, the Madonna pal and ex-Miami club king moved to Los Angeles where he spent years running a successful pizzeria—which was shuttered at the end of 2009 with a handwritten note from "Cristoni," Paciello's latest identity. "Cristoni" was a party animal. Once again the Brooklynite had become a bold-faced name in L.A., where journalists noted he was spotted at the Xenii party Saturday night at 3 A.M. with Doron Ophir and Allison Melnick. The *New York Post* quoted a source—who recalls, "He once picked me up by my neck after I said something drunk and silly back in '97"—as saying, "He was all smiles. We talked and he said he's hanging in L.A. 'indefinitely.' "

Paciello only spent seven years in what wise guys call the "rat jail," a federal prison built especially to house government cooperaters. The mere fact that Paciello is able to hit the party scene in Los Angeles (he was also sighted in Las Vegas grinding on a dance floor with Lindsey Lohan) without fear of reprisal from the hierarchy of the New York City Mafia says more about the decline of the power of the Mob than it does about the prowess of Chris Paciello.

The era of whacking witnesses is a time gone by, as Mafia bosses are just as likely to "turn bad" and give up their underlings as the wannabe thugs that deal drugs for them. Bonanno crime family boss Joseph Messina—on whom I once wrote a front-page story for the New York *Daily News* with the headline "The Last Don"— cooperated against his former criminal cohorts, as did Vincent "Vinny Ocean" Palermo, the head of the New Jersey mob which was the model for the hit HBO show *The Sopranos*. With those defections, it was only a matter of time before the five families of the New York City Mafia were decimated from within. And they were. The old-school mob dons are decrepit with age and illness. The young guns are impulsive, greedy drug lords. In 2001, not long after Chris Paciello pleaded guilty and was transferred to federal prison for cooperating witnesses, there were 3,118 indictments against organized crime figures. Of those, more than 2,000 were convicted and are currently serving long prison sentences. By 2008, federal indictments crippled all five crime syndicates in New York City—including the Colombo clan that Paciello was affiliated with during his last days out on the streets as a wise guy.

All of that must be little comfort to Chris Paciello, though. He will likely live out his life looking over his shoulder, jumping at anyone who makes a sudden move. Sure, he rubs elbows with Hollywood types including Brett Ratner and Leonardo DiCaprio. Within months of his 2006 release, Paciello was romantically linked with raven-haired supermodel Erin Naas and photographed canoodling with Grammy-nominated singer Natalie

Imbruglia. (Paciello was set up with the British singer through his ex-girlfriend Madonna, tabloids around the world reported breathlessly.) But as he parties with the beautiful people, it cannot be far from Paciello's mind that one of the men he helped send to prison for life is Alphonse "Allie Boy" Persico, the boss of the Colombo crime family. Persico may be a man of polish with a law degree, but he is also a savage brute given to holding a grudge—a grudge that he has nothing but time now to nurse. In November 2007, Persico was convicted in the murder of William "Wild Bill" Cutolo. The conviction helped him once again follow in the footsteps of his father, Carmine "the Snake" Persico. The elder Persico and his son once held the title of boss of the Colombo crime family and lived the lifestyle that title afforded them. And now both of them will die in prison.

History has shown that bars have never prevented either Persico from reaching an enemy to exact revenge. In 1992, the younger Persico was believed by the FBI to have ordered a hit on a 28-year-old Staten Island nightclub owner named Michael Devine, who dated the jailed mob boss' wife, Teresa. Devine's bullet-riddled body was found in his Nissan Pathfinder, his head a mess of large-caliber weapon wounds, sprawled over the steering wheel with the engine still running. The FBI found photographs of Teresa and Devine in the victim's home, fueling speculation that the nightclub owner was shot dead on orders from the jailed Colombo acting boss. He was never charged in the case, though, but rumors to this day continue to swirl that Persico was responsible for the unsolved slaying.

Paciello knew all too well what kind of muscle Persico had on the streets. After all, he was the man caught in a cash war between Persico and William "Wild Bill" Cutolo. Both Mafiosi wanted a cut of Paciello's lucrative

South Beach nightclub interests. In fact, Paciello had a sit-down on Persico's yacht, a secret meeting during which he brought along an undercover Miami Beach cop, Andy Dohler, to talk about how much money he was paying up to Cutolo. "Cutolo was coming on like a freight train, acting like he had his own mob," Assistant United States Attorney Deborah Mayer would say of the hit. "Alphonse Persico had to act."

It was months later that Cutolo vanished after strolling along the Brooklyn waterfront. Prosecutors also said the hit was carried out by gangsters Vincent "Chickie" DeMartino and Thomas "Tommy Shots" Gioeli—who got $50,000 for the murder—and that Cutolo's corpse was dumped from a boat into the Atlantic Ocean. Persico paid for the hit and was convicted in 2007. Persico is currently appealing that sentence, saying that one of the witnesses against him—Marguerite Cutolo, Wild Bill's widow—perjured herself on the stand.

If Persico's bid for release is successful, Paciello has a lot to worry about. The power of the Mafia may have been dampened by unrelenting federal indictments against even bit players in the game. But Paciello cannot underestimate the one rule that continues to exist among old-style wiseguys. Losing money is one thing. Losing honor is something else altogether. Losing freedom is unspeakable. Chris Paciello's cooperation with the government cost Alphonse "Allie Boy" Persico, a very dangerous man, to lose all three.

As dangerous as that is, Paciello does not seem that worried. He has a Facebook page—with the most famous of his monikers, Chris Paciello. (He did not confirm a friend request I sent to his Facebook account.) And the New York *Daily News* would report that he was still in the sights of law enforcement: in 2009 he was accused of using a cop buddy to seek revenge on a business partner in a now-defunct West Hollywood eatery called Murano.

It was not exactly out of character for him to seek revenge on an enemy. Sandy Sachs, who was Paciello's partner in West Hollywood's Murano restaurant, is ready to file a multi-million-dollar lawsuit against the L.A. County Sheriff's Department, charging that Paciello vengefully persuaded a cop buddy to have her busted on a phony drunken-driving charge. Sachs' lawyer, Gerson Horn, says Paciello set her up after she sued him for allegedly failing to make good on a promised $600,000 investment. Horn tells us that, on April 16, cops received a call from off-duty deputy Sheriff Ralph Garay, who claimed Sachs was drunk at the restaurant and about to drive home. According to Horn, Paciello can be heard on a dispatch tape coaching Garay to tell on-duty cops Sachs should be arrested.

Horn says a deputy who came to the restaurant "saw no evidence that Sandy was drunk." But, after Paciello's girlfriend at the time, Erin Naas, also allegedly told police Sachs was drunk, Sachs was confronted at her home by several officers. Horn says they "threw her to the ground, handcuffed and pummeled her. Her body was covered with bruises." A forced blood test determined Sachs' alcohol level was within legal limits. The L.A. district attorney's office has declined to file charges against her. Horn says Sachs' suit will accuse police of wrongful arrest, battery and civil rights violations. The case remains pending.

And Paciello, apparently, is still acquainted with the part of his personality that prompted his nickname "the Binger."

Michele R. McPhee
2010